VICO AND HERDER

VICO

AND

HERDER

TWO STUDIES
IN THE HISTORY OF IDEAS

ISAIAH BERLIN

THE VIKING PRESS NEW YORK

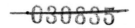

Published in 1976 by The Viking Press
625 Madison Avenue, New York, N.Y. 10022

Library of Congress Cataloging in Publication Data
Berlin, Isaiah, Sir.
Vico and Herder.

Includes index.
1. Vico, Giovanni Battista, 1668-1744.
2. Herder, Johann Gottfried von, 1744-1803.
I. Title.
B3583.B46   901   75-33299
ISBN 0-670-74585-5

Printed in the United States of America

*Acknowledgment is made to the following
for permission to use material:*
Cambridge University Press: From *Herder on Social and
Political Culture* by F.M. Barnard.

Cornell University Press: From *The New Science of Gianbattista
Vico*, translation of the 3rd edition (1744) by Thomas Goddard
Bergin and Max Harold Fisch. Copyright © 1968 by Cornell University.
Copyright © 1961 by Thomas Goddard Bergin
and Max Harold Fisch. Copyright © 1948 by Cornell
University. Reprinted by permission of Cornell
University Press.

Indiana University Press: From *The Rise of Modern Mythology
1680-1860* by Burton Feldman and Robert D. Richardson, Jr.
Copyright © 1972 by Indiana University Press. Reprinted by
permission.

The Johns Hopkins University Press: From *Aspects of the
Eighteenth Century*, edited by Earl R. Wasserman.
Copyright © The Johns Hopkins University Press, 1965.
Reprinted by permission.

To the Memory of
LEONARD WOOLF

Contents

Preface

THE essays in this book originate in lectures delivered respectively to the Italian Institute in London in 1957-58 and to Johns Hopkins University in 1964. The original version of the essay on Vico was published in *Art and Ideas in Eighteenth-Century Italy* (Rome, Edizioni di Storia e Letteratura, 1960); that on Herder appeared in Earl R. Wasserman (ed.), *Aspects of the Eighteenth Century* (Baltimore, Johns Hopkins University Press, 1965) and was later reprinted with minor modifications in *Encounter*, July 1965. Both essays have since been revised, and the first has been considerably expanded. I should like to take this opportunity of thanking Dr Leon Pompa for discussing with me his views of Vico, particularly Vico's conception of science and knowledge, and Professor Roy Pascal for an illuminating letter about Herder—from both of these I have greatly profited. Dr Pompa's book on Vico[1] unfortunately appeared only after my book was already in proof, too late to enable me to make use of it here.

As will be plain from the references in the text, I have relied on the admirable translation of Vico's *Scienza Nuova* by Professors T. G. Bergin and M. H. Fisch for the quotations from, and references to, it in this book. My thanks are also due to Professors B. Feldman and R. D. Richardson, Roy Pascal, and F. M. Barnard, for the use of their renderings of texts by Herder quoted in this work. My debt to Professor Barnard's excellent anthology, *Herder on Social and Political Culture*, is particularly great: some of his renderings are reproduced verbatim, others in a form somewhat altered by me. I also wish to thank Mr Francis Graham-Harrison for his valuable help in reading the proofs of this book, Mr Hugo Brunner of the Hogarth Press, for the care, courtesy and above all infinite patience displayed by him in his dealings with me, and finally Mrs Patricia Utechin, my secretary, for generous and unflagging help when it was most needed.

I. B.

July 1975

[1] Leon Pompa, *Vico: A Study of the 'New Science'* (Cambridge University Press, 1975).

Introduction

HISTORIANS are concerned with the discovery, description and explanation of the social aspects and consequences of what men have done and suffered. But the lines between description, explanation and analysis, selection and interpretation of facts or events or their characteristics, are not clear, and cannot be made so without doing violence to the language and concepts that we normally use. Goethe remarked long ago that no statement of fact is free from theory; and even though some conceptions of what shall count as fact are less theory-laden than others, yet there is no complete consensus on this. Criteria of what constitutes a fact differ between fields of knowledge and between those who engage in them. Even within one field, history for instance, there are obvious differences in this regard between Christian and pagan historians, or post-Renaissance historians of different outlooks; what was incontrovertible evidence for Bossuet was not so for Gibbon, what constitutes a historical fact is not identical for Ranke, Michelet, Macaulay, Guizot, Dilthey. It is not the same past upon which nationalists and Marxists, clericals and liberals, appear to be gazing: the differences are even wider when it comes to selection and interpretation. This is equally true of the methods of those who rely principally upon quantitative and statistical methods as opposed to those who engage in imaginative reconstruction; of writers guided, not always consciously, by the maxims of this or that school of social psychology, or sociology, or philosophy of culture, or those who find illumination in the doctrines of functional anthropology or psychoanalysis or structuralist theories of language or imaginative literature.

This book examines the work of two thinkers whose ideas played a major part in transforming the canons of selection and interpretation of historical facts, and thereby affected the view of the facts themselves. Both wrote in the eighteenth century, but their doctrines did not achieve their full effect until the nineteenth, in both cases mainly through the labours of their disciples. These studies are not intended as an examination of the entire *oeuvre* of either Vico or Herder: only of those among their theses which seemed to me the most arresting, important and suggestive. For this reason I have made no attempt to submit the more technical philosophical ideas of either thinker to critical examination, even though some among them raise issues of considerable importance; so—to take but three examples—Vico's notion of *scienza*, which involves the conception of explanation *per caussas*, seems to embody a view of causality which differs from those of Descartes or Hume or Kant or modern positivists, and leads him to a doctrine of motives and causes *par excellence* which is highly relevant to problems that are in hot dispute today. So, too, is the distinction he draws between *scienza* and *coscienza*, *verum* and *certum*, which, in its turn, is highly relevant to much Hegelian and post-Hegelian—materialist, Marxist, Freudian —discussion and controversy about historical and sociological methods. Again, Herder's conceptions of teleological or cultural explanation made, or at least widened, conceptual and psychological paths not open to tough-minded and consistent materialists, positivists and mechanists —and this, too, leads to the widely varying positions of, among others, thinkers influenced by Marxism, by the doctrines of Wittgenstein, by writers on the sociology of knowledge or phenomenology. But a discussion of these philosophical developments, like that of anticipations of modern linguistic structuralism in Vico's *New Science*, although both interesting and seminal, would take one too far from Vico's and Herder's own discussions of issues on which they propounded their most original and influential theses—the nature and growth of human studies in general, and the nature of history and culture in particular. I have not attempted to trace the origins of these ideas, save in a somewhat tentative fashion, nor to give an account of the historical or social circumstances in which they were conceived, nor their precise role in the *Weltanschauung* of the age, or even that of the thinkers themselves. No one stressed the importance of comprehensive historical treatment more boldly or vehemently than Vico; no one argued more eloquently or convincingly than Herder that ideas and outlooks could be understood adequately only in genetic and historical terms, as expressions of the particular stage in the continuing development of the society in which they originated. A good deal of light has been shed on the intellectual and ideological sources of these ideas by scholars far more erudite than I can ever hope to be: Benedetto Croce, A. Corsano, Max H. Fisch, Nicola Badaloni, Paolo Rossi, A. Gerbi and, above all, Fausto Nicolini, have done much of this for Vico; Rudolf Haym and, more recently, H. B. Nisbet, G. A. Wells, Max Rouché, V. Zhirmunsky and Robert Clark (to choose the most important) have provided an indispensable framework for Herder's teaching. I have profited greatly by their labours even where I disagreed with some of their assessments of the ideas themselves. Ideas are not born in a vacuum nor by a process of parthenogenesis: knowledge of social history, of the interplay and impact of social forces at work in particular times and places, and of the problems which these generate, is needed for assessing the full significance and purpose of all but the strictly technical disciplines and, some now tell us, even for the correct interpretation of the concepts of the exact sciences. Nor do I wish to deny the importance of considering why it is in the Kingdom of the Two Sicilies, and still more in East Prussia, usually described as cultural backwaters in an age of intense intellectual and scientific activity, that original ideas of major importance were generated. This is a historical problem for the solution of which knowledge of social, ideological and intellectual conditions is clearly indispensable, and which, so far as I know, has not been adequately examined. But it is not directly relevant to the purpose of these essays. But even though such historical treatment is required for full understanding, it cannot be a necessary condition for grasping the central core of every historically influential doctrine or concept. The neo-Platonists in the later Roman Empire or during the Renaissance may not have interpreted Plato's doctrines as faithfully as more erudite and scrupulous commentators of a later period, who paid due attention to the relevant social and historical context of his thought, but if Plato's main doctrines had not transcended their own time and place, they would scarcely have had expended on them—or, indeed, deserved—the labours of gifted scholars and interpreters; nor would the imagination of distant posterity—of Plotinus or Pico della Mirandola or Marsilio Ficino or Michelangelo or Shaftesbury—have been set on fire by them; nor would they have had enough life in them to provoke major controversies in our own time. Accurate knowledge of the social, political and economic situation in England in the second half of the seventeenth century is certainly required for a full understanding of a particular passage in Locke's *Second Treatise* or of a letter to Stillingfleet. Yet what Voltaire (who did not go into such details), or the Founding Fathers of the American Republic, supposed him to mean, nevertheless derives from his writings, and not solely, or even mainly, from their own minds or problems. The importance of accurate historical knowledge to the understanding of the meaning, force and influence of ideas may be far greater than many unhistorical thinkers, particularly in English-speaking lands, have recognized, but it is not everything. If the ideas and the basic terminology of Aristotle or the Stoics or Pascal or Newton or Hume or Kant did not possess a capacity for independent life, for surviving translation, and, indeed, transplantation, not without, at times, some change of meaning, into the language of very disparate cultures, long after their own worlds had passed away, they would by now, at best, have found an honourable resting place beside the writings of the Aristotelians of Padua or Christian Wolff, major influences in their day, in some museum of historical antiquities. The importance of historical hermeneutics has been greatly underestimated by historically insensitive British thinkers in the past—with the result that the swing of the pendulum sometimes makes it appear an end in itself. These are mere truisms, which need stating only because the notion of the possibility of a valid examination of the ideas of earlier ages, unless it is steeped in a rich cultural, linguistic and historical context, has been increasingly called into question in our day. Even though the shades of Vico and Herder are invoked in support of this doctrine, the importance of past philosophers in the end resides in the fact that the issues which they raised are live issues still (or again), and, as in this case, have not perished with the vanished societies of Naples or Königsberg or Weimar, in which they were conceived.

What, then, it may be asked, are these time-defying notions? In the case of Vico, let me try to summarize those which appear to me the most arresting in the form of seven theses:

(1) That the nature of man is not, as has long been supposed, static and unalterable or even unaltered; that it does not so much as contain even a central kernel or essence, which remains identical through change; that men's own efforts to understand the world in which they find themselves and to adapt it to their needs, physical and spiritual, continuously transform their worlds and themselves.

(2) That those who make or create something can understand it as mere observers of it cannot. Since men in some sense make their own history (though what this kind of making consists in is not made entirely clear), men understand it as they do not understand the world

of external nature, which, since it is not made, but only observed and interpreted, by them, is not intelligible to them as their own experience and activity can be. Only God, because he has made nature, can understand it fully, through and through.

(3) That, therefore, men's knowledge of the external world which we can observe, describe, classify, reflect upon, and of which we can record the regularities in time and space, differs in principle from their knowledge of the world that they themselves create, and which obeys rules that they have themselves imposed on their own creations. Such, for example, is knowledge of mathematics—something that men have themselves invented—of which they therefore have an 'inside' view; or of language, which men, and not the forces of nature, have shaped; and, therefore, of all human activities, inasmuch as it is men who are makers, actors and observers in one. History, since it is concerned with human action, which is the story of effort, struggle, purposes, motives, hopes, fears, attitudes, can therefore be known in this superior— 'inside'—fashion, for which our knowledge of the external world cannot possibly be the paradigm—a matter about which the Cartesians, for whom natural knowledge is the model, must therefore be in error. This is the ground of the sharp division drawn by Vico between the natural sciences and the humanities, between self-understanding on the one hand, and the observation of the external world on the other, as well as between their respective goals, methods, and kinds and degrees of knowability. This dualism has continued to be the subject of hot dispute ever since.

(4) That there is a pervasive pattern which characterizes all the activities of any given society: a common style reflected in the thought, the arts, the social institutions, the language, the ways of life and action, of an entire society. This idea is tantamount to the concept of a culture; not necessarily of one culture, but of many; with the corollary that true understanding of human history cannot be achieved without the recognition of a succession of the phases of the culture of a given society or people. This further entails that this succession is intelligible, and not merely causal, since the relationship of one phase of a culture or historical development to another is not that of mechanical cause and effect, but, being due to the purposive activity of men, designed to satisfy needs, desires, ambitions (the very realization of which generates new needs and purposes), is intelligible to those who possess a sufficient degree of self-awareness, and occurs in an order which is neither

fortuitous nor mechanically determined, but flows from elements in, and forms of, life, explicable solely in terms of human goal-directed activity. This social process and its order are intelligible to other men, members of later societies, since they are engaged in a similar enterprise which arms them with the means of interpreting the lives of their predecessors at a similar or different stage of spiritual and material development. The very notion of anachronism entails the possibility of this kind of historical understanding and ordering, since it requires a capacity for discriminating between what belongs and what cannot belong to a given stage of a civilization and way of life; and this, in its turn, depends on an ability to enter imaginatively into the outlook and beliefs, explicit and implicit, of such societies—an enquiry that makes no sense if applied to the non-human world. That the notion of the individual character of every society, culture, epoch is constituted by factors and elements which it may have in common with other periods and civilizations, but each particular pattern of which is distinguishable from all others; and as a corollary of this, that the concept of anachronism denotes lack of awareness of an intelligible, necessary order of succession which such civilizations obey. I doubt if anyone before Vico had a clear notion of culture or historical change in this sense.

(5) That the creations of man—laws, institutions, religions, rituals, works of art, language, song, rules of conduct and the like—are not artificial products created to please, or to exalt, or teach wisdom, nor weapons deliberately invented to manipulate or dominate men, or promote social stability or security, but are natural forms of self-expression, of communication with other human beings or with God. The myths and fables, the ceremonies and monuments of early man, according to the view prevalent in Vico's day, were absurd fantasies of helpless primitives, or deliberate inventions designed to delude the masses and secure their obedience to cunning and unscrupulous masters. This he regarded as a fundamental fallacy. Like the anthropomorphic metaphors of early speech, myths and fables and ritual are for Vico so many natural ways of conveying a coherent view of the world as it was seen and interpreted by primitive men. From which it follows that the way to understand such men and their worlds is by trying to enter their minds, by finding out what they are at, by learning the rules and significance of their methods of expression—their myths, their songs, their dances, the form and idioms of their language, their marriage and funeral rites. To understand their history, one needs to understand

what they lived by, which can be discovered only by those who have the key to what their language, art, ritual mean—a key which Vico's *New Science* was intended to provide.

(6) From which it follows (in effect a new type of aesthetics) that works of art must be understood, interpreted, evaluated, not in terms of timeless principles and standards valid for all men everywhere, but by correct grasp of the purpose and therefore the peculiar use of symbols, especially of language, which belong uniquely to their own time and place, their own stage of social growth; that this alone can unravel the mysteries of cultures entirely different from one's own and hitherto dismissed either as barbarous confusions or as being too remote and exotic to deserve serious attention. This marks the beginning of comparative cultural history, indeed, of a cluster of new historical disciplines: comparative anthropology and sociology, comparative law, linguistics, ethnology, religion, literature, the history of art, of ideas, of institutions, of civilizations—indeed, the entire field of knowledge of what came to be called the social sciences in the widest sense, conceived in historical, that is, genetic terms.

(7) That, therefore, in addition to the traditional categories of knowledge—*a priori*-deductive, *a posteriori*-empirical, that provided by sense perception and that vouchsafed by revelation—there must now be added a new variety, the reconstructive imagination. This type of knowledge is yielded by 'entering' into the mental life of other cultures, into a variety of outlooks and ways of life which only the activity of *fantasia*—imagination—makes possible. *Fantasia* is for Vico a way of conceiving the process of social change and growth by correlating it with, indeed, viewing it as conveyed by, the parallel change or development of the symbolism by which men seek to express it; since the symbolic structures are themselves part and parcel of the reality which they symbolize, and alter with it. This method of discovery which begins with understanding the means of expression, and seeks to reach the vision of reality which they presuppose and articulate, is a kind of transcendental deduction (in the Kantian sense) of historical truth. It is not, as hitherto, a method of arriving at an unchanging reality via its changing appearances, but at a changing reality—men's history—through its systematically changing modes of expression.

Every one of these notions is a major advance in thought, any one of which by itself is sufficient to make the fortune of a philosopher. Vico's work lay unheeded, save among scholars in his native city, until that most indefatigable of transmitters of ideas, Victor Cousin, brought it to the attention of Jules Michelet. The effect on the great French historian was immediate and transforming, and it was he who first spread Vico's fame throughout the length and breadth of Europe.

Even though Michelet, at the end of his life, claimed that Vico was his only master, like every strongly original thinker he took from the *New Science* only that which fitted in with his own, already formed, conception of history. He derived from Vico a vision of men as moulders of their own destinies, engaged in a Promethean struggle to achieve their own moral and social freedom, wresting from nature the means to serve their own human goals, and, in the course of this, creating and destroying institutions in the perpetual struggle to overcome obstacles, social and individual, to the full realization of the moral energies and creative genius of entire peoples and societies. What does not fit into Michelet's ardent populist vision, for example, the notion of a divine providence, which, unknown to them, shapes the ends of individuals and societies—Vico's version of the Hidden Hand, or the Cunning of History, or of Immanent Reason—Michelet, in effect, half translates into secular terms and half ignores, as he ignores Vico's Platonic moments, his theory of historical cycles, his anti-democratic bias, his admiration for devout, authoritarian, semi-primitive societies, which is the very antithesis of Michelet's passionate faith in popular liberty.

This is an instance of a recurring phenomenon—that the importance and influence of ideas do not invariably depend on the validity or value of the systems in which they occur. That Plato or Spinoza or Leibniz or Kant were thinkers of genius has seldom been denied even by those who reject the central tenets of their metaphysical systems, or look on them as deleterious; this is so because they recognize that these philosophers advanced ideas the depth and power of which have permanently altered the history of thought, or (which comes to the same) that they raised issues which have exercised the minds of thinkers ever since; and this remains true even when some of the most ambitious and celebrated of the systems of thought which initially gave rise to these issues have long lost whatever life they may have had and are looked upon as being, at best, of purely historical interest. So it is with the two thinkers discussed in this book. Vico certainly supposed himself to have discovered a new science: that is, general principles capable of yielding rules the correct application of which could, at least in principle, explain the order of the phases in the recurrent cycles of human history as completely as the triumphant natural sciences of his day could account for the regularities of the positions and movement of physical matter. I am not here concerned with weighing the justice of this claim against the claims of rival systems made by earlier and later thinkers. All I have attempted to do is cast light on some of the building blocks in this vast, sprawling, at times fantastic, baroque edifice: stones that are valuable on their own account, capable of being used in the construction of firmer, if more modest, structures. This holds of such novel notions as, for example (to recall them once again), Vico's distinction between the realm of nature, which obeys (knowable but not intelligible) laws, and the man-made, which is subject to (intelligible) rules; his theory of the function of myth and symbolism and above all of language; his conception of a central style which characterizes and expresses (he does not say that it determines or renders coherent) the varied activities of societies or entire epochs, which in its turn suggests the notion of a variety of human cultures; of the radical implications for aesthetics, anthropology, and, of course, the entire range of the historical sciences, of such an approach to human activity.

So, also, with Herder. He, too, tried to embrace the entire province of knowledge of his time: science and art, metaphysics and theology, epistemology and ethics, social life, history, anthropology, psychology, all that men were most deeply concerned with in the past and the present and (with far greater emphasis than Vico) the future. Like the English thinkers by whom he was deeply influenced, like Young and Percy and the Wartons and Sterne (and Lavater in Zürich), he was a divine and a man of letters, and, in an age of increasing specialization, aimed at universality. He was a poet, a philosopher, a literary scholar and historian, an amateur philologist, an aesthetic theorist and critic, an eager student of the biological and physical sciences of his day: he wished to bring all the sciences of man and of his environment, his origins, his history, into a single integrated whole. He regarded the frontiers between the human sciences as pedantic and artificial devices, irksome hindrances to self-understanding by human beings in all their illimitable variety and spiritual power which the tidy categories of philosophers vainly sought to contain. In the course of this vast undertaking, for which he had neither the capacity nor the knowledge, he originated and gave life and substance to ideas some of which have entered permanently into the texture of European thought and feeling.

Among the concepts which Herder originated or infused with a new life are at least three central ideas, which have grown in strength and influence since they were launched: the idea that men, if they are to exercise their faculties fully, and so develop into all that they can be, need to belong to identifiable communal groups, each with its own outlook, style, traditions, historical memories and language; the idea that the spiritual activity of men—expressed in art and literature, religion and philosophy, laws and sciences, play and work—consists not in the creation of objects, of commodities or artefacts, the value of which resides in themselves, and is independent of their creators and their characters and their purposes—but in forms of communication with other men. The creative activity of men is to be conceived not as the production of objects for use or pleasure or instruction, additions to, or improvements on the world of external nature, but as voices speaking, as expressions of individual visions of life, to be understood not by rational analysis, that is, dissection into constituent elements, nor by exhaustive classification under concepts, subsumption under general principles or laws, incorporation in logically coherent systems or the use of other technical devices, but only by what Herder calls *Einfühlen*— empathy—the gifts not of a judge, a compiler or an anatomist, but of an artist endowed with historical insight and imagination. 'Every court, every school, every profession, every sect', wrote Herder's mentor, Johann Georg Hamann, 'has its own language', which can be grasped only 'by the passion of a lover, a friend, an intimate'; abstract formulae, general theories, scientific laws, are keys that open no individual door. Only a combination of historical scholarship with a responsive, imaginative sensibility can find a path into the inner life, the vision of the world, the aspirations, values, ways of life of individuals or groups or entire civilizations. Finally, it was Herder who set in motion the idea that since each of these civilizations has its own outlook and way of thinking and feeling and acting, creates its own collective ideals in virtue of which it is a civilization, it can be truly understood and judged only in terms of its own scale of values, its own rules of thought and action, and not of those of some other culture: least of all in terms of some universal, impersonal, absolute scale, such as the French *philosophes* seemed to think that they had at their disposal when they so arrogantly and blindly gave marks to all societies, past and present, praised or condemned this or that individual or civilization or epoch, set some up as universal models and rejected others as barbarous or vicious or absurd. To judge, still more to mock at, the past according to one's own—or some other alien—lights, must lead to grave distortion. The ancient Hebrews must not be judged by the standards of classical Greece, still less by those of Voltaire's Paris or of his imaginary Chinese mandarins; nor should Norsemen or Indians or Teutons be looked at through the spectacles of an Aristotle or a Boileau. He is as critical of Europocentrism as his enemy Voltaire. For him men are men, and have common traits at all times; but it is their differences that matter most, for it is the differences that make them what they are, make them themselves, it is in these that the individual genius of men and cultures is expressed.

The denial, at any rate in Herder's earlier writings, of absolute and universal values carries the implication, which with time has grown increasingly disturbing, that the goals and values pursued by various human cultures may not only differ, but may, in addition, not all be compatible with one another; that variety, and perhaps conflict, are not accidental, still less eliminable attributes of the human condition, but, on the contrary, may be intrinsic properties of men as such. If this is so, then the notion of a single, unchanging, objective code of universal precepts—the simple, harmonious, ideal way of life to which, whether they know it or not, all men aspire (which underlies the central current of the Western tradition of thought) may turn out to be incoherent; for there appear to be many visions, many ways of living and thinking and feeling, each with its own 'centre of gravity', self-validating, uncombinable, still less capable of being integrated into a seamless whole. It is worth remarking that—apart from this revolutionary corollary which undermined the ancient notion of the moral unity of the human race, or, at least, of that of its rational members— the notion that variety is either inescapable, or valuable in itself, or both at once, was itself novel. Herder may not be its only begetter, but the idea that variety is preferable to uniformity, and not simply a form of human failure to arrive at the one true answer, and consequently a form of error or imperfection—the rejection of the traditional belief in the necessary harmony of values in a rational universe, whether as the reality beneath the appearances, or as the ideal presupposed both by reason and faith—this radical departure is altogether modern. The ancient world and the Middle Ages knew nothing of it.

These ideas—that all explanation, all understanding, indeed, all living, depends on a relationship to a given social whole and its unique past, and that it is incapable of being fitted into some repetitive, generalized pattern; the sharp contrast between qualitative as opposed to quantitative approaches; the notion that art is communication, a form of doing and being, not of making objects detachable from the maker; the notion that change and variety are intrinsic to human beings; that truth and goodness are not universal and immutable Platonic forms in a super-sensible, timeless, crystalline heaven, but many and changing; that the collision of equally compelling claims and goals may be unavoidable and incapable of rational resolution, so that some choices may be at once unavoidable and agonizing; all these notions, which entered into many varieties of Romanticism, relativism, nationalism, populism, and many brands of individualism, together with corresponding attacks upon the methods of the natural sciences and rational enquiry based on tested empirical evidence, have their fateful beginnings here. To ascribe some of these views to either of the thinkers treated in these pages would be false and unjust. Men are not responsible for the careers of their ideas: still less for the aberrations to which they lead.

Both Vico and Herder tended to overstate their central theses. Such exaggeration is neither unusual nor necessarily to be deplored. Those who have discovered (or think they have discovered) new and important truths are liable to see the world in their light, and it needs a singular degree of intellectual control to retain a due sense of proportion and not be swept too far along the newly opened paths. Many original thinkers exaggerate greatly. Plato and the Stoics, Descartes, Spinoza, Hume, Kant, Rousseau, Hegel, Marx, Russell, Freud (not to mention later masters) claimed too much. Nor is it likely that their ideas would have broken through the resistance of received opinion or been accorded the attention that they deserved, if they had not. The moderation of an Aristotle or a Locke is the exception rather than the rule. Vico was not answering questions posed by earlier thinkers. His vision of men and their past involved him in conceiving, in some excitement (to which he owns), new categories and concepts, and his struggle to adapt traditional terms to convey the basic structure of the new discipline to his contemporaries resulted in sudden leaps of thought and a convoluted and obscure terminology. Herder often wrote with a rhapsodic intensity not conducive to clear reflection or expression. The vehement zeal with which both Vico and Herder thought and spoke inevitably blinded them to the great cardinal merits of the methods of the thinkers against whom they inveighed. In a radical conflict of beliefs and methods on this scale, both sides were bound to attack too violently and to reject too much. It is plain to us now that insight, no matter how brilliant and intuitive, and attempts to reconstruct the main lines of entire cultures by sheer imaginative genius, based on scattered erudition, are not sufficient. In the end it is only scrupulous examination of the evidence of the past and the systematic, self-critical piecing together of whatever can be empirically established, that can confirm one hypothesis and weaken or rule out others as implausible or absurd. History needs whatever it can obtain from any source or method of empirical knowledge. As antiquarian research, archaeology, epigraphy, palaeography, philology have altered historical writing in previous centuries, so quantitative methods, the accumulation and use of statistical information to support economic, sociological, psychological, anthropological generalizations, have added to, and transformed, our knowledge of the human past, and are doing so to an increasing extent. The use of chemical and biological techniques has added materially to the knowledge of the origins of men and the dating and identification of the monuments on which our knowledge is founded. Without reliable empirical evidence, the most richly imaginative efforts to recover the past must remain guesswork and breed fictions and romances. Nor is there any assignable limit to the influence upon historical studies of disciplines yet unborn. Nevertheless, without such inspired insights, the accumulated data remain dead: Baconian generalizations are not enough. The revolt against, on the one hand, the labours of antiquaries and compilers (Voltaire was among the first to cover them with ridicule), and the ideological dogmas of the Enlightenment, on the other, transformed both literature and history.

Vico, even after Michelet, remained an esoteric interest. But the influence of Herder's writings, acknowledged and unacknowledged, direct or indirect, was wide and permanent. After him the feeling grew that human history was not a linear progression, but a succession of distinct and heterogeneous civilizations, some of which influenced each other, but could, nevertheless, be seen to possess an inner unity, to be individual social wholes, intelligible in their own right and not primarily as so many steps to some other, more perfect, way of life. Such cultures could not be reconstructed fragment by fragment in accordance with mechanical rules supplied by a generalizing science: their constituent elements could be grasped adequately only in relation to each other—this indeed was what was meant by speaking of a civilization, a way of living and an expression of a society characterized by an identifiable pattern, a central style which informed, if not all, yet a great many of its activities, and so revealed, even in its internal tensions, its differences and conflicts, a certain degree of unity of feeling and purpose. This style or character was not something that could be abstracted from its concrete expressions or used as a reliable method of infallibly reconstructing missing facts and filling gaps in our empirical knowledge; it was not governed by discoverable laws, nor could it yield a formula defining some metaphysical essence from which the attributes or history of men were logically deducible. It was an intelligible, empirically recognizable, pattern—a network of relationships between human beings, a way of responding to their environment and one another, a form—some said a structure—of thought, feeling and action. This could only be grasped by the use of the imagination, by a capacity to conceive the life of an entire society, to 'feel oneself into' its mode of thought, speech, feeling; to visualize the gestures, to hear the voices, to trace the changing moods and attitudes and in this way to follow the fortunes of its members.

Both these thinkers perceived—Herder more vividly than Vico—that the task of integrating disparate data and interpretations of events, movements, situations, of synthesizing such heterogeneous material into a coherent picture, demands gifts very different from those required for rational methods of investigation or formulation and verification of specific hypotheses: above all, the gift of breathing life into the dead bones in the burial grounds of the past, of a creative imagination. In the absence of sufficient empirical evidence, such accounts of total social experience may remain no more than historical romances; but unless one is able in the first place to imagine such worlds in concrete detail, there will be little enough that is worth verifying: without the initial intuitive vision of a world about which one wishes to learn, the data remain lifeless, the individuals mere names, at most stylized figures in a procession, a pageant of operatic characters clothed in historical garments, or at best idealized personages in a classical drama. The rational methods of reconstruction of the past—whether human or non-human—zoological, palaeontological, geological—lead to conclusions that are precise or vague, valid or invalid, accurate or inaccurate, correct or incorrect, and are so certified by the application of methods accepted by reputable experts in the relevant field. But such attributes as 'profound' and 'shallow', 'plausible' and 'implausible', 'living' and 'lifeless', 'authentic' and 'unreal', 'rounded' and 'flat' and the like, are not often ascribed to the achievements of logic or epistemology or scientific method but are more often used to characterize the arts and works of scholarship, which require a capacity for insight, responsiveness, understanding of what men are and can be, of their inner lives, perception of the meaning and implications, and not only of the appearances, of their observable gestures. These are terms used to describe works of humane learning—histories, biographies, works of criticism and interpretation, some branches of philosophy, and indeed, the more precise labours of the reconstruction of the monuments of the past—social, religious, literary—works of art, buildings, cities. It was the psychological gifts required for imaginative reconstruction of forms of life—ideally to read the symbols with which societies and civilizations express themselves as a graphologist reads handwriting—if not as they were, at least, as they could have been, as well as the intellectual capacity for weighing the empirical evidence for and against the authenticity of such accounts that were demanded by the new kind of history, and so sharply divided its founders—Boeckh and Niebuhr, Augustin Thierry and Guizot, Ranke and, above all, Burckhardt and after him Dilthey—from even the best writers of the Renaissance or the Enlightenment. 'Even a half-mistaken historical perspective is worth a great deal more than no perspective at all', wrote Burckhardt in a letter in 1859.[1] To have opened doors to this great enlargement of the human spirit is the achievement of the two thinkers with whom this book is concerned.

---

[1] Quoted by Peter Gay in *Style in History*, p. 179 (Jonathan Cape, London, 1975).

The Philosophical Ideas of
GIAMBATTISTA
VICO

*Singulière destinée de cet homme! Lui, qui fut si intuitif,
il sort du tombeau lorsqu'il n'a plus à enseigner.*[1]
*Historici utiles non qui facta crassius et genericas caussas
narrant, sed qui ultimas factorum circumstantias
persequuntur, et caussarum peculiares reserant.*[2]

[1] Pierre-Simon Ballanche, *Essai de Palingénésie Sociale*, 1830.
[2] This may be translated as follows: 'The useful historians
are not those who give general descriptions of facts and explain
them by reference to general conditions, but those who go
into the greatest detail and reveal the particular cause of each
event.' Giambattista Vico, *De Antiquissima Italorum Sapientia
ex Linguae Originibus Eruenda*, Cap. 2 (Opere, ed. Fausto
Nicolini, I, Laterza, Bari, 1914, p. 135).

PART ONE

General Theory

I

VICO's life and fate is perhaps the best of all known examples of what is too often dismissed as a romantic fiction—the story of a man of original genius, born before his time, forced to struggle in poverty and illness, misunderstood and largely neglected in his lifetime and (save among a handful of Neapolitan jurists) all but totally forgotten after his death. Finally, when after many years he is at last exhumed and acclaimed by an astonished nation as one of its greatest thinkers, it is only to be widely misrepresented and misinterpreted, and even today to be accorded less than his due, because the *anagnorisis* has come too late, and during the century that followed his death ideas similar to his were better expressed by others, while he is best remembered for the least original and valuable of his doctrines. It is true that Vico's style tends to be baroque, undisciplined and obscure; and the eighteenth century, which came close to taking the view that not to say things clearly is not to say them at all, buried him in a grave from which not even his devoted Italian commentators have fully succeeded in raising him. Yet his ideas are of an arresting novelty, a half-abandoned quarry of fascinating, if ill-developed, ideas unique even in his own intellectually fertile age.

Vico's claim to originality will stand scrutiny from any point of vantage. His theories of the nature and development of the human mind, of culture, society and human history are audacious and profound. He developed a novel theory of knowledge which in the hands of others played a decisive rôle. He distinguished for the first time a central type of human knowledge, which had been misunderstood or neglected by previous thinkers. He was a bold innovator in the realms of natural law and jurisprudence, aesthetics and the philosophy of mathematics. Indeed his conception of mathematical reasoning was so revolutionary that full justice could scarcely have been done to it until the transformation effected by the logicians of the twentieth century, and it has not been fully recognized for what it is even now. More than this, Vico virtually invented a new field of social knowledge, which embraces social anthropology, the comparative and historical studies of philology, linguistics, ethnology, jurisprudence, literature, mythology, in effect the history of civilization in the broadest sense. Finally, he put forward a cyclical view of human history, which, although it is significantly different from those of Plato, Aristotle, Polybius, and their followers in the Italian Renaissance, and has had some influence on later thinkers, is probably the best known and the least valuable among his achievements.

One can readily understand that in the case of a thinker so rich and so confused, and above all so genuinely seminal—the forerunner of so many of the boldest ideas of later, more celebrated, thinkers—there is a permanent temptation to read too much into him, especially to sense intimations, perceive embryonic forms and prefigured contours of notions dear to the interpreter himself. Michelet, Dilthey, Croce, Collingwood (and less certainly Herder and Hegel) are among his progeny, and some among them, notably Michelet and Croce, consciously or unconsciously tried to repay their debt by attributing too many of their own most characteristic ideas and attitudes, sometimes at the cost of patent anachronism, to Vico's writings. To attribute one's own opinions to an earlier thinker is doubtless a sincere form of admiration. It is one of the attributes of intellectual depth that very different minds fancy that they find their own reflection in it. But this characteristic is purchased at a price, and has rendered Vico a disservice. Neither the romantic humanist of Michelet's fervid imagination, nor the more plausibly drawn quasi-Hegelian metaphysician celebrated by Croce (still less Gentile's bold variation of this), nor Professor Paci's protoexistentialist, nor Professor Nicola Badaloni's naturalistic forerunner of Feuerbach, reveal enough of Vico's own original shape and colour. The devoted labours of the most scrupulous, scholarly and dedicated of the editors and glossators of Vico, Fausto Nicolini, provide a marvellous monument of lucid learning, but no more.[1] There is, as in the case of all authentic thinkers, no substitute for reading the original. This is no easy labour, but—here one can only speak from personal

[1] Neither the later Italian scholars, with A. Corsano and Paolo Rossi at their head, nor the admirable German critics Erich Auerbach and Karl Löwith, nor the English-speaking students of Vico, among whom Professor Max Harold Fisch is the most distinguished, widely as their interpretations differ, can, for the most part, be charged with a tendency to transform Vico into a vehicle for their own ideas.

experience—the reward is great. Few intellectual pleasures are comparable to the discovery of a thinker of the first water.

Giovanni Battista Vico was born in 1668, the son of a bookseller in Naples. He died there in 1744. Apart from the few years which he spent in nearby Vatolla in Cilento, as a tutor to the sons of Domenico Rocca, Marchese di Vatolla, he never left his native city. All his life he had hoped to be appointed to the principal chair of Jurisprudence in his native city, but only succeeded in holding various lower posts in the related field oᶠ 'rhetoric', ending with an inferior professorship which he held from 1699 until 1741. It provided him with a modest salary, and obliged him to deliver a number of inaugural lectures, some of which contain his most original ideas. He eked out his low income by accepting commissions from the rich and the grand to write Latin inscriptions, official eulogies and laudatory biographies of important persons. The best known of these are his life of Antonio Caraffa, a Neapolitan *condottiere* in the service of the Emperor, and an account of the unsuccessful Macchia conspiracy in Naples. Caraffa's campaigns involved Vico in the study of inter-state relations, and it is probably this that caused him to read Grotius and other philosophical jurists. This had a decisive effect on his own ideas. The story of the Macchia was concerned with an attempt made at the turn of the century to replace Spanish by Austrian rule in Naples. The plot was uncovered, and in 1701 the ringleaders were executed by the Spaniards. In 1702 Vico published an account of the conspiracy denouncing the participants as criminals and traitors. Five years later the Austrians acquired Naples and held it for the next twenty-seven years. In 1708 Vico issued a memorial volume which made no reference to the earlier work and celebrated the two chief conspirators as patriots and martyrs. In 1734 Naples was reoccupied by Spain. The new ruler, Charles de Bourbon, was duly offered humble congratulations by Vico at the head of a delegation sent by the University of Naples, and, in the following year, graciously appointed Vico historiographer royal. Political courage was no more characteristic of Vico than of Leibniz or a good many other scholars and philosophers of the age; nor did the political issues seem to be as clear, or as profoundly felt, as those of earlier or later times.

In 1692 Vico wrote a poem, in a conventional *genre*, on despair and the vanity of human wishes. None of these works are today of more than biographical interest. The poem (*Affetti d'un Disperato*) expresses Lucretian-Epicurean sentiments which he was later exceedingly anxious to disclaim. It contains no trace of orthodox Christian belief, and constitutes important evidence of the preoccupations in the last decade of the century of Vico and his free-thinking friends, to whom he appears to have been closer than his autobiography would lead one to believe. The first work by him containing original ideas appeared in 1709, in the form of his last routine inaugural lecture in Latin, and attracted little attention. It was entitled 'On the Method of the Studies of Our Time'[1] and contains important adumbrations of his later work. This was followed a year later by a major Latin treatise 'On the oldest wisdom of the Italians',[2] which attracted more attention. Both these works, one in the guise of an educational programme, the other of a linguistic and legal investigation of a fancifully conceived tradition of ancient Italian thought, advanced some of his boldest hypotheses in the philosophy of history. Some ten years later, in 1719, he published, also in Latin, an oration on Universal Law, and, in the following two years, an expansion of this, called 'About the Single Principle of Universal Law and Its Single Purpose',[3] the second part of which deals with specific topics in jurisprudence. This was almost certainly his bid for the First Chair of Jurisprudence at the university that he long and passionately hoped for. The election had been pre-arranged long before, and he was not appointed. He claimed, not without some bitterness, that this was a blessing in disguise, for it enabled him to devote himself freely to the new philosophical ideas which took possession of him. Four years later, in 1724, he completed a treatise refuting the views of some of the most admired thinkers of the age—the jurists Grotius, Selden and Pufendorf, the philosophers Hobbes, Spinoza, Locke and Bayle, the scholars Casaubon, Saumaise and Voss. His patron, Cardinal Corsini, later Pope Clement XII, to whom it was dedicated, declined to provide the sum which he had promised for its publication. In despair, Vico sold his only valuable possession, a ring, but this covered only a quarter of the required amount. Thereupon

[1] De Nostri Temporis Studiorum Ratione, delivered in 1708 and published by Mosca in Naples in the following year. There is an English translation of this work, with an illuminating introduction by the translator, Professor Elio Gianturco, entitled On the Study Methods of Our Time (The Library of Liberal Arts, Bobbs-Merrill, New York, 1965).

[2] The full title is De Antiquissima Italorum Sapientia ex Linguae Latinae Originibus Eruenda—'On the oldest wisdom of the Italians recoverable from the origins of the Latin language', commonly referred to as De Antiquissima.

[3] De Universi Juris Uno Principio et Fine Uno (Il Diritto Universale), 1720-22.

Vico cut out the entire 'negative' part of the work—the attack on the Natural Law theorists, contractualists, neo-Stoics, neo-Epicureans, Aristotelians, Cartesians—the most influential schools of the age—and retained only his own positive doctrine. The excised portion is lost. The book, shrunk to a quarter of its original size, was published a year later. This was his crowning masterpiece, 'The New Science'. The first edition appeared in 1725; the second and altered version—virtually a new composition—in 1730, reprinted with additions in 1744, the year of his death.

In the same year, he wrote down an account of his own intellectual development. He composed it at the invitation of a rich Venetian dilettante, Count Gian Artico di Porcía, to whom the notion of inviting learned men to record the most important steps in their intellectual development may have been suggested by his friend the Abbé Conti, a well-known man of letters. Conti was a friend and correspondent of a number of German scholars and intellectuals, one of whom, the great Leibniz, had written to their common friend, Louis Bourguet, expressing his regret that men who had made great discoveries often left no record of the steps by which they had arrived at them. Porcía invited the leading scholars and thinkers of Italy to contribute accounts of their mental development to be published in a single anthology. In this casual fashion the art of intellectual autobiography was born. The editors expressed their delight with Vico's contribution, which, they were enlightened enough to realize, was a perfect model of the *genre* which they sought to establish. Indeed, to his extreme annoyance, they circulated it as a model to other contributors. Vico, who never ceased altering and correcting, made some additions to it later.

The *Autobiography* is a vivid and arresting record of the life of a man wholly preoccupied with philosophical issues. When Vico said that he was a solitary traveller in territory hitherto traversed by no one, this often repeated classical cliché for once expressed the literal truth. Vico knew that he had made discoveries unlike any that had been made before, and he knew that these discoveries were of cardinal importance. The violent intensity of his intellectual life, and its remoteness from the pathetic worries and humiliations of his lowly academic existence, was to some degree a compensation for his degraded status as a client of clerical and secular patrons. He lived in embittered poverty; he had little contact with the life round him; he was a cripple all his life as a result of a fall in childhood. His elder son became a criminal, one of his daughters was diseased from birth, all his devotion went to his younger son for whom he managed to secure the succession to his chair. After his son, he loved his library best. Like Machiavelli, he escaped from his miseries into the world of books: Plato, Varro, Mucius Scaevola, Lucretius, Tacitus, Ulpian, were more real to him than the writers of his own time, except, perhaps, Bacon, whom he adored, and Descartes, against whom he turned. All his life he lacked the most precious possessions of a scholar—tranquillity and leisure. He was a timid, obsequious, poverty- and anxiety-ridden scholar, who wrote too much and in haste, 'in the midst of the conversation of his friends, and the chatter and clatter of his children', but he knew that he had made a major discovery and had opened a door to a world of which he alone was master, and the thought, so he tells us in his autobiography, made him happy and serene.[1]

One of his listeners described him as a man 'lean, with a rolling eye, ferule in hand', who lectured with an intensity of eloquence which fascinated his students. He was much respected by his learned Italian contemporaries. The great historiographer Muratori procured his election to the Academy of the Assorditi; the eminent jurist Gravina admired his learning. But it is clear that neither of these great lights of their age (Gravina, it is true, died before the publication of the *Scienza Nuova*), nor even Conti, had any inkling that their admired friend possessed gifts of an altogether different order from their own. Certainly there is no evidence that any of his fellow scholars had begun to realize that Vico was a man of genius, and that his ideas about history and about natural law would one day render many of their own assumptions obsolete.

He had been taught by priests, and received a strictly traditional education in the, at that time, deeply clerical kingdom of Naples. But despite this almost exclusively mediaeval diet, scholastic philosophy left

[1] This was not as true as he wished, and, perhaps, believed, it to be. To the end of his life he longed for recognition, which had so signally been refused him in Naples. His letter to the Protestant French editor of a learned journal is revealing in this regard. He begs this man of letters, Jean Leclerc, who had written him a laudatory letter, for the favour of a word in his publication, which would, he feels sure, make the name of Vico resound throughout Europe. (F. Nicolini: 'Due Lettere inedite di G. B. Vico a Giovanni Leclerc'. *Revue de Littérature Comparée*, vol. IX, p. 737, 1929, quoted by Paul Hazard in *La Crise de la Conscience Européenne*, Paris, 1935, translated into English under the title *The European Mind*, Meridian Books, p. 76.)

comparatively little trace upon his thought, and merely saddled him for life with a ponderous and pedantic manner of writing. His interest was excited by the new philosophy, which had, half a century before, been initiated by Grotius and Descartes, and had been developed and applied by their followers with revolutionary results to the natural sciences and legal, political and metaphysical thought. Vico fully understood the aims and methods of this revolution. It liberated him and his entire generation from Aristotle and the schoolmen. He began by accepting its method, but then rebelled against it; indeed, he was the most original figure in what may be called the Counter-Reformation in the history of early modern philosophy. Vico was not interested in mathematics or in the natural sciences as such. Despite the efforts of Vincenzo Cuoco in his own century, and Fausto Nicolini in ours, to acclaim his geophysical and medical discoveries, Vico was remote from the scientific revolution of his time; his physics was the physics of Zeno, only remotely touched by imperfect acquaintance with Leibniz. He seems to have had no notion of what Galileo had achieved, and did not begin to grasp the effect of the new science upon the lives of men. He grew progressively more hostile to the assimilation of all knowledge to mathematical and physical models, and became preoccupied by problems of jurisprudence, humane learning and social psychology. Above all he grew more and more deeply convinced that earlier philosophy had failed to do justice to the methods and power of the sort of knowledge which he came to regard as central to human studies: in particular, the study of history. He conceived this study in the widest and most philosophical fashion—as being concerned with what it was for men to constitute a fully human society, more particularly, how men came to think, feel, act, live as they did. This sprang from his growing conviction that not a timeless analysis, but a genetic approach, that is, historical investigation, could alone discover and describe the relationships between various aspects of human experience and activity. Certainly no philosophy that failed to provide a method and criteria of truth for dealing with these matters, could, in his view, have any claim to authority in the field of human knowledge.

The starting point of Vico's revolt against Descartes was his conviction, articulated fully in 1708-9, that the Cartesian criteria of clear and distinct ideas could not profitably be applied outside the field of mathematics and natural science. The paradigm of true knowledge, according to the Cartesian school, consisted in beginning from truths so clear and so distinct that they could be contradicted only on pain of falling into absurdities; and in proceeding thence, by strict deductive rules, to conclusions whose truth was guaranteed by the unbreakable rules of deduction and transformation by which, as in mathematics, they were derived from their unassailable, eternally true, premisses. It was obvious to Vico, as indeed it had been to Descartes himself, that this model was inapplicable to the field of what today we call humane studies. Where in history, or in classical scholarship, or in literature, can we find strict definitions, rigorous proofs, concepts exhaustively analysed into their ultimate atomic constituents, demonstrated theorems, luminous and self-evident premisses leading with inexorable logic to unalterable conclusions? The application of such an *a priori*, deductive schema to any piece of narrative, or critical analysis of a work of art, or a historical or legal work or monument, or an account of the moral or intellectual development of an individual or a society, will not yield results. Descartes had seen this all too clearly, and had, in consequence, bluntly asserted that, while history, like travel, might do little harm as a casual source of entertainment, it was plainly not a branch of knowledge in which what had once been established did not need to be proved again, that is to say, in which scientific progress, universally recognized as such by rational thinkers, was possible. 'Memorable actions . . . elevate the mind . . .' he declared, and they might even help 'to form judgment', but otherwise they were of small value. Why study the chaotic amalgam of childish stories about the past, still less the passions and crimes of our dark beginnings, when reason can provide true and final answers to the problems which had puzzled our irrational ancestors? Valid knowledge is to be obtained only by the methods of the sciences, which Descartes and his followers contrasted with the unscientific hotch-potch of sense perception, rumour, myth, fable, travellers' tales, romances, poetry and idle speculation that in their view passed for history and worldly wisdom, but did not provide material amenable to scientific, that is, mathematical, treatment. Hence, history and humane studies generally were relegated by Descartes to the province of miscellaneous information with which a serious man might while away an hour or two, but which was an unworthy object of a lifetime of study and meditation.[1] Vico was not prepared to accept

1 Descartes' view of humane learning may be gathered from such remarks as 'A man needs Greek or Latin no more than Low-Breton, to know the history of the Roman Empire no more than of the smallest country there is' (*La Recherche de la*

this. His Catholic piety alone was sufficient to turn him against so positivist an approach, beside which must be set his passion for legal history and antiquarian learning as such. Yet the arguments which he uses against Descartes are neither theological nor rhetorical nor subjective. He became convinced that the notion of timeless truths, perfect and incorrigible, clothed in universally intelligible symbols which anyone, at any time, in any circumstances, might be fortunate enough to perceive in an instantaneous flash of illumination, was (with the sole exception of the truths of divine revelation) a chimera. Against this dogma of Rationalism, he held that the validity of all true knowledge, even that of mathematics or logic, can be shown to be such only by understanding how it comes about, i.e. its genetic or historical development. In order to demonstrate this, he attacked the claims of the Cartesian school in the very field in which it felt itself strongest and most impregnable.

II

Descartes' new criterion of truth is that the judgments claiming to be true must be seen to consist of clear and distinct 'ideas', ultimate constituents which are 'simple', that is, not further analysable. These ultimate atomic entities of thought are conceived as being connected with one another by 'necessary' logical links, that is, such that to attempt to sever them by contradicting their nexus would lead to self-contradiction, since each atom is logically bound to none but a particular set of other atoms, each set being logically an island, distinct or separate from other similar systems of interconnected atoms. The doctrine further holds that the structures of such systems, and of movements in, or by, them, can be clearly, that is, logically or mathematically, described. What cannot in principle be stated in such terms is automatically defined as less or more delusive. This applies notably to the unstable, melting data of the human senses—sights, sounds, smells, tastes—with their frequently vague outlines and indefinite, kaleidoscopically altering hues or tones, and equally to that other realm of

---

Vérité: Oeuvres, ed. Adam et Tannery, X, p. 503), or the better known passage in the *Discours de la Méthode* on the unimportance of travel and the exaggerations of historians; to which must be added the contemptuous remarks about the study of the classics in the beginning of his essay on the 'Passions of the Soul'. It is principally against the *Discours*, with its, as it seemed to him, baseless claim to take all knowledge for its province, that Vico's polemic appears almost exclusively to be directed.

qualitative distinctions—'inner' psychical states, muscular sensations, states of feeling, dreams, images, memories, imprecise thoughts, wishes, purposes, and the like. This must apply to attempts to examine historical data, however scrupulously and however narrow their compass, where the factual evidence may indeed be plentiful, but cannot be formulated in precise quantitative terms. True intellectual progress clearly depends, as the natural sciences have shown, on the reduction of the matter to be studied to clear and distinct, i.e. mathematically expressible, concepts and judgments. Thus the devoted labours of antiquarians and historians to reconstruct, say, the events of the last years of the Roman Republic, can at best (as Descartes contemptuously remarked) furnish us with no more information than such as might have been possessed by Cicero's servant girl. Was this to be dignified by the name of science? Would anyone but an ignoramus or a bigot venture to deny that mathematical knowledge was the paradigm of all knowledge attainable by human beings, the collection of the clearest and most certain propositions thus far discovered by man's own efforts, the nearest approximation to infallible knowledge to which man had yet attained?

This is the triumphant thesis that Vico at first accepted and echoed, and then audaciously attacked. He rejected it after he had become convinced that whatever the splendours of the exact sciences, there was a sense in which we could know more about our own and other men's experiences—in which we acted as participants, indeed as authors, and not as mere observers—than we could ever know about non-human nature which we could only observe from outside. It seemed to him clear that the external world must remain opaque to men in a sense (which he endeavoured to make clear) in which it could be said that their own thoughts, feelings, purposes and volitions were not opaque, but capable of being understood. This is the position which he set himself to defend in 1708, in his seventh Inaugural Lecture. The distinction he draws is between 'outer' and 'inner' knowledge, what later came to be distinguished as *Naturwissenschaft* and *Geisteswissenschaft*. It was the opening shot in a battle which from that moment has never ceased.

Vico concedes that mathematical knowledge is indeed wholly valid and its propositions are certain. But the reason for this is only too clear: 'We demonstrate geometry because we make it';[1] similarly, sixteen years later, he says that geometry 'while it constructs out of

[1] *De Nostri Temporis Studiorum Ratione, op. cit.*, Section IV. The passage in question will be found on p. 23 of the English translation.

its elements or contemplates the world of quantity itself creates it'.[1]
This is a particular application of a wider principle, that full knowledge
can be only knowledge 'through causes', *per caussas* (in Vico's spelling);
according to this principle we can be said fully to know a thing if,
and only if, we know why it is as it is, or how it came to be, or was made
to be, what it is, and not merely that it is what it is, and has the attributes
it has.

The view that knowledge *per caussas* is superior to any other is an
old idea, frequently found in scholastic philosophy. Thus God knows
the world because He has made it in ways and for reasons which He
alone knows;[2] and we cannot know it in that full sense, because we
have not made it—because we find it 'ready made'—it is given to us
as a 'brute fact'. To the maker of a thing, particularly if (as in the case
of God) in addition to making the artefact, he has also made the material
out of which he constructs a thing, and, in addition, has invented the
rules in accordance with which he made it, nothing can in principle
be opaque. He is responsible for it all, and has made it in accordance
with his own will, out of stuff the reason for the existence and behaviour
of which he knows, since he has created it for purposes of his own,
which he alone (since he is the author) fully understands. This is the
sense in which, for instance, the novelist can be said to be capable of
fully understanding the characters of his novel, or the painter or composer the painting or the song. It is true that in the case of the writer
or the composer not everything has been made by him—the words
he uses, the sounds he employs, have not, for the most part, been
invented by him, and to that extent there is something that is even for
him 'brute fact'—a given medium which he is, within limits, free to
choose, but to which, having chosen it, he must submit, without
necessarily understanding the 'reasons for' its properties—without
knowing it *per caussas*—and which he can only alter within certain
limits. Only in the ideal case, where we make or design something out

---

[1] *Scienza Nuova* 349. All references to the *Scienza Nuova*, unless otherwise
indicated, are taken from the numbered paragraphs of the excellent English translation by Professors T. G. Bergin and M. H. Fisch (Cornell University Press, 1948).

[2] Indeed, for God, knowing and making are one act, as Augustine and Aquinas
had taught. (Aquinas, *Summa Theologiae*, I, 14, 8.12 quoting Augustine, *De
Trinitate*, XV, 13. On this see K. Löwith, *Verum et Factum Convertuntur* in *Omaggio
a Vico*, Napoli, 1968, which seems to me far more convincing than Croce's account
in his lecture on Vico's sources printed as Appendix III to R. G. Collingwood's
translation of his important and influential book on the philosophy of Vico.)

of literally nothing, can we be said fully to understand what we have made; for in that situation to create, and to know what and why we are creating, is a single act. This is how God creates. The nearer artistic creation approaches this limiting case—the greater the element of sheer creation and the smaller that of 'brute' matter obeying 'external' laws of its own—the more we can be said to understand *per caussas*, the more we truly know. This is virtually the case with algebra and arithmetic. The shapes of the symbols, auditory or visual, that we employ, are, it is true, made of sense-given material. But they are arbitrarily chosen, and are used as counters in a game that we ourselves have freely invented.

Geometrica demonstramus quia facimus. Vico was certainly familiar with Hobbes' *De Corpore*, in the beginning of which these words are contained. But he draws a further implication from it: '*Si physica demonstrare possemus, faceremus*':[1] if we could literally demonstrate the propositions of physics, we should be making it—i.e. we should be creating its object, the material world. But we cannot do this. Only God can do so, for 'in Him alone are the true forms of things after which nature is modelled . . .', and it is the quest for this reality that draws us towards God, who alone is the Truth and the Way. This is a form of Christian Platonism or neo-Platonism, and leads us back to the Renaissance doctrine that to know something is to become it: at any rate to dominate it. Thus Campanella declares that to know is to become what is known,[2] and Patrizzi says that to know is to be united with what one knows,[3] there being a mystical play on the notion of union—*coitus*—in *cognoscere*: 'co-knowing' is being made one with the thing known. This stems, perhaps, from the ancient metaphysical (and mystical) doctrine, of which Plato's Symposium contains the most memorable version, that in the beginning, subject and object, man and nature, sensation and thought, were one; then a great catastrophe divided them; since when they everlastingly seek reunion—re-integration—which can be achieved in 're'-cognition. Hence the belief in magic as the acquisition of power by the subject over the object, by re-entering it, immersing oneself in it, and so reassimilating it to oneself, a notion which is at the heart of much Renaissance natural philosophy. This is the meaning of Pico della Mirandola's celebrated

1 *De Nostri*, *op. cit.*, Section IV.
2 *Cognoscere est fieri rem cognitam.*
3 *Cognoscere est coire cum suo cognobili.*

proposition in his *Apologia* that 'Magic is identical with wisdom'.[1] There is no doubt that there is something in Vico of this doctrine of perfect knowledge as identical with creation, but for him only God can know reality in this sense; men cannot intuit it, they cannot contemplate Platonic essences, at any rate so far as the external world—the world of nature—is concerned. He does not believe, with Leonardo, for example, that reason obviates the need for experience.[2] Far from it: experience—empirical knowledge, above all study of the monuments of the past—is everything. But Janus-like, Vico faces both worlds; his anti-mathematical bias blends oddly with his genuine empiricism, and Meinecke's characterization of him as basically a *Barockmensch*, despite the arresting modernity of his central doctrines, is not inept: although it describes only the face turned to the past. However this may be, more important is his central doctrine which takes him far, at times too far, beyond Hobbes' thesis—namely, that mathematical knowledge is, in principle, not identical with knowledge of the real world: not even with that of physics, no matter how susceptible to mathematical treatment this science has proved to be. For we cannot literally manufacture the physical world as he supposes that we can that of algebra and geometry.

In an age when mathematics was almost universally considered to be a form of factual knowledge about nature, the deepest, most revealing and certain of all the sciences, the object of metaphysical insight of a power denied to the grosser senses, the special glory of human reason, able to reveal the real attributes of things as against their often blurred and always misleading appearances, it was a momentous step to declare that mathematics is indeed most clear, most rigorous and wholly irrefutable, but only because it is the free creation of our own minds, that mathematical propositions are true only because we ourselves have made them. This is the meaning of Vico's famous formula 'the true (*verum*) and the made (*factum*) are convertible'.[3] It may be doubted

---

[1] *Magia idem est quod sapientia.* For some of these neo-Platonic formulae see Ernst Cassirer, *Individuum und Kosmos in der Philosophie der Italienischen Renaissance*, English translation (Blackwell, Oxford, 1953), pp. 169 ff.

[2] *Intendi la ragione, e non ti bisogna esperienza* (quoted by Cassirer, *op. cit.*, p. 168, from the *Codice Atlantico*, fol. 147ᵛ).

[3] *Verum et factum convertuntur.* This bold statement was first published in 1710 in the treatise allegedly concerned with the ancient wisdom of the Italians (see p. 6, n. 2), hereafter referred to as *De Antiquissima*. The question of whether the doctrine of the interchangeability of *verum* and *factum* has mediaeval roots has been much

whether the eminent persons present on this occasion, e.g. the Vice-roy of Naples, or Cardinal Grimani, who listened to Vico's enunciation of this principle, were aware of the momentous nature of what was being said. In this they did not differ from most men of learning in their own or later times.

Algebra is an unshakeable deductive edifice, but it cannot give us factual information, any more than a game or a piece of fiction which we have made up can, as such, describe the world to us. Mathematics is not determined by reality outside itself, to which it has to conform, but only by our own fancy or creative imagination, which moulds the

---

disputed. Benedetto Croce, in a lecture published in the *Atti dell'Accademia Fontaniana*, March 10, 1912, argues that it does not come from the Thomists or scholastic philosophy in general, and establishes a good case against the deriva-tion from Ficino, Cardano, Scotus, or even Occam (in the version given to it by Sarpi), and others. These writers, and many others, had indeed remarked that what one creates one can fully know, but not the converse—that one can fully know only what one has created; the doctrine that perfect knowledge, whether rational, or resting on faith, is confined to what one has oneself made, does not appear to be an orthodox scholastic doctrine. The one actual formulation of this doctrine before Vico, among the authors examined by Croce, seems to be that of Sanchez, whom, as Croce notes, Vico certainly read, since he quotes from his *Opera Medica* of 1636 in a wholly different connection. But in Sanchez it seems to occur as a casual observation, with a sceptical intent common enough in the sixteenth and early seventeenth century writers: since men have created so little, their real knowledge is very small. The revolutionary implications of this formula were for the first time drawn by Vico, when he set himself to distinguish what man has created and could know, from what he cannot create, and consequently cannot know.

The relation of Vico's doctrine to Spinoza's doctrine of the relation of the *ordo et connexio rerum* to the *ordo et connexio idearum*: 'The order of ideas must follow the order of things', to which some commentators refer, is a good deal less plausible. There is more to be said for the parallel with the Renaissance doctrine of man as a microcosm of *natura naturans*—just as God alone understands the world he has created (which is identical with Nature) so man can understand in this 'divine', i.e. perfect, sense, only the world he himself creates. He possesses a derived, but nevertheless genuine capacity for creativity—a divine attribute. Moreover, in the unity—and parallelism—which obtains between the necessary succession of the phases of a civilization and the development of mental attributes and powers in the growing individual—Vico's *idée maîtresse*—the Renaissance notion of the relation-ship between the macrocosm and the microcosm is clearly central. The fullest development of this conception is, of course, to be found in Hegel's *Phenomenology*. It forms the basis of the historical theories of Marx, Comte and Croce, and bears directly on the phylogenesis-ontogenesis parallel in some versions of psycho-analytic theory. On Vico's possible sources see Part Two.

material (in this case, the symbols and rules) as it pleases. Once you try
to apply mathematics to the world, for example in the way in which
it is applied in the science of mechanics, the results are *pro tanto* less
certain than those of pure mathematics, because there enters an element
not freely created by us, namely the 'brute' matter of the external
world, resistant to our minds, of which mechanics seeks to be the
science. Then, in order of decreasing certainty, there come, according
to Vico, physics, psychology, history.[1] Certainty increases in inverse
ratio as the proportion of matter not made but merely found by us;
the smaller the element of free manipulation imported by ourselves, the
less certain our knowledge. *Mathesis* is a *scientia operatrix*: 'The
criterion of the truth', he declares in *De Antiquissima*, 'is to have made
it.'[2] 'Demonstration is operation; truth is what has been made, and
for this very reason we cannot demonstrate physics *per caussas* because
the elements which compose nature are outside us.'[3] We can no more
generate a pebble out of nothing than an entire universe. History, at
this point, is still rather low in the table of the sciences headed by
mathematics: physics, indeed, has been demoted—this is directed at
the presumption of the Cartesians—but the humanities come lower
still in terms of *verum*. This is Vico's semi-Cartesian position in middle
life, in about 1710. The degree of knowability of any subject matter
is determined both by the degree of the stability and regularity of its
'elements', and of the 'clarity' or 'opaqueness' of the object of investigation: thus *physica sunt opaca, nempe formata et finita*.[4] Hence we get
an order of the sciences determined by the extent to which the mind
is capable of penetrating them. Thus physics is more 'opaque' than
mechanics, mechanics than geometry and arithmetic; morality is even
less certain than physics, because it is concerned with unstable sentiments, something that is subject to the wayward waves of *libido*,
irregular 'movements of the inner spirit tossed about by passions'.
History is to be found in this somewhat chaotic region, somewhere
at the level of morality. In other words, physics has been demoted from
its Cartesian pinnacle, but history has not been promoted yet; that

[1] *De Antiquissima, op. cit.* (*Opere* I, ed. G. Gentile and F. Nicolini, Laterza, Bari,
1914, p. 150.)
[2] *Veri criterium est ipse fecisse.*
[3] *Demonstratio eadem ac operatio fit, et verum idem ac factum. Atque obidipsum
physica a caussis probare non possumus, quia elementa rerum naturalium extra nos sint.*
[4] This is the central doctrine of *De Antiquissima*.

radical move is still to come.[1] At this stage of his thought he has not moved from the deeply Cartesian position which he held eight years before, in 1702, when in his third Inaugural Oration, he mocked his fellow humanists with the words: 'You boast, philologist, of knowing everything about the furniture and clothes of the Romans, of being more intimate with the streets, tribes and quarters of Rome, than with those of your own city; why this pride? You know no more than did a potter, a cook, a cobbler, a summoner, an auctioneer in Rome'.[2] This is an echo of Descartes' gibe about the fact that historians of Rome can know at best no more than Cicero's servant girl. Ten years later, however, in 1712, in the Second Reply to criticisms of De Antiquissima, Vico complains that philological studies are regarded as useless nowadays 'on the authority of Descartes', and repeats the remark about the servant girl, this time with obvious disapproval.[3]

If the only perfect knowledge is *per caussas*—the creator's own knowledge of his creature—what becomes of Descartes' crucial criterion of clear and distinct ideas? Vico boldly takes the war into the enemy's country. He declares that factual propositions can be exceedingly clear—in the sense of seeming wholly self-evident—and yet be false.[4] If there is only a single criterion of the truth or the validity of a proposition, namely, that such a proposition consists of or can be analysed into 'simple', indivisible ingredients, this would instantly rule out the greater part of our most common experience, that is, whatever is not susceptible to quantitative treatment. Such knowledge may not

---

[1] *Scientiae minus certae, prout aliae aliis magis in materia corpulenta immerguntur: uti minus certa mechanice quam geometrica et arithmetica, quia considerat motum sed machinarum ope: minus certa physice quam mechanice … minus certa moralis quam physica.* This is so because the '*motus animorum qui penitissimi sunt*' are very unstable whereas physics is concerned with '*motus interni corporum qui sunt a natura quae certa est*'. (*De Antiquissima, Opere, op. cit.*, I, p. 132 and pp. 136-7.)

[2] *Gloriaris, philologe, omnem rem vasariam, vestiariam, Romanorum nosse et magis Romae quam tuae urbis vias, tribus, regiones callere. In quo superbis? Nihil aliud scis, quam figulus, coquus, sutor, viator, praeco Romanus.* (*Oratio*, III, *Opere*, vol. I, pp. 35 ff.)

[3] See Introduction to *The Autobiography of Giambattista Vico*, translated and edited by M. H. Fisch and T. G. Bergin, p. 37 (Great Seal Books, Cornell University Press, 1962).

[4] Vico seems to suspect that Descartes' criterion of clarity and distinctness is, in the end, not logical by psychological, and therefore subjective and liable to error—see his letter to Esperti of 1726 (*L'Autobiografia, il cartiggio e le poesie varie*, ed. B. Croce, Laterza, Bari, 1911, p. 186).

be of *verum*—of what can be logically demonstrated—but it is knowledge nevertheless, of *certum*, based on direct experience of the world,
what is common to all men, everywhere, at all times—on which all
empirical knowledge is based. Such 'certainty' may not be incorrigible, but it is what men necessarily live by: to relegate it to the
sphere of mere opinion, as Descartes appears to do, is to imply that
ideally men could live by true knowledge—*verum*—alone. Vico per-
ceives that if his view of *a priori* knowledge is correct, this cannot
possibly be so. For the only objects we can know through and
through—in the sense required by Descartes—are what we have
wholly created. Even geometry, on reflection, if it is interpreted as a
metric of space (and not as pure algebra) remains only a tool leading to
no more than tentative results; for we have not created physical space.
If the only true knowledge is knowledge of necessary connections,
then it is knowledge only of what obeys the rules that we have ourselves made: for nothing else can be known *a priori*.[1] We can wholly
guarantee the validity, of necessity, only of what we have ourselves
wholly invented: but this would plainly exclude the entire world of
men and nature. We cannot know this *a priori*, it cannot be *verum*
for us; yet we cannot begin to do without it, for it constitutes the
basic data of all human experience. Only the Creator looking at, or
rather 'within', himself, that is, at the Universe which is identical
with his own self, can be said to have knowledge in this sense.
Being author of all, he contemplates only the fruit of his own creative
activity. Men can fully know only what they (being made in the
image of God, and consequently creative within limits), in their turn,
have made. But they are not gods; they must begin with material
not made by themselves, and so not fully knowable by them.

Hobbes, following Bacon, had said something along these lines: 'Of
arts, some are demonstrable, others indemonstrable; and demonstrable
are those the construction of the subject whereof is in the power of the
artist himself, who, in his demonstration, does no more but deduce the
consequences of his own operation. . . . Geometry therefore is demonstrable, for the lines and figures from which we reason are drawn and
described by ourselves; and civil philosophy is demonstrable, because we
make the commonwealth ourselves. But because of natural bodies we
know not the construction, but seek it from the effects, there lies no

---

[1] It is, perhaps, this doctrine that led Jacobi, and later, Franz von Baader, to see
Vico as a forerunner of Kant.

demonstration of what the causes be we seek for, but only of what they may be.'[1] Vico develops this by drawing a crucial distinction between the fullest and clearest knowledge in physics, and full demonstration, to which even proofs in physics are not equivalent. For 'the things which are proved in physics are those to which we can perform something similar, and ideas about natural things which are thought to have the most perfect clarity, and on which there is the completest consensus, are those to the support of which we can bring experiments by which we so far imitate nature'.[2] But experiment is not creation, yet it gives knowledge because by its means we recreate the processes of nature. What we can take to pieces and reassemble, we know—know the 'working of'—in a more genuine sense than that of which we, as it were, see only the surface and the outward changes. Yet to the extent to which we do not ourselves create physical matter or its laws, physics is not a demonstrative science and therefore not fully knowable. Only so far as it yields to experiment and is susceptible to mathematical treatment can it be, to that limited degree, called a science at all.

On this topic Vico is eloquent and unequivocal. 'The rule and criterion of truth is to have made it. Hence the clear and distinct idea of the mind, i.e. the Cartesian criterion, not only cannot be the criterion of other truths, but it cannot be the criterion of the mind itself; for while the mind apprehends itself, it does not make itself, and because it does not make itself, it is ignorant of the former mode by which it apprehends itself.'[3] And, still more boldly: 'Those who try to prove that God exists *a priori* are guilty of impious curiosity. For to do that is tantamount to making oneself the god of God, thereby denying the God one seeks.'[4]

If I can be said to know beyond the possibility of error only what I myself have—or could have—created, only mathematics can be called knowledge. This is evidently regarded by Vico as too paradoxical. For it would follow that not only natural, i.e. scientific, knowledge can no longer be called knowledge, but metaphysics and theology, if they are not to be regarded as man-made fictions, fall too. We should be forced to rule out the greater part of what even Descartes regarded as valid

---

1 Thomas Hobbes, *English Works* (ed. W. Molesworth), VII, 183 f., quoted in the Introduction by Professor M. H. Fisch to *The Autobiography of Giambattista Vico*, op. cit., Great Seal edition, p. 211, n. 39.

2 *De Antiquissima*, op. cit., I, p. 136.

3 ibid. (See Vico, *Autobiography*, op. cit., 1944 edition, pp. 38-39.)

4 op. cit., I, p. 150.

knowledge. Vico is not a sceptic nor an irrationalist, and looks on this as a kind of *reductio ad absurdum*. Hence Descartes is dismissed, firstly because of the inadequacy of his (psychological) criteria of truth, and secondly for not realizing that mathematics is rigorous only because it is arbitrary, that is, consists in the use of conventions freely adopted as in the playing of a game; and is not, as had hitherto been generally supposed, a set of innate and objective rules, or a discovery about the structure of the world. This theory of mathematics as the manipulation of counters lay unregarded until our own time, when it became a leading doctrine.[1] It must not be confused with the view that mathematical propositions are analytic or tautologous. Tautologies are statements, though they may not describe anything; inventions, like rules or moves in games, do not state at all. It is one thing to regard deductive reasoning as giving us no new information (an ancient commonplace), and quite a different one to say that it is, like music, an activity. Similarly, it is one thing to warn against confusing the causes of things with their definitions, or facts with symbols (which nominalists had done even before Occam), and much more startling to suppose, as Vico did, that formal sciences, like mathematics or logic, are not forms of discovery at all but of invention, so that if they are to be called true and false, it must be in a sense widely different from that in which these words are applied to statements.[2]

III

Vico's next large step was a thesis which undermined the accepted division of all knowledge into three kinds: metaphysical or theological, i.e. based on rational intuition or faith or revelation; deductive, as in logic or grammar or mathematics; and perceptual, based on empirical observation, refined and extended by hypotheses, experiment, induction, and the other methods of the natural sciences. There exists, for him, yet another type of awareness, unlike *a priori* knowledge in that it is empirical, unlike deduction in that it yields new knowledge of facts, and unlike perception of the external world, in that it informs us not merely of what exists or occurs, and in what spatial or temporal

[1] *This footnote is printed on p. 142.*

[2] Let me give an illustration. When Torricelli asserted that to say of a horse that it is rational is like uttering a mathematical contradiction, this might have seemed valid to an Aristotelian, perhaps even to a Cartesian. But for Vico it would constitute a confusion of two wholly distinct types of truth (and of nonsense), and therefore be an utterly misleading analogy.

order, but also why what is, or occurs, is as it is, i.e. in some sense *per caussas*. This species is self-knowledge: knowledge of activities of which we, the knowing subjects, are ourselves the authors, endowed with motives, purposes and a continuous social life, which we understand, as it were, from inside. Here and only here we are not passive observers looking on from the outside, as when we contemplate the external world, where all that we can see are events, or the 'surfaces' of things about the inner lives or goals of which—or whether, indeed, they have, or in principle could be said to have, goals, or inner lives— we can only darkly speculate.

In the case of the external world the naturalists are right: all that we know is based on what the senses report. We can classify their contents into regular uniformities, apply mathematical techniques, decompose them into smaller parts, re-combine them, but the result of our investigations will be no more than a report of what stands in what spatial relation to what, or what follows, or is simultaneous with, what else. Yet to say that this is all we can know about human beings, and that the techniques of our ways of apprehending the external world are, therefore, all that we can use in learning about each other, would be a grave understatement, a denial of what we know to be true. In the case of human behaviour we can surely ask why men act as they do; ask not merely what mental states or events, e.g. feelings or volitions, are followed by what acts, but also why; not only whether, but also why persons in this or that mental or emotional state are or are not likely to behave in a given fashion, what is, or what would be, rational or desirable or right for them to do, how and why they decide between various courses of action, and so on. In short, we judge human activity in terms of purposes, motives, acts of will, decisions, doubts, hesitations, thoughts, hopes, fears, desires, and so forth; these are among the ways in which we distinguish human beings from the rest of nature. We expect to obtain answers, less or more satisfactory, to such questions. To conceive of non-human nature in such terms is irrational: a misapplication of categories, called anthropomorphism or animism, characteristic of primitive times, the ages of 'the Gods' or of 'the heroes', or, when it was used by poets in more sophisticated times, liable to be called the pathetic fallacy.

These things were affirmed by Vico before Herder and the Romantics made them their own. There are adumbrations of this position in the Italian Renaissance, particularly among the neo-Platonists, and in

French historiography in the sixteenth century, but they are no more than adumbrations. No one before Vico declared that if our knowledge of human beings is not demonstrative in the way in which mathematics (or divine omniscience) is so, neither is it that of perception or the natural sciences, based on the senses, as our knowledge of material objects or plants and animals must be. We can perceive and describe a table, a tree, an ant, accumulate information about their behaviour, establish laws such as those of physics, botany, entomology and so on, but all this, even at its fullest, will tell us only what it is to look like a table, a tree, an ant, or to move, or be causally affected like one. What we still cannot tell is what it is like to *be* a table, a tree, an ant, in the sense in which we do know what it is not merely to look or behave like, but to be, a human being. If, following Descartes' rigorous rule, we allowed only that to be true knowledge which could be established by physics or other natural sciences, we should be confined to behaviourist tests, and this would result in the opposite fallacy to that of anthropomorphism, namely the uncritical assimilation of the human world to the non-human—the restriction of our knowledge to those characteristics of men which they share with the non-human world; and consequently the attempt to explain human behaviour in non-human terms, as some behaviourists and extreme materialists, both ancient and modern, inspired by the vision (or mirage) of a single, integrated, natural science of all there is, have urged us to do. It may be that a good deal more can be said in such purely 'physicalist' language than its opponents have, at times, thought possible; but certainly not enough. For we should find ourselves debarred by such self-imposed austerity from saying or thinking some of the most natural and indispensable things that men constantly say or think about other human beings. The reason is not far to seek: men can think of others only as being like themselves.

Just as we can say with assurance that we ourselves are not only bodies in space, acted upon by measurable natural forces, but that we think, choose, follow rules, make decisions, in other words, possess an inner life of which we are aware and which we can describe, so we take it for granted—and, if questioned, say that we are certain—that others possess a similar inner life, without which the notion of communication, or language, or of human society, as opposed to an aggregate of human bodies, becomes unintelligible. Anthropomorphism is the fallacy of attributing specifically human characteristics to non-human entities—gods or rivers or planets or abstract notions. It follows that there must exist a region in which anthropomorphism is valid, where these characteristics are not misapplied but correctly attributed, namely the world of men. To speak as if even men did not possess these attributes, or that they can be 'reduced' to characteristics shared with non-human entities which alone can form the subject matter of any reputable natural science, is to ignore the distinction between human beings and non-human nature, between material objects and mental or emotional life. Why has this knowledge been so strangely ignored in comparison with that of the external world? Because men, Vico declares, find it difficult to think of anything in other than bodily terms, in as much as bodies are the most familiar entities in the world of their common experience. Vico stresses over and over again how difficult it is to concentrate on, discriminate and describe mental activity. 'The human mind is naturally inclined to see itself externally in the body, and only with great difficulty does it come to understand itself by means of reflection.'[1] Hence there is a powerful tendency to describe mental phenomena in corporeal terms, which leads to crude materialism on the one hand, and fetishism and animism on the other.

The emphasis on this contrast, which runs through all Vico's thought, is, in effect, the original formulation of the familiar and much controverted distinction between the methods and goals of *Naturwissenschaft* and *Geisteswissenschaft*—natural science as against humane studies, *Wissen* and *Verstehen*. If some of the central categories of interpretation of human behaviour are in principle different from those used in explaining facts about animals or plants or things, this is a fact of cardinal importance. For it points to a type of knowledge which, in at least some respects, differs in kind from deduction, from sense perception as well as generalizations based upon it, and from scientific or immediate sense-based kinds of knowledge, as they are normally understood. Vico plainly regards such cognition as being superior to anything based on mere observation, since it is knowledge of what we ourselves have in some sense created and of which we consequently possess an intimate knowledge *per caussas*—'from within'—a capacity with which men have been endowed from their earliest beginnings without consciously realizing this: like Monsieur Jourdain, who did not know that he was speaking prose.

This distinction is not wholly absent from the thought of earlier

---

[1] N.S. 236.

Italian thinkers. In 1452 Gianozzo Manetti in his *De Dignitate et Excellentia Hominis* proclaims 'ours, that is, human, because made by men, are what we gaze upon: all houses, all towns, all cities, all the buildings in the world. Ours are paintings, ours are sculptures, ours are the arts, ours the sciences ... and all the inventions, ours the varieties of different languages and of diverse letters ...'[1] Ours, that is, as against those of Nature. So, too, Marsilio Ficino declares 'We are not slaves of nature, we emulate her'.[2] And this is echoed by Pico, Bouelles, Bruno. The conception of man as an autonomous being, a creator and moulder of himself and the world, is a notion often found in the Renaissance and indeed both before it and in the sixteenth century in France. Vico's momentous step is to have combined this notion with the older idea of the Schoolmen, that we can truly know only what we create;[3] and—the most audacious step of all—to apply this not only to the works of man in general, conceived in timeless fashion, the *urbes* and *artes* and *scientiae*, but to his history conceived as a collective, social experience extended through time; that is, not as a passive acceptance of 'ideas' showered upon men (as both Descartes and Locke in their different ways conceived human consciousness), but as a perpetual 'intentional' activity, a ceaseless employment of historically changing conceptions, categories, interpretations, mythical, symbolic, metaphysical, logical, empirical, an endless probing, questioning, ordering and moulding and goal-seeking, which characterize the restless human mind.

This is the revelation to the exposition of which Vico dedicated the second and most creative part of his long life. Descartes is the great deceiver, whose emphasis on knowledge of the external world as the paradigm of all knowledge has set philosophy on a false path. I know what it is to look like a tree, but I cannot know what it is to be a tree. But I do know what it is to be a mind, because I possess one, and create

---

[1] *Nostra namque, hoc est humana, sunt, quoniam ab hominibus effecta, quae cernuntur, omnes domus, omnia oppida, omnes urbes, omnia denique orbis terrarum aedificia. Nostrae sunt picturae, nostrae sculpturae, nostrae sunt artes, nostrae scientiae ... omnes adinventiones, nostrae omnium diversarum linguarum ac variarum litterarum genera ...*" (quoted by Giovanni Gentile in his *Concetto dell'Uomo nel Rinascimento*, reprinted in his *Giordano Bruno ed il Pensiero del Rinascimento* [Vallachi, Florence, 1920], pp. 111 ff).

[2] *Non servi sumus naturae, sed aemuli* (Theologia Platonica, XIII, p. 295).

[3] On the superior knowledge of those who play an active, as opposed to a passive, role in a process, see Part Two, pp. 106-7.

030835

with it. 'Create the truth which you wish to cognize, and I, in cognizing the truth that you have proposed to me, will "make" it in such a way that there will be no possibility of my doubting it, since I am the very one who has produced it.'[1] Vico is here speaking of scientific, in this sense, mathematical ideas. But it applies to all human invention. Men 'create' in doing or knowing or desiring; in this they are active, they do not simply record passively. Because, by action, they 'create', or mentally live through the creations of others, they have a more direct and intimate acquaintance with action than with the natural data that they merely observe outside themselves. This is Vico's reason for believing that human studies, inasmuch as they are concerned with both the content and the form of the entire field of men's activity—arts and sciences, custom and law, indeed every form of life and human relationship, expressed as they are in monuments, rites, in forms of symbolism and articulation, rudimentary and developed, emotional and reflective, abstract and concrete, collective and individual—that this great realm is intelligible to men, who are its authors, in a way in which nothing else can be. It is the nearest approach attainable by his creatures to divine knowledge which only the Creator of all things has of all things.

The truly revolutionary move is the application of the *verum/factum* principle to the study of history. Vico probably found a clue to this in Hobbes.[2] But Hobbes' statement that 'civil philosophy is demonstrable, because we make the commonwealth ourselves' seems to refer to conscious plans and arrangements: constitutions or blueprints, and other constructions of human minds: like geometrical figures, for example, that are fully intelligible or 'demonstrable' because they are literally invented. Vico transformed this notion and gave it immensely greater scope and depth (and increased its dangerously speculative character) by extending it to the growth in time of the collective or social consciousness of mankind, particularly at its pre-rational and semi-conscious levels, to the dreams and myths and images that have dominated men's thoughts and feelings from his earliest beginnings. Vico stated this bold thesis, of which he seems to be the only true

---

1 Quoted from the English version of Vico's reply to Article X of Volume 8 of the *Giornale dei Letterati d'Italia* (Venice, 1711), cited in *On the Study Methods of Our Time, op. cit.*, p. xxxi.

2 Did Vico read Hobbes in the original? Professor M. H. Fisch plausibly conjectures that he did not. (See Vico, *Autobiography, op. cit.*, Great Seal edition, p. 40).

begetter, in a famous passage in the *New Science*: 'In the night of thick
darkness enveloping the earliest antiquities, so remote from ourselves,
there shines the eternal and never failing light of a truth beyond all
question: that the world of civil society has certainly been made by
men, and that its principles are, therefore, to be found within the
modifications of our own human mind. Whoever reflects on this cannot
but marvel that the philosophers should have bent all their energies to
the study of the world of nature, which, since God made it, He alone
knows: and that they should have neglected the study of the world of
nations or civil world, which since men had made it, men could come
to know'.[1] By 'modifications' he appears to mean what we should mean
by the stages of the growth, or of the range or direction, of human
thought, imagination, will, feeling, into which any man equipped with
sufficient *fantasia* (as well as knowledge acquired by rational methods)
can 'enter'. Vico nowhere, so far as I know, fully or exactly explains
the way in which men understand other men—'know their minds',
grasp their goals, outlooks, ways of thinking, feeling, acting. He does
not account for our knowledge of other selves—individual or collective,
living or dead—by invoking the language of empathy, or analogical
reasoning, or intuition or participation in the unity of the World Spirit.
That has been left to his interpreters. He rests his case on his conviction
that what men have made, other men, because their minds are those of
men, can always, in principle, 'enter into'.[2]

This is the proclamation of the autonomy of historical studies and
of their superiority over those of nature. The first adumbration of this
step occurs in the *Diritto Universale* of 1720. Vico's views have under-
gone a radical shift. History is promoted from the comparatively lowly
place it still occupied in his hierarchy of types of knowledge in 1709-10
—the period of *De Nostri* and *De Antiquissima*, and because it is seen
to be a form of self-knowledge, has now risen above the place assigned
to natural science. Vico cannot claim for it the certainty of mathematics:

---

[1] N.S. 331.

[2] But see p. 32, n. 1. This view can be developed in many directions, of which the
Absolute Idealism of Hegel and of his Italian disciples, Croce and Gentile (and the
peculiar variant advocated by their English follower, R. G. Collingwood), is only
one, deeply metaphysical, form, for which some authority may be sought in Vico's
text (see, e.g., p. 75, n. 2), not in my view with great plausibility. The influence of Vico's
central principle on the German philosopher Wilhelm Dilthey and on the French
historian Jules Michelet, and, less directly, on social anthropologists, philologists and
historians of culture, has, as a rule, taken more empirical and less speculative forms.

but it has in it something of the 'divine' pleasure which that creative discipline, not trammelled by 'opaque' facts, provides. It is the queen of all the studies that are concerned with reality, with knowledge of what there is in the world.

Since it is their minds that are so harnessed, men can grasp what they and other men are at; for they know what a mind is, what a plan and a purpose are, whether one's own or another's. Above all, men know what it is to be a man—not merely a solitary individual, but a man in society, in reciprocal relations, co-operating consciously, with other similar men. Such self-knowledge, because it is knowledge *per caussas*—knowing why, and not merely knowing that, or knowing how—is the nearest that man can attain to divine knowledge. If ever I can understand myself at all, even though I may do it imperfectly, and could learn to do it better (as a trained critic must have learned, if he sees more in a work of art, 'knows why', better than I do), I am no longer merely recording or classifying or deducing from external data. This kind of knowing is what German thinkers later distinguished as understanding. It is different from knowing facts, however systematically and scientifically. Understanding other men's motives or acts, however imperfect or corrigible, is a state of mind or activity in principle different from learning about, or knowledge of, the external world. We observe, we learn facts about, but we cannot understand, stones or the death-watch beetle. Since I did not create my own personality—my psychological characteristics or the contents of my mind—I cannot be said to know myself through and through, as I can know mathematics which I, or other men, have created; or as my Creator can know me. On the other hand, mathematics, compounded as it is of fictions, of counters made by men, and played according to man-made rules, cannot give knowledge of reality. Because I have not made myself, self-knowledge is less 'transparent' than mathematics or logic (or, one might add, chess or heraldry or fiction); but because I, or other men, are not mere passive spectators but actors, and understand, 'enter into', the purposes, states of mind or will, of which actions are the expression, such knowledge, because its principles, being *modificazioni* of the human *mente*, are common to men in widely different cultures, is more 'transparent', nearer to the mathematical knowledge *per caussas*, than mere contemplation of the successions and compresences of things in nature can ever be. Such historical insight thus seems to stand half-way between the deductive or formal *scienza* of pure artefacts, and the scientific, inductive or experimental, perceptual *coscienza* of given, irremovable, opaque, 'brute' Nature. I understand the human past—the experience of my society or of other societies—'what Alcibiades did and suffered',[1] —in a sense in which, in principle, I cannot understand the history of stones or trees or animals. For this reason, stones, trees, animals, have a knowable past, but no history. Historical knowledge is not mere knowledge of past events, but only of events so far as they enter into human activity, and are an element in the biography of an individual or a group.[2] They are intelligible only to creatures who know what it is like to be a man. Whatever has been made by men, or thought, willed, imagined by sentient beings, because they follow certain rules, obey certain principles (which can be discerned and formulated), and only that (even though God is the ultimate source of it all), can be grasped by the similarly rule-guided imaginations of other men.

How, otherwise, could communication occur? How are sentences spoken to one man by another, or any other mode of direct expression, understood? Not by inductive reasoning. Knowledge of other human beings is supplemented, rendered less or more probable, systematized, corrected, justified by scientific method, but is not gained by it. For Vico, such knowledge is the result of a human capacity for imaginative understanding. The task of historians cannot be performed without this faculty, and their success will, in part, depend on how richly endowed with it they are, and how well they use it. Just as I can attempt to comprehend what the man who is at this moment speaking to me seeks to convey, which involves some understanding of his outlook, his social *milieu*—his past, the likelihood of this or that kind of behaviour on his part—so, too, must I be able to grasp (if I try hard enough, and possess the kind of genius needed) what it must have been like to have been a primitive man: for example, not to have lived in an organized society, or (harder still) to have been without language. This, Vico freely acknowledges, may require an 'incredible effort'. It is almost, but not quite, impossible to work back from the present, think away society and civilization, and imagine what it must have been like to be a primitive savage wandering in the 'vast forest of the earth', scarcely able to communicate, with a vocabulary of gestures or pictures much smaller than even that of a modern child. We cannot hope to recover it

---

[1] Aristotle's illustration of the subject-matter of history.

[2] This is at the root of Hegel's celebrated distinction of *an sich* and *für sich*. But see p. 32, n. 1.

all. 'It is beyond our power to enter the vast imagination of these first men.'[1] Yet (Vico comes back to this obstinately and repeatedly) history has, after all, been made by men, and therefore in the end it must always be penetrable to other men, as that which is not made by men—rocks, trees and animals—is not. The very same imaginative faculty which makes it possible for me to conceive the feelings, thoughts, acts of human beings of my time, but distant from me in space, or of different habits or language or mentality, ultimately makes it possible for me to understand remote cultures too.

How in practice is this to be done? How can I grasp what was thought or willed by the aggressive brutes described by Hobbes, or 'the helpless simpletons of Grotius, or Pufendorf's waifs and strays', or the other stock figures of the theorists of the state of nature? Vico had been deeply influenced in his youth by Lucretius' account of human origins; he had had an Epicurean and a Cartesian phase, and his Catholic orthodoxy has been strongly doubted; but it was a genuinely devout Christian who wrote the *Scienza Nuova*. Consequently, it may be that Vico's belief in an omnipresent creative spirit—God, who made him and in whom he lived, the central fire of which he was a spark—led him to the metaphysical belief that a man could have a direct relationship in some non-empirical fashion with spiritual activity in times and places other than his own. For, as has often been remarked, it is some sort of pantheism or panpsychism, rather than orthodox Catholicism, that is constantly suggested by his language. But whether or not Vico was in any degree a pantheist or, as Croce and his disciples hold, an Absolute Idealist, and whatever the psychological roots of his beliefs, his view of historical knowledge does not, in fact, require such transcendentalist assumptions. All that he demands is a vivid capacity for imaginative reconstruction, for conceiving the *modificazioni* of the human mind, for knowing what human beings could, and what they could not, have done or thought. One can grasp what it is like to be a savage, or at least believe, whether correctly or not, that one can succeed in doing this, without mystical or non-empirical presuppositions. When, for example, Vico argues that it cannot be true that the Romans borrowed the Twelve Tables (the original Roman code of laws) from the Athens of Solon's day (as Roman tradition maintained), he is asserting not that he positively knows that they did not in fact do

---

[1] N.S. 378, see also 338. On this see p. 44 below.

so—he does not claim to know the past by a direct act of metaphysical clairvoyance—only that the Romans could not have done so, because such barbarians as the Romans must, to judge by the evidence, at that time have been, could scarcely have known where Athens was, or that it possessed the kind of culture which had something specific to give Rome, or the nature or value of Solon's activities. He knows, too, that even if one makes the absurd assumption that the prehistoric Romans somehow divined all this, they could scarcely have translated the Attic words into the most idiomatic Latin, without a trace of Greek influence upon it, using such a purely Latin word as *auctoritas*, for example, for which no Greek equivalent existed. When Vico argues that the Romans could not have done these things, that the story is intrinsically too implausible, his argument rests not so much on an empirical accumulation of evidence about human behaviour in many places and situations from which such conclusions can be drawn by normal scientific reasoning (although, no doubt, this too is necessary), as upon some more immediate apprehension of what it is to be civilized and how this differs from being barbarian, on some acquaintance with the stages of the growth of self-consciousness in individuals or societies, based, in its turn, on some notion of what constitutes a man, some awareness of the way and the time order in which the interplay of natural and spiritual factors is likely to give birth to different human faculties, or modes of feeling or expression, and to the evolution of various concepts and categories, and the institutions, habits and 'styles of life' bound up with them, at various times and in various conditions. Unless we possess some knowledge gained by orderly, i.e. scientific or 'common sense', methods of acquiring information of what in fact occurred, such general notions will lack content— indeed could not arise at all. But neither factual information nor reasoning power is enough.[1] Without the grasp of what it is to possess a mind, what it is like to respond to stimuli, and how this differs from following rules or pursuing a policy, from love or hate, worship or

[1] He fully recognizes that deductive techniques are indispensable for examining and criticizing sources, but he is, as might be expected, apprehensive of the scepticism which such destructive critics of the Scriptures as Spinoza and Père Simon thereby breed. (On the relationship to Spinoza, see the interesting article by Arnaldo Momigliano entitled 'Vico's Scienza Nuova' in *History and Theory*, V, 1966.) He supposes that the power of *fantasia*, imaginative insight, was an antidote to this subversive and, in his day, fast growing intellectual fashion. He was ironically enough accused of this very vice by orthodox Catholic critics not long after his death. See p. 78.

recognition of authority, of what it is to be imaginative or critical, childlike or mature, unworldly or possessive, religious or atheistic, a master or a servant—without this understanding, acquaintance with empirical facts will be of little avail. Only sentient beings can have this basic understanding, and only of creatures similar to themselves— angels of angels, men of men. We begin with this capacity for understanding. We may possess it only in embryo, but we could not even begin, and should not be recognizably human, without it. Possession of its rudiments is intrinsic to being a man.[1]

1 On this, however, see 'Vico's Science' by Leon Pompa, *History and Theory*, X, No. 1, 1971, pp. 49-84. In this well argued, though to me not altogether convincing, exposition, which seeks to demonstrate that Vico's 'science' is truly scientific, Dr Leon Pompa advances the view that by *modificazioni* (one of the crucial terms on the interpretation of which a very great deal turns) Vico means not individual but social 'purposes, necessities, utilities; those of the social world', and treats *mente* as a kind of general social consciousness governed by the laws on which the new science is founded. This may well be correct; Vico discusses the purpose of societies and classes and scarcely at all of 'world-historical' individuals. But this interpretation still seems to me to leave exceedingly obscure the exact way in which Vico supposes that men of a later age can 'enter'—only, he tells us, with the utmost difficulty—the remote 'social purposes, necessities', etc. of earlier, barbarous times. The laws that determine the successive stages of the *corsi e ricorsi* are too few and too general to make it possible to reconstruct specific social or cultural phenomena: the scientific method employed in the natural sciences is excluded inasmuch as it yields only 'external' knowledge, whereas we have an 'inside' view of the acts and works of man. If the method is not connected with the capacity for intercommunication whereby men are enabled to understand and misunderstand one another, both within the same culture, and historically, across stretches of time and varieties of culture—Dilthey's *Verstehen*—then what does Vico mean? His *fantasia*—capacity for imaginatively 'entering' worlds different from our own, or perhaps even any experience that differs from the most familiar—may be fallible, and, in any case, is not a sufficient condition for arriving at historical truth, which needs verification by the ordinary methods of research; but may it not be a necessary condition, since without it we should not be capable of even so much as conceiving what it is that we are looking for—a possible world, the 'portrait' of a society or an age— and not a mere collection of data or propositions? Doubtless we cannot understand ourselves save by understanding others, or our own present state save by becoming aware of whence we came and how; but equally we cannot understand others save in terms of their relation to ourselves and our world, nor the human past unless we trace it backwards from our present. If this is correct, is Vico entitled to speak of a 'science', even as the term was understood in his own time? But Dr Pompa may not wish to press the appropriateness of this term—in which case there may not be much disagreement between us. On this entire topic see also the excellent discussion in P. Winch, *The Idea of a Social Science*, Routledge, London, 1958.

A sense of historical perspective—for that is Vico's new and revolutionary discovery—cannot, unaided by empirical data, 'intuit' what actually occurred; it can at best rule out what could not have occurred. It works with such vague basic concepts as change, causality, growth, the pattern of a culture, time sequence, anachronism—concepts by which we order the data, attribute characteristics and perceive irreversible relationships. When we say that the social (or economic, or religious) condition of England in the fifteenth century could not have been what it was if the events which constitute, say, the history of the fourteenth and thirteenth centuries in England, had not taken place; and therefore that someone who knows, no matter how minutely, only the history of the twelfth century could not understand, or account for, what took place in England in the fifteenth; or if we say that it is wholly impossible for *Hamlet*, or anything like it, to have been composed in the kind of society which inhabited Outer Mongolia in the third century A.D., and look on any theory which rests on the opposite assumption as too absurd to be worth a moment's notice; these 'could nots' and 'impossible' are categories of the historical sense, of the sense of what goes with what, and of what is incompatible with it. The recognition of an irreversible process of infancy, youth, maturity, old age, final decline in the lives of societies, no less than of individual men, and of what types of language or ritual or economic relations belong to each stage of social growth, is something, it seemed to Vico, that the philosophers or jurists of his own and of other times did not sufficiently possess or understand, otherwise they would not have credited early man with their own sophisticated mental processes.[1] This blind-

---

[1] Dr Pompa, *op. cit.*, has taken me to task for supposing that according to Vico the capacity to think historically was the condition of any thinking whatever about ourselves, involving as it does such basic concepts as coherence and implausibility, since if this were so, he could scarcely have charged modern scholars with the very kind of unhistorical thinking which he denounces as a cause of anachronism and misinterpretation. But neither Vico nor I seem to me to be guilty of this fallacy: a man's sense of what is and what is not likely or even thinkable within a particular society need not rest on what fits into his own world; only the general category or notion of coherence is required: the data needed for grasping the activities of a given society are to be discovered by the methods of ordinary empirical research: observation, hypothesis, confirmation, etc. To interpret the data correctly, however, the historian needs the aid of the set of principles of what Vico claims to be his new science, which indicates by means of universally applicable and intelligible 'laws' the necessary succession of stages that each culture must go through. This discovery seems to be founded on an analogy with the irreversible pattern of individual

ness vitiated their work and made it necessary to reconstruct the entire science of man from the foundations. He meant by this science the study of all that pertained to men as such, as contrasted with that which they shared with the non-human world, such as their bodies, or the physical properties of the physical matter by which their lives were sustained.

The theorists whom he singled out for attack were those who seemed to him to have perpetrated unhistorical anachronisms: like the upholders of theories of Natural Law or social contract, who credited primitive men with some of the civilized attributes of their own 'magnificent' age; and those rationalists like Descartes and Spinoza, or utilitarians like Hobbes and Locke, or 'Epicureans' like Gassendi, who, however deeply they differed from one another, all assumed the existence of a fixed, unchanging human nature, common to all men, everywhere, at all times, a fully developed moral and psychological structure from which rights, obligations, laws, flowing from universal goals, identical for all men, could be logically deduced. Vico attacks the great jurists Grotius, Selden, Pufendorf, whose gifts and erudition he admired, and to whose notions of social laws (especially Grotius') he acknowledged a profound debt, for their blindness to the idea of development, *nascimento*, coming to birth, from which *natura* is derived, whereby one generation, or culture, grows into another. Blind to this, they cannot see the organic interconnection which unites the various fields of activity which belong to any one particular stage of social growth. Above all, he charges them with ignoring the cardinal truth that all valid explanation is necessarily and essentially genetic, in terms either of human purposes, which change with changing circumstances, or of the alteration of circumstances by these purposes themselves, that is, by human action, or the interplay of purposes and 'blind' circumstances or environment, which often leads to consequences unintended by men. The central idea at the heart of Vico's thought is that, in the individual

---

lives or of the short span of the more or less immediate past of a man's own society. We cannot think of our own lives (he seems to assume) or of the immediate past of our own societies, or of those sufficiently close to them in space and time, save in historical terms—as structured processes, some formed by our own lives, others formed by the social patterns out of which we emerge. The fault of the scholars who perpetrate anachronisms is not to apply this (evidently given or inescapable) notion of a fixed order—e.g. of the primitive stage succeeded by the mature, the mature by the decadent—to the remoter past. I owe this highly plausible interpretation of Vico's thesis to Dr Pompa, to whom I gladly acknowledge this debt.

and society alike, phase follows phase not haphazardly (as the Epicureans thought), nor in a sequence of mechanical causes or effects (as the Stoics taught), but as stages in the pursuit of an intelligible purpose—man's effort to understand himself and his world, and to realize his capacities in it. History for him is the orderly procession (guided by Providence, working through men's capacities) of ever deepening types of apprehension of the world, of ways of feeling, acting, expressing, each of which grows out of, and supersedes, its predecessor. To each type or culture necessarily belong some characteristics not found in any other. So begins the conception of the 'phenomenology' of human experience and activity, of men's history and life as determined by their own, at first unconscious, then progressively more conscious, creative moulding, that is, mastery of nature both living and dead. In the forms given it by Hegel and Marx and their followers, this idea dominates the modern world. It is for this that Marx praised him. Of this view of men and history, for better and for worse, Vico is the pioneer.

How are we to discover how we came to be what we are, why we think and act as we do, and what we truly need or want? Only by the study of our own development. The ancient analogy between the individual and society, microcosm and macrocosm, ontogenesis and phylogenesis, dominates Vico's thought as much as that of the Renaissance. The task is to uncover the actual story of how and, above all, why cultures come to be, rise and fall. This is what the New Science is to tell us: how is this to be achieved? We have the means within our grasp. They have not been used only because men have not realized their marvellous potentialities.[1] The key lies in the past experience of the human race, which, from its earliest origins, may be read in its mythology, its language, its social and religious institutions. In particular it may be perceived in the evidences still extant of earlier forms of life, discoverable in ancient monuments and the accounts of the early customs and institutions of peoples, as well as their occasional survival—living or fossilized—in isolated places, among backward or simple folk, especially in the poetry, the magical rites, the legal structures of primitive societies. To suppose this process to be intelligible, is to find an order

[1] Bodin and Bacon had both noted that fables and myths provided evidence of the beliefs and social structure of primitive peoples, but did not develop this insight with anything resembling the breadth and depth of Vico. Nevertheless, he is probably more indebted to them and others, e.g. Jean de Clerc, and, perhaps, Lafitau and the Chevalier Ramsay, in this respect, than he chooses to acknowledge.

in the apparent chaos—an Ariadne's thread that will not merely lead us out of the labyrinth, but will explain its complexities. This Vico affects to find in the Platonic idea of man as he should be—not in Plato's static ideal pattern, but in a dynamic principle of 'growth', a principle of movement, itself immutable, which governs human evolution. The unfolding—the succession of states—is a process; but the pattern is always the same. Vico expands this Platonic truth by saying that the intelligible 'substance' is one, although the 'modes' of its development are diverse.[1]

This single, unvarying, central truth, apprehended with varying degrees of clarity and fullness in its many 'modes' or appearances— from the *certum* of insufficiently developed societies to the *verum* of high cultures, from concrete imagery of poetry that is plunged in the senses to metaphysical soaring towards abstractions[2]—is to be grasped by the use of systematic comparisons 'between the beginnings and last phases' of ancient and modern nations. It is this method that, by abstracting what is common to various phases of culture—what Vico calls 'induction'—reveals the unalterable inner pattern, the Platonic law, that shapes not only our world, but, since 'the rise, progress, maturity, decay and fall' is a universal principle, is eternally valid for all possible societies.[3] This marks the birth of full-fledged modern historicism—a doctrine that in its empirical form has stimulated and enriched, and in its dogmatic, metaphysical form, inhibited and distorted, the historical imagination.

The work of Providence, Vico's anticipation of Hegel's 'Cunning of History' (or of 'Reason'), obeys (or imposes) this Platonic pattern. It is Providence that turns men's instincts and purposes to the creation of institutions which do indeed minister to their true ends on earth, but which, primitive and vicious savages that they are, they are in no condition to conceive, let alone aim at; and Providence is identified with this Platonic pattern, the laws that govern the *storia ideale eterna* of the peoples. Seen in retrospect, men, or, at any rate, Vico, can discover how the vicious desires of the *ferini* (on which Tacitus, who paints 'men as

---

1 N.S. 1096. See the excellent exposition of Vico's Platonism by Professor Werner Stark, the best and most convincing known to me ('Giambattista Vico's Sociology of Knowledge', in *Giambattista Vico, an international symposium*, ed. G. Tagliacozzo and H. White, Johns Hopkins University Press, Baltimore, 1969, pp. 297-309).

2 N.S. 821.

3 N.S. 348.

they are', is regarded by him as the supreme expert) have been turned to the profit of justice and truth, the seeds of which, buried by sin, nevertheless live on in the most degraded savages.[1] Above all we must not search for the nature of man as some unaltering static 'core' within the flux of experience, but perceive it in the flux itself—'of what comes into being, at what times, in what fashions'.[2] All that can be gathered about the past and present of the moral, religious, aesthetic outlook of human groups, or their social, economic, linguistic habits as they gradually alter and grow; in short, all that comparative mythology, philosophy, jurisprudence, anthropology, ethnology, sociology, and the other sciences of man duly came to investigate, falls into this province. But one must have eyes to see and ears to hear. Small wonder if Vico found difficulty in conveying to his contemporaries a vision so transforming and so universal.

IV

Men make their own history, that is, they shape their own lives, both deliberately and without conscious intention, in response to physical environment and to unintended, 'providential' changes in their own natures. To understand their present condition, to be able to answer the most urgent problems which trouble men, political, moral, social, legal, religious, is to understand how these men came to be in a situation where alone these problems have arisen in this or that specific shape. Why, for example, should we obey our constituted superiors? All kinds of conflicting answers have been given; each, in the end, appeals to a specific model of what a human being is, usually a figment compounded from characteristics which the theorist has met in his own limited and transient world, or those which he needs for his theory, or both together. But do these abstractions, whether the natural man of Grotius, or Hobbes's ruthless egoist, or Spinoza's free and rational mind, correspond to anything actual or possible? Natural law theorists, social contract theorists, utilitarians, individualists, materialists and rationalists of various types, have, according to Vico, gone hopelessly astray because they do not understand the systematically developing and altering succession of outlooks and motives, dictated by the changing needs of human nature, a nature which is a *nascimento*—a process; for him

[1] See Alain Pons, 'Nature et Histoire chez Vico', in *Les Etudes Philosophiques*, No. 1 (janvier-mars 1961, Paris).
[2] N.S. 147.

human nature, in the course of seeking to satisfy its needs, cannot help transforming itself, and so constantly generates new characteristics, new needs, new categories of thought and action. The leading theorists of the age—lawyers and philosophers—are blind to this because they do not understand the nature of history or society or the individual soul. They love to speak of the 'matchless wisdom of the ancients',[1] as if early men could conceivably have known more than their descendants who have inherited all the discoveries and inventions of the past and improved upon them; or, more absurdly still, as if these early men were fully rational beings, or lived (or could have lived) in a world similar to our own, or faced the kind of problems that necessarily belong to our own unique phase of historical growth. If we do not study origins, we shall never know to what problems the thought or behaviour of our ancestors were a continuous response; and since their response ultimately shaped not only them but us, too, we shall not understand ourselves unless we trace our own growth to its roots. 'Theories must start from the point where the matter starts whereof they treat'.[2] Then, and then only, shall we understand how men came to be what they are, and how the problems which torment us have come to be problems for us at all.

This is the whole doctrine of historicism in embryo. Knowledge of genetic psychology, of the history of social consciousness, the retracing of our steps, light cast upon the path that we have traversed—these alone can settle the controversies of the dogmatic jurists and political thinkers. Problems are intelligible—and soluble—only within their own socio-historical context. It is plainly ridiculous to assume, in the teeth of all historical evidence, that in early, barbarous societies there sprang forth, fully armed like Athena from the head of Zeus, poets and lawgivers, beings of vast knowledge and consummate wisdom who owed nothing to the primitives among whom they were bred but, possessing esoteric sources of information and intellectual and moral attributes and insight undreamt of by the societies of their time, proceeded to dispense eternal laws and timeless wisdom to their peoples. Yet, Vico asks, is not this precisely what is attributed to Lycurgus, Draco, Homer, Solon, and all the mythological sages of antiquity?[3]

---

1 N.S. 128.

2 N.S. 314, 394.

3 Yet, of course, it is precisely this that he supposes to have been the case with the Jews, to whom the truth was directly revealed by God. Vico cautiously leaves the case of sacred history largely undiscussed; he is mainly concerned to deny that

Are we seriously to suppose that 'the first men, the stupid, insensate, horrible great beasts'[1], the impious progeny of Noah, wandering in the vast forests of the earth—that these creatures found not the slightest difficulty in conceiving a set of eternal, unalterable, universal principles (*quod semper, quod ubique, quod ab omnibus*) binding on all men at all times, and laying down once and for all both what men do, and what they ought to do: principles concerning which the most profound philosophers and the most learned jurists notoriously do not agree, but which, nevertheless, are said to be engraved on the hearts of all men from all eternity?[2] It was a stroke of genius to deny, as Vico did in the face of the highest authorities of his time, and of Aristotle, Seneca, and the central Western tradition, the existence of an unaltering human nature whose properties and goals are knowable *a priori*.

It has been argued that although such models of human nature may be historically or psychologically unreal, yet they may have value as analytic fictions (like the atom or the economic man) in terms of which a science can be built—entities which may, indeed, be imaginary or idealized, but, despite this, perform an indispensable function by constituting standards or types in terms of deviation from which natural objects can be measured or classified. Vico's reply to this is contained in his criticism of the theories of Natural Law and of the social contract, which is designed to show that to leave out history is to render the model of man too remote from reality to be of use. When, in addition, the plasticity of men, and especially their capacity for transforming themselves by their own creative activity, is omitted from the model, it becomes a caricature and, if applied to reality, leads only to errors and absurdities. Vico argues that the theory of the social contract, for

---

the principles of Natural Law, or any other esoteric knowledge, were to be found among the primitive gentile peoples—hence his denial that the pagans derived Natural Law from the Jews and corrupted it, as maintained by Huet, Bochart, Witsius and others; or that hieroglyphs concealed secret Christian truths, as asserted by Athanasius Kircher. So far as God shaped the lives of the pagans, he did so by purely naturalistic means (on this see Arnaldo Momigliano, 'La Nuova Storia Romana di G. B. Vico', pp. 779-81, *Rivista Storica Italiana*, Anno LXXVII, Fascicolo IV, 1965).

[1] *Primi uomini, stupidi, insensati, ed orribili bestioni* (N.S. 374).

[2] This was not wholly fair, since these thinkers did not maintain that all men were necessarily able to formulate explicitly the principles they were following—although they could always, in theory, have done so; nor does Vico concede that savages followed these principles even unconsciously.

example, which dominated his own age, takes it for granted that the original solitary wanderers who came out of the woods to make a compact to live together already understood what a compact was. But he points out that this is patently absurd; for such men could not have understood so complex a notion—or even used it—unless they were already living in society governed by rules, since only within such a social whole could the concept of compact or promise—an elaborate piece of social machinery or convention—have originated or been understood. Men could not have invented social organization by means of a promise given by all to all, or by all to one man—democratic or monarchical—for if the social nexus—rules, conventions, compacts and all—had not already existed, the notion of a promise would have meant nothing to them. To found the state on a promise, and not the other way about, is thus a logical absurdity. This demonstrates not merely that the institution called the social contract cannot have been the historical origin of later social habits, but that it is useless even as an analytical device to explain why today we have come to behave (or to think it right to behave) as we do: why we do not rebel, condemn resistance to authority, pay debts, think it right to serve in the army, allow ourselves to be taxed, and so on.[1] Moreover to say that although no contract was ever in fact made, yet we now behave (as Hobbes or Rousseau maintained) exactly as if such a contract, overt or tacit, existed, is to ignore or misinterpret the fact that human beliefs, conduct, character, experience, are today what they are not in obedience to a historical fiction, but only because they once were what they were, that is, as a stage in a continuous evolution in time. It follows that no one can understand either how or why men act as they do, without knowing by what steps they came to be what they are. A static model like the social contract omits sociological and psychological facts—the survival of the past into the present, the influence of tradition, of inherited habits and the shapes they assume; it ignores or distorts the true view of society as something compounded out of many interlaced, altering strands of conscious, semi-conscious and buried memories, of individual and collective reactions and sentiments, of patterns of social

1 Something similar, but not identical, is to be found in Hume's later objections to the view that political arrangements rest on contract (that is a solemn promise), when he argues that whatever explains the sacredness of promises (in his opinion, social utility) is by itself sufficient to account for those social institutions which promises are brought in to explain and justify.

life which we speak of as the character of a family, a tribe, a nation, an historical period, the roots of which are all but lost, yet to some degree still remain traceable in the opaque and tantalizing past. Only those who have the imagination and knowledge to trace this process to its origins, and so reconstruct it, can understand its effects in the present or assess its value and prospects. Implausible myths like the contract, or obedience to universal reason, or calculation of rational self-interest, placed at the centre of their systems by Hobbes and Spinoza, are, for Vico, merely the refuge of ignorance. If we understand what we come out of, the perplexing problems of why we are as we are—and whether it is desirable or right to continue to be so—we will be nearer solution. Whatever accounts for our character and institutions will also account for our values, which themselves belong to, and are effective and intelligible at, only their own specific stage in human history. The notion of absolute standards, moral, aesthetic, social, in terms of which the entire human past is largely a story of mistakes, crimes, deception— the very cornerstone of the outlook of the Enlightenment—is the absurd corollary of the fallacious belief in a fixed, ultimate, unchanging human nature. But Vico is not primarily concerned with morality, or value judgments. Like Spinoza—the adversary often in his thoughts[1] —he seems content to understand. He does, of course, in fact make moral judgments, and in them unhesitatingly takes for granted the validity of the values embodied in his own faith and civilization; but this is quite consistent with his 'historicist', conservative thesis. He does, at times, remind himself that Christian values are timeless and absolute; but for the most part he forgets this, and speaks as if necessarily *autres temps, autres moeurs.*

If knowledge of the past is so vital to our understanding of ourselves, what methods are we to use to obtain it? The evidence lies scattered about us, yet historians have steadily ignored it, and tell us stories which, besides contradicting one another, must often appear inherently implausible to anyone who has grasped in what ways human beings in fact develop. Yet the remedy lies at hand. There are, Vico declares, three incorruptible sources of true historical knowledge of man: language, mythology, antiquities; these cannot lie. He develops this thesis with learning, imagination and audacity.

---

[1] See Arnaldo Momigliano, *ibid.*, esp. p. 781. Also his 'Vico's Scienza Nuova', *op. cit.*

V

Men embody their feelings, attitudes, and thoughts in symbols. These symbols are natural means of self-expression; they are not forged for the purpose of misleading or entertaining future generations. Consequently they are dependable evidence of the minds and outlooks of which they are the vehicles, if only we knew how to read it. Language is not a deliberate invention on the part of men who think thoughts, and then look around for means of articulating them. Ideas, and the symbols in which they are expressed, are not, even in thought, separable. We do not merely speak or write in symbols, we think and can think only in symbols, whether words or images; the two are one.[1] From words and the way they are used we can infer the mental processes, the attitudes and outlooks of their users, for 'minds (*ingenia*) are formed by the character of language, not language by the minds of those who speak it'.[2] This is an observation of great suggestiveness: men are born into traditions of speech and writing which form minds as much as minds form them. Although probably merely occasioned by a famous controversy, in Vico's own day, about the superiority of French as against Italian literary style claimed by the Abbé de Bouhours and others, this insight embodies a point of central importance—the denial of the very possibility of an unaltering, logically perfect language, constructed to reflect the basic structure of reality—the famous revolutionary thesis adumbrated by Leibniz and developed in modern times by Russell and some of his disciples. For Vico there is no such structure, at any rate in the human world, no world of perfect, unaltering essences. What kind of words have human beings used to express their relation to the world, to each other, and to their own past selves? Vico speaks of what he calls the 'poetical' cast of mind— poetical language, poetical law, poetical morals, poetical logic, and so on. By 'poetical' he means—what, following the Germans, we tend to attribute to the people or 'folk'—modes of expression used by the unsophisticated mass of the people in the early years of the human race,

---

[1] Cp. Joseph de Maistre's remark, still novel enough when it was made a hundred years later, that '*la pensée et la parole sont un magnifique synonyme*'. This probably derives from Vico, of whose works Maistre was one of the few readers in his day, and not from Hamann or Herder, whose views reached Paris (and Piedmont) somewhat later.

[2] *De Nostri, op. cit. (Opere*, I), 1.95; cp. Gianturco, *op. cit.*, p. 40.

not by the children of its old age—self-conscious men of letters, experts or sages. The earliest human beings, primitive savages, in order to communicate, used natural signs and gestures: what Vico calls 'mute acts'[1]—the designating of some one actual thing to stand for or signify other things which it resembles, or the pictorial representation of something to stand for a whole class of entities which it resembles; this, for example, is done by hieroglyphs or ideograms, which, Vico surmises, were once in use everywhere, but have survived only in Egypt and China (and among the Indians of the New World), because the civilizations of these countries have long been insulated from the main stream of human culture. For this reason he believed that writing preceded speech. Such objects, signs, pictures, or gestures can refer not merely to material objects, but to what we should now call mental qualities as well, for which there have emerged as yet no separate terms, so that, in view of what Vico (mistakenly) supposed to be the extreme poverty of primitive language, these few gestures or pictures are obliged to stand for abstract notions too. This is so because in early times, 'words are carried over from bodies and from the properties of bodies to express the things of the mind and spirit'.[2] This evolutionary view has proved more fruitful than the better known theories which dominated the earlier eighteenth century, e.g. Condillac's contractual-utilitarian theory which bases language on agreed conventions, or the opposing view which traced language to the imitation of sounds in nature, or Süssmilch's doctrine of the divine origin of language, or the emotive theory of Rousseau and others. The next stage in the ascent of humanity is marked by the use of metaphors, similes, images and the like, which characterizes the language that we now (in the normal, not in Vico's, sense) call poetical. Primitive men, Vico tells us, do not denote things each by its own 'natural' name (Adam did, indeed, give each thing its own unique name, but the Flood obliterated the high civilization that he founded[3]) but by 'physical substances endowed with life'. Fables and myths, or rather the characters who

[1] N.S. 32.

[2] N.S. 237.

[3] N.S. 401-2. This is Vico's way of preserving orthodox Christian doctrine, and avoiding the Epicurean-evolutionist heresy for which the Inquisition, in the last years of the seventeenth century, had inflicted terrible punishment on some of his Neapolitan friends and contemporaries. Yet, although he may have feared charges of heresy, there is no reason for thinking that he is necessarily insincere in this or any other affirmation.

occur in them, are 'imaginative universals'[1]—attempts to refer to whole classes of entities without, as yet, the aid of proper general terms (for the capacity for abstraction is not, at this stage, sufficiently developed), and, therefore, by means of some magnificently conceived example of the class (not yet clearly conceived as a class) which stands both for itself and for the entire class. Thus 'Jove' is at one and the same time the name of the sky, of the father of the Gods and ruler of the universe, and of the source of thunder, terror and duty—he is both the embodiment and the wielder of all the compulsive forces before which men must, at their peril, bow down. 'Hercules' is the name of a heroic individual, the performer of vast and beneficent labours, but also of the class of all the heroes of all the various mythologies: hence every people worships its own Hercules. 'Neptune' refers to a trident-carrying divinity, but also to all the seas of the world; 'Cybele' symbolizes the earth and at the same time a woman, mother of the giants.[2] Vico calls this 'credible impossibility'[3], which he regards as the 'proper material' of 'poetry'. Such images may later come to seem logical monstrosities, yet Vico is convinced that this is not mere confusion: these are categories in which early men thought. He warns us that unless we make a gigantic effort to enter into this type of mentality, we shall never penetrate into the remote world of our ancestors which alone holds the key to our own. 'It is impossible that bodies should be minds, yet it was believed that the thundering sky was Jove'.[4] The sky is a huge and terror-inspiring person—Jove. This is what Virgil means when he says *Jovis omnia plena*[5] (*Eclogues*, III, 60). We think in abstractions, but they were immersed in the senses. For this reason 'it is . . . beyond our power to enter into the vast imagination of those first men whose minds were not in the least abstract, refined, or spiritualized, because they were entirely immersed in the senses, buffeted by the passions, buried in the body'. Nevertheless, we must do what we can to 'enter into' these vast imaginations ('*entrare nella vasta immaginativa di que' primi uomini*').[6] We must 'descend to' or 'understand' the minds of these 'savage monsters' who identify causes with persons.[7] Sometimes they even said that they saw these divine beings[8], for instance Jove, and believed that he 'commanded by signs, that such signs were real words and that nature was the language of

---

[1] N.S. 381, 403.   [2] N.S. 402, 549.   [3] *L'impossibile credibile* (N.S. 383).
[4] N.S. 383.   [5] N.S. 379.   [6] N.S. 378-9.   [7] N.S. 338, 375.
[8] N.S. 375.

Jove'.[1] Hence sprang divination, 'the science of the language of the Gods', which 'the Greeks called theology'; and not the Greeks only, but later mystics and indeed Vico's younger contemporaries, Berkeley and Hamann. At the same time Jove, the sky, was 'a vast animate body' which 'feels passions and effects',[2] while nature was personified as 'a mistress', as 'Sympathetic Nature', something that we could surely no longer comprehend;[3] yet this is the world we must seek to 'enter', to 'go down to', to 'comprehend', if we are to grasp what early societies were like. Vico claimed as his cardinal achievement this anthropological approach: 'to discover the way in which this . . . arose in the gentile world, we encountered exasperating difficulties which have cost us the research of a good twenty years . . . to descend from these human and refined natures of ours to those quite wild and savage natures, which we cannot at all imagine and can apprehend only with great effort'.[4] This we must do not by looking for evidence outside our minds, but 'as the metaphysicians do' who look 'within the modifications of their own minds—of him who meditates'[5]—that is, by a species of self-analysis, by tracing the phases of the development of one's own individual mind from childhood to maturity.

We normally distinguish between the literal and the metaphorical use of language. To be literal is to call things by their appropriate names, and describe them in plain, simple terms; to use metaphor is a sophisticated or poetical way of embellishing or heightening such plain usage for the sake of giving pleasure, or of creating vivid imaginative effects, or of demonstrating verbal ingenuity; this is usually considered the product of conscious elaboration which could, with enough effort, always be translated back into the plain or literal sense of which it is merely an artificially heightened expression. Metaphor and simile, even allegory, are not, for Vico, deliberate artifices. They are natural ways of expressing a vision of life different from ours. Men once thought, according to him, in images rather than concepts, and 'attributed senses and passions to bodies as vast as sky, sea and earth'.[6] What is for us a less or more conscious use of rhetorical devices, was their sole means of ordering, connecting and conveying what they sensed, observed, remembered, imagined, hoped, feared, worshipped, in short their entire experience. This is what Vico calls 'poetic logic', the pattern of language and thought in the Age of Heroes. The metaphorical use

[1] N.S. 379.   [2] N.S. 377.   [3] NS. 378.   [4] N.S. 338.   [5] N.S. 374.
[6] N.S. 402.

precedes—and must precede—the 'literal' use of words, as poetry must come before prose, as song is earlier than spoken speech. 'The sources of all poetic locutions are two; poverty of language and the necessity of making oneself understood'.[1] Early man, animist and anthropomorphist, thought in terms of what we now call metaphor as naturally and inevitably as we now think in 'literal' phrases. Hence a great deal of what now passes for literal speech incorporates dead metaphors, the origins of which are so little remembered that they are no longer felt—even faintly—as such. Since the changing structure of a language 'tells us the histories of things signified by the words',[2] we can glean from it something of how their world looked to our ancestors. Because primitive men cannot abstract, 'metaphor makes up the great body of the language among all nations'[3] at that time. Vico supposed that such men used similes, images and metaphors much as people, to this day, use flags, or uniforms, or Fascist salutes—to convey something directly; this is a use of sign which it would today seem unnatural to call either metaphorical or literal. Vico maintains that when a primitive man said, 'the blood boils in my heart',[4] where we should say, 'I am angry', his 'metaphorical' phrase is a uniquely valuable evidence of the way in which such a man thought, perceived and felt. What he felt when he spoke of blood boiling seemed to him —and indeed was—more directly related to his perception of water in a heated cauldron than our sensation of anger would seem to us today. The marvellous images, the immortal phrases coined by early poets are, according to Vico, due not to conscious flights of fancy, but to the fact that the imaginations of such men and their capacity for direct sensation were so much stronger than ours as to be different in kind, while their capacity for precise analogies and scientific observation was far less developed. Hence, if we are to understand their world we must try to project ourselves into minds very remote from our own and endowed with these unfamiliar powers. A world in which men naturally talk of the lips of a vase, the teeth of a plough, the mouth of a river, a neck of land, handfuls of one thing, the heart of another, veins of minerals, bowels of the earth, murmuring waves, whistling winds, and smiling skies, groaning tables and weeping willows[5]—such a world

---

1 N.S. 34.   2 N.S. 354.
3 N.S. 444.   4 N.S. 460, 935.
5 N.S. 405. Vico's examples are drawn from metaphors taken from the human body.

must be deeply and systematically different from any in which such phrases are felt, even remotely, to be metaphorical, as contrasted with so-called literal speech. This is one of Vico's most revolutionary discoveries.

According to Vico, words, like ideas, are directly determined by things—the concrete circumstances in which men live—and are therefore the most reliable evidence for them. As so often, he illustrates his most original and important perceptions with highly fanciful examples: he points to the fact that life in the 'great forests of the earth' is earlier in date than life 'in huts', earlier still than the civilization of villages, cities or academies; this seems to him borne out by linguistic evidence: thus Latin, which Vico regards as a very ancient language, springs from life connected with forests; to demonstrate this he devotes one of his many essays in genetic etymology to grouping together words like 'lex' (acorn), 'ilex', 'aquilex', 'legumen' and 'legere', as typical 'sylvan' words drawn from life in the woods, which then come to be used to denote quite different activities, states and objects.[1] Language 'tells us the history of things signified by the words',[2] beginning with the original meanings of words in the earliest of all periods, and illustrating historical change by its modifications in—and in response to—the successive phases of civilization. Language reflects these phases: 'First the forests, then the huts, thence the villages, next the cities, finally the academies'.[3] Like many thinkers, Vico is fascinated by the magic of the number three. Humanity has passed through three stages.[4] First comes the 'divine' period dominated by 'the senses', when the 'poetic' language was that of 'natural symbols', hieroglyphs or ideograms—'mute' signs. Thunder and other natural phenomena are a language in which the gods speak: so are the entrails of animals or

---

[1] 'For example, lex. First it must have meant a collection of acorns. Thence, we believe, is derived ilex ... the oak (and certainly aquilex means the collector of waters); for the oak produces acorns, by which swine are drawn together. Lex was next a collection of vegetables, from which the latter were called legumina. Later on, at a time when vulgar letters had not yet been invented for writing down laws, lex or law that solemnized [their] wills ... finally, collecting letters ... in a sheaf for each word, was called legere, reading' (N.S. 240).

[2] N.S. 354.

[3] N.S. 239.

[4] Comte's law of the three phases—the theological, metaphysical and positive—is clearly influenced by Vico's ages of Gods, heroes and men, a notion, he tells us (N.S.173), that 'had come down to us from Egyptian antiquity'.

the flights of birds, symbols which the experts—priests or augurs—can read. The next period—the 'heroic'—is dominated by oligarchies of 'heroes', of which language rich in simile and metaphor—created by an imagination still directly related to nature—is characteristic. Finally comes the 'human' period in which *ragione* (reason) and language as we now know it, that of purely conventional signs invented and altered at will—'language of which men are absolute lords'[1]—predominate. Vico tries to be more specific still. He says that first came onomatopoeic monosyllables, then polysyllables, followed by interjections, pronouns, prepositions, nouns, and finally verbs. This is not accidental, but springs from the fact that the concepts of 'before' and 'after', and of movement, which verbs convey, necessarily came later than the apprehension of things—lumps of material stuff—objects denoted by nouns, which in their turn came later than the sense of personal identity, or the states conveyed by primitive cries. He provides equally fanciful arguments for the view that the earliest forms of verbs must have been in the imperative.

But these fantasies should not obscure Vico's central and vastly suggestive notion that the development of the morphology of a symbolic system is one with the growth of the culture of which it is the central organ. Moreover, he believes that since men are everywhere men, it follows that although 'there are as many languages as types of custom and outlook, yet there must, in the nature of things, be a mental language common to all nations which uniformly grasps the essence of things feasible in human social life, and expresses it with as many diverse modifications as the same things have aspects'.[2] This unifying factor, which makes history the story of the development of a single species—mankind—seems to Vico demonstrated by the similarity of proverbs in many tongues, and he thinks a dictionary could be composed of basic ideas (*voci mentali*) common to all peoples, although each of these cultures might perhaps have evolved at a different tempo in different environments. Such central ideas (or words—for he insists that it is a mistake to try to distinguish the two) are 'gods', 'family', 'heroes', 'auspices', *'patria potestas'*, 'sacrifices', 'rights' (to a piece of land), 'command', 'authority', 'conquest', 'courage', 'fame'. These are, as it were, basic terms or ideas which all human beings must have conceived and lived by at some time or other; from their evolution the

---

[1] N.S. 32 (cf. also 935).   [2] N.S. 161.

story of the societies in which they were current can, according to Vico, be reconstructed.[1] This is perhaps too simple and bold a programme, but it has in it the seeds of what, under the impact of German historicism, ultimately revolutionized the writing of history. That day, however was not yet. Vico went a considerable way towards it with his new method which he applied with brilliant effect to the issue over which a famous war was fought in his day, of whether the wisdom of the ancients was superior to that of the moderns.

Vico notes the deep, recurrent, nostalgic human tendency (revived in his day by Bacon and the Natural Law theorists) to assume that once upon a time there existed a marvellous science which, owing to our sins or ill luck, we have lost, a science which can, perhaps, be recovered from ancient monuments that might have preserved something of it.[2] This underlies the conviction that ancient myths must enshrine some profound lesson for our own time, inasmuch as they embody the pure knowledge possessed by our antediluvian ancestors, governed, as they surely were, by an *élite* of sages, whose poems, oracles and maxims—the ancient lays and legends of the tribe— contain esoteric truths long lost or forgotten, or distorted by their degenerate descendants. Vico's outright rejection of this almost universal belief is one of his many claims to originality. History reveals no golden age to him. He gets over the difficulty presented by his orthodox Christian faith by explaining that the Flood has obliterated all earlier culture, including that of the Garden of Eden.[3] After it men were once again brutish, solitary savages wandering in 'the great forests of the earth'. Ancient poetry does indeed require wise minds

[1] Professor Enzo Paci in his study of Vico—*Ingens Sylva* (Mondadori, Milan, 1949, 1970)—draws attention to the parallel between Vico's conception of deep, recurrent themes in the history of the collective human consciousness (and its subliminal regions), and the great myths of the German romantics, Schelling, Novalis and, above all, Richard Wagner. Fafner and Fasolt, Siegmund and Sieglinde do indeed, as Professor Paci remarks, belong to the grim, early world of Vico's *grossi bestioni* and *giganti*; Vico would have understood Wagner's cosmic myths.

[2] A century later, Joseph de Maistre defended against the *philosophes* the special status which the Church accorded to Latin (which he, too, thought a very ancient language) on the ground that it was the matchless repository of the accumulated wisdom of the human race.

[3] It is worth noting that a century earlier Jean Bodin, whose works Vico certainly knew well, had rejected the idea of a Golden Age on much the same grounds (e.g. in his *Methodus*, see *Oeuvres philosophiques de Jean Bodin*, ed. Pierre Mesnard [Paris, 1951], p. 2268).

to interpret it, but it is not a path to forgotten eternal truths: it is a window into a crude and barbarous world, into laws and customs remote from our own. 'Ancient jurisprudence is a severe kind of poetry'.[1] *Genres* that we distinguish now, prose and verse, law and history, are still one and undivided. Roman law 'is a grave poem'.[2] 'Poetical' is Vico's term for 'primitive', formalized, social imagery which tells us how men saw themselves and their social relationships at the time when it was created; 'poetical' law is the language 'natural' to that specific moment of evolution, and is full of animism and fetishism. This is so because 'mind makes itself the rule of everything it does not know' and 'when men are ignorant of the natural causes producing things, and cannot even explain them by analogy with similar things, they attribute their own nature to them. So the vulgar, for instance, say that the magnet loves iron'.[3] For Vico this is not a consciously exaggerated or deliberately fanciful use of words, but the natural language of a particular stage of evolution, symptomatic of a particular type of immature apprehension that occupies its own unique and unalterable place in a recurrent, intelligible pattern of the development of the human spirit.

His sensitiveness to words and the philosophical significance of their use can be very modern. So, for example, he notes what has only in our day been analysed and classified as the 'performative function of words',[4] namely the fact that words themselves need not merely describe or attract attention to something outside themselves, but may themselves be acts or intrinsic elements in action, as, for example, in the part that they play in legal transfers, or religious ceremonial. That words are not invariably used to describe, or command, or threaten or ejaculate or convey images or emotions, but can themselves be a form of action, is certainly a new and important idea, whenever it may first have been enunciated. Vico declares that, just as peasants still think that their rights, say to a piece of land, lie in the actual words of the contract—because words themselves have a compulsive power—

---

[1] N.S. 1037.

[2] *Ibid.* See Momigliano's interesting suggestion ('La Nuova Storia Romana di G. B. Vico', *op. cit.*) that Vico may have tried to look on the Twelve Tables as the Roman equivalent corresponding to the Homeric poems.

[3] N.S. 180.

[4] By J. L. Austin. Something of this kind was adumbrated by Hobbes, and later by Hume, but its full significance was brought out only in our own time.

so in primitive societies such important acts as the manumission of slaves, or taking possession of a property, or retaliation for an injury, were acts performed by means of words which themselves had the force of the original acts. Agamemnon and Jephtha (who belonged to the age of 'the gods') sacrificed their daughters because the very action of uttering the oaths had the force of natural causality, and the words directly altered (and were recognized as acts which could not but alter) the *status quo* simply in virtue of having been spoken. For Vico a society where words can function in this way must see, feel, think, act, in ways unlike those of any society in which words are not so employed, but are used, let us suppose, only to describe, or explain, or express, or pray, or command, or play certain verbal games and the like.

Whether this—or any other among Vico's many specific hypotheses—is correct or not, is less important than what he did achieve. Much of his genetic etymology and philology is clearly faulty or naïve or fantastic. But it is equally clear that he was, so far as I know, the first to grasp the seminal and revolutionary truth that linguistic forms are one of the keys to the minds of those who use words, and indeed to the entire mental, social and cultural life of societies. He saw much more clearly than anyone before him, even the great Valla (a century and a half earlier) and his disciples, that a particular type of locution, the use and structure of a language, has a necessary, 'organic' connection with particular types of political and social structure, of religion, of law, of economic life, of morality, of theology, of military organization, and so on. He was convinced that this 'organic' connection can always be traced between all the various aspects of the activity of the self-same men; that these interconnections, which in their totality form ways of life or cultures, do not follow each other in a haphazard order, but in a pattern, so that each phase flows out of, and is at once a development of, and a revolt against, its predecessor; moreover, that the pattern is intelligible, inasmuch as it flows from the nature—interpreted as *nascimento*—of man, from those developing faculties which alone make men human and go through an objective universal order of stages of growth in the lives of individuals and societies, a process which can be not merely recorded, but understood. It can be understood because (although he was perhaps not the first thinker to perceive this) men are conscious of their own powers, types of motives, reactions, social relationships, as participants, and not as spectators—from, as it were, within; and, so he believed, can see in their own experience not only the workings of their own purposes, but glimpse those of their Maker. Providence, he declares, shapes our lives, at times against our conscious purposes; but it is our desires, our goals, our motives, our acts, through which it works its will. In this sense at least, it is we who make our own history. This is analogous to Hegel's view of human passions as the dynamic forces used by the Cunning of Reason, and Marx's conception of class interest as the engine of progress.[1] The proper study of man is his own evolving character and the pattern of cultures in which it is made concrete. He can understand what he has, in some sense, himself created, in a different and profounder way than 'external' nature which is his environment and his raw material. The study of language is one of the paths to this kind of self-knowledge. These were ideas of exceptional originality and fertility.

The second great door to the recovery of the past is mythology. Mythology is neither, as was held by neo-classical theorists in the Renaissance, the picturesque invention of the poets seeking to stimulate our imagination, nor, as rationalists maintained, lying fables spread by unscrupulous priests or other self-interested charlatans, to deceive or lull the ignorant masses. Nor are they, as the Euhemerists declared, confused memories of extraordinary men, promoted by popular imagination to divine or heroic status. Myths, according to Vico, are systematic ways of seeing, understanding, and reacting to the world, intelligible fully perhaps only to their creators and users, the early generations of men. 'In their fables the nations have in a rough way, and in the language of the human senses, described the beginning of the world of the sciences, which the specialized studies of the scholars have since clarified for us by reasoning and generalization.'[2] Mythologies are 'civil histories of the first peoples, who were poets',[3] that is to say, they are natural modes of expression for those who felt, thought, spoke in ways which we can now grasp only with the greatest effort of the imagination. How can we fully enter, Vico asks, into a world in which it was normal to see the sky as incarnate Jove (for what can such phrases as *Jovis omnia plena* mean to us? how can Jupiter be at once the father of the gods and also the whole of heaven?)[4] and Nature as an immense woman or 'a vast animate body which feels passions and effects'.[5] We are reminded again that for us it is almost impossible to think and feel in 'corporeal'

---

[1] On this, see Part Two, pp. 113-4. [2] N.S. 779.
[3] N.S. 352 (see p. 46 above). [4] N.S. 379. [5] N.S. 377, 379.

categories, 'to enter the vast imaginations of those first men'.[1] The gods of the ancient peoples—of the Greeks and Romans, for instance —are not devils (as the early Christian theologians taught), nor are their attributes and histories poetic constructions, deliberate products of a long period of elaboration created for aesthetic contemplation, but the 'poetic' (that is, generated by the *Volksgeist*) creations of early human consciousness, now dead, fossilized, and ready for dissection and analysis by experts. Myths are the concrete mode of expression of the collective imagination of early mankind, and for modern critics the richest of all sources of knowledge of the physical and mental habits and the social ways of life of their creators. 'Fables are true histories of customs.'[2] Homer in particular is a rich treasure-house of information about the Hellenic past.[3] 'Fables are the first histories of the gentile peoples',[4] hence 'mythology is the first science to be learnt'. They reflect the realities of the time in which they were born. So, for example, the relationships of the gods must be understood in terms of the primitive society of which they are symbolic: to be shocked by their 'immorality', or to be amused by it, or to look upon them as material for poetical treatment, as was done by Greek or Roman poets, philosophers and critics, rests on a misinterpretation of the Olympian religion by later, sophisticated writers, lacking in historical sense, who misunderstood the past by applying their own social and moral categories to worlds remote from their own. As for the allegorical fancies of modern writers, they bear no relation to genuine myths—indeed they stand at the farthest possible remove from them.

Where there are laws of development, there must be the possibility of a systematic science. Armed with his new principles, Vico tries to reconstruct long lost worlds out of the myths of which the grammarians who preserved them did not begin to grasp the 'true' meaning. What

---

[1] N.S. 378.   [2] N.S. 7.   [3] *Ibid.*

[4] N.S. 51. Only of the 'gentile peoples', because the history of the Jews, who had been made rational by divine revelation (N.S. Prima, *iii*, 18), has been directly revealed by God in the Scriptures, and does not need archaeological reconstruction. Vico plainly tried to avoid giving examples from the 'sacred history' of the Jews to illustrate his thesis. For obvious reasons he deliberately averted his gaze from this rich treasury of myth and fact, yet his eye occasionally and perhaps inevitably strays towards it. The notion that fables and legends are evidences of the *moeurs* of the past and that the 'first historians were poets' is to be found in French historiography in the sixteenth century, e.g. in Bodin and La Popelinière, as well as in Bacon (see Part Two, pp. 131 ff).

kind of society, he asks again and again, could have given rise to this or that fable or image? He is the father of the economic interpretation of ancient legends, which, striking enough in his own day, at times foreshadows the approach of later anthropological, particularly Marxist, writers. The story of Theseus and Ariadne, for example, is, according to him, primarily concerned with early seafaring life. The Minotaur represents the pirates who abduct Athenians in ships, for the bull is a characteristic ancient emblem on a ship's prow, and piracy was held in high honour both by the Greeks and the ancient Germans. Ariadne is the art of seafaring, her thread is navigation, the labyrinth is the Aegean Sea. Alternatively, the Minotaur, when he is not the embodiment of piracy, is a half-caste child—a foreigner come to Crete —indicating that immigration from the mainland was prevalent at the time. No myth is safe from Vico's zeal: every legend is so much grist for his socio-economic mill. Cadmus is primitive man, and his slaying of the serpent is intended to convey the notion of the clearing of the vast forest. He sows the serpent's teeth in the ground—the teeth are in reality the teeth of the plough; the stones he casts about him are the hard clods of earth which the nobility—the oligarchy of the heroes —retain against the land-hungry serfs; the furrows are the orders of feudal society; the armed men who spring up from the teeth are heroes, but they fight not each other as the myth relates (at this point Vico, like many a higher critic or the less restrained followers of Freud and Jung, feels impelled to 'correct' the evidence), but attack robbers— the still unsettled vagabonds who threaten the lives of the settled agricultural folk. The wounding of Mars by Minerva is the defeat of the plebeians by the patricians. Minerva, who conspired against Jupiter, is the nobility that bands together against tyrants, and so on. The notion of early class war preoccupied Vico. R. W. Vaughan[1] has compiled a useful catalogue of some of Vico's symbols for the rebellious plebeians fighting for their rights against the aristocracy. It includes the Sirens, the Sphinx, Marsyas, Circe, Ixion, Tantalus, Midas, Phaeton, Antaeus, Orpheus torn limb from limb by the Maenads, Vulcan hurled down by Jupiter, and Penelope's suitors. All these he takes to be memories, symbols, and later rationalizations of traumatic collective experiences—the critical turning points (and the wounds sustained in the course of them) in the lives of entire societies. Pegasus, on the other

---

[1] In the essay on Vico in his *Studies in the History of Political Philosophy*, vol. 1.

hand, has quite a different, and a logically more interesting, function: *prima facie*, Vico tells us, he might be taken to represent the invention of riding; but one can delve deeper. Since in early times universal notions had not been attained, complex ideas were represented by means of spatial combinations of the relevant characteristics, resulting in physical monsters. In the case of Pegasus, wings represent the sky, and the sky represents the birds the flight of which yields the all-important auspices. Therefore, wings plus a horse is equivalent to the horse-riding nobility with the right of taking auspices and, on the strength of that, in authority over the people. Myths represent powers, institutions, radical changes in the social order; hence, according to Vico, nothing can be more absurd than to try to fit an obviously mythological creature like, say, the lawgiver Draco, the symbol of authority, a serpent found in China and Egypt as well as among the Greeks, or, for that matter, Minos or Hercules or Aeneas, into the real chronology of history. Gods, heroes, mortals, are each a myth and symbol. The descent of Aeneas to Avernus is a symbol of sowing. Pythagoras and Solon turn out to be pure myths— Solon, for example, simply represents the aspirations of the Athenian lower class for equal rights. Apollo[1] symbolizes historically successive human and social functions—first he is the hunter, then a tree-trunk wielder, then an inventor and a rider, and always the immortal, long-haired youth (for these are all social habits or ideals at various moments of history). Three-quarters of a century before Wolf and his school, Vico saw in Homer not an individual who wrote the *Iliad* and the *Odyssey*, but the national genius of the Greek people itself, as it articulates its vision of its own experience over the centuries.[2] Seven Greek cities vied for the honour of being the birthplace of Homer, not because he was born in one of them, but because he was born in none—'the Greek peoples were themselves Homer',[3] he is the creative poetic imagination of all the Greeks, the symbol of the 'many centuries' which divided the *Iliad*, written by a poet of North-Eastern Greece who sings of 'pride, wrath, lust for revenge . . . Achilles, the hero of violence'[4], from the *Odyssey*,[5] written by a man of the South West, who celebrates 'the luxury of Alcinous . . . the pleasures of Calypso, the song of the Sirens' and 'Ulysses, the hero of wisdom'[6]—the Homeric poems are what certain classical scholars at the beginning of our own century used to call a 'floating mass of *epos*'.

[1] N.S. 533-38.   [2] N.S. 873.   [3] N.S. 875.
[4] N.S. 879.   [5] N.S. 879-80.   [6] N.S. 879-881, 789, 904.

Some of Vico's ideas are patently extravagant, but some are of the greatest pregnancy. The notion that there are abiding symbols in the imagination—in the semi-conscious mental processes of individuals and groups (some of which evolve at a different pace from others); that certain images persistently recur in the history of mankind—such as salvation and resurrection, cataclysm and rebirth; that myths and magic and formal ritual may be a natural—indeed, the only historically possible—way of describing their experience on the part of human beings at a given stage of linguistic, and *eo ipso* of social and psychological development; that attitudes, beliefs, cultures, are products of a given stage of social change, indeed of class structure and class warfare, and could not have arisen at any other stage (a hypothesis which in its Hegelian and Marxist forms led to the modern schools of the sociology of knowledge and of culture)—these ideas, derived for the most part from other authors and schools of thought, have affected our own views both of men and of the writing of history. The light cast since Vico's day by comparative mythology, philology, anthropology, archaeology, art history, by all the interrelated studies of human antiquities pursued under the influence of contending theories and systems—of Hegel, Marx, Comte, Durkheim, Weber, Freud; the very idea of using empirical methods to find order and meaning beneath the vast variety of social experience in its historical movement; the notion that there stretches a gulf, or at least a great distance, between us and the early centuries of man, so that a powerful, but not impossible, leap of the imagination must be made by anyone who seeks to explain to himself that remote world; these transforming conceptions ferment in what Michelet admiringly called 'the little pandemonium of the New Science'. Vico is the author of the idea that language, myths, antiquities, directly reflect the various fashions in which social or economic or spiritual problems or realities were refracted in the minds of our ancestors; so that what may appear as profound theological conflicts or impassable social taboos are not what mechanically-minded thinkers have taken them to be—by-products of material processes, biological, psychological, economic, and so on, although they may be that too—but primarily, 'distorted' or primitive ways of recognizing social facts and of reacting to them. He is the author of the view that a rite or symbol or object of worship, from fetishism to modern nationalism, is most correctly interpreted as an expression of resistance to some social pressure, or joy in procreation, or admiration for power, or craving for unity or security or victory over a rival group (what later theorists were to call ideologies) which may take diverse forms, mythological, metaphysical, aesthetic—different types of spectacles through which reality is apprehended and acted upon. He was the first to conceive the notion that in this fashion it was possible to achieve a kind of window into the past—an 'inside' view—to reconstruct, not simply a formal procession of the famous men of the past, clad in their stock attributes, doing great deeds or suffering some fearful fate, but the style of entire societies which struggled and thought, worshipped, rationalized, and deluded themselves, put their faith in magical devices and occult powers, and felt, believed, created in a fashion which may be strange to us, and yet not wholly unintelligible. All these astonishingly bold hypotheses Vico conceived and applied in a world which was then, and for many years, acutely hostile to this 'psychologizing', anti-Cartesian, anti-'physicalist', approach.[1] It is scarcely credible that Vico could have achieved all this in the intellectual solitude and squalor of the conventional, timid and narrow society which he accepted completely, and in which he lived out his long, oppressed, unhonoured life.

The principles of the new method can now be re-stated more fully. The search for the truth is for the most part a genetic and self-analysing enquiry. Wherever man is more than a mere spectator, wherever he takes part as an actor, that is, outside the province of the natural sciences, of the objective laws of which he is an observer, and of mathematics, which he invents, and which cannot, therefore, by itself yield information about the real world, he is examining the activity of his own spirit in its interaction with the external world. This activity shapes and leaves unmistakable evidence of itself in human institutions —the chief amongst which are language, customs, religious rites, legends, myths, moral and legal systems, literature, the arts—everything that together constitutes a culture or way of life. Examination at first hand of surviving monuments is a direct door into the human past, and casts a steadier light both on what men were and did, and on their reasons and motives for it, than the stories of later chroniclers and historians, many of whom lacked knowledge and, above all, historical imagination, and were often guilty of anachronisms, crude and shallow

[1] See Part Two, Section I.

psychology, undisciplined fancy, and innocent or corrupt personal bias. Men must write history afresh in the light of the new critical principles, using as material the long familiar data, but subjecting them to questions of a novel kind: what kind of men can have talked, written, worshipped, governed themselves, created, as these men did? What must the natures and lives of such men have been, and what kind of social experiences must have shaped them, to have generated the successive stages through which they developed?[1] Can a fixed order or pattern of such stages be shown to follow by causal or metaphysical necessity from the changing natures of these men, or, it may be, of all men and societies as such? If there are such patterns, are they linear and non-repetitive or cyclical and recurrent? All 'popular' traditions must have 'grounds of truth', that is, some direct vision of the world, of which they are incarnations, preserved by entire peoples for long periods of time: the function of Vico's new science was to recover these grounds.[2] This was the programme, and the *New Science,* especially in the second, recast version of 1730, was Vico's attempt to realize it.

It was clear to him that, whatever the correct solution of the problem of development, the fashionable theories of his time were false. It is not conceivable that men have reached their latest state as a result of a single, collective act of will, starting from 'the ferine wanderings' of Hobbes' licentious and violent men, or Grotius' 'solitary, weak and simple, needy simpletons', or Pufendorf's 'waifs, cast into this world without divine care or help'.[3] Nor does Spinoza's psychology begin to explain men as they are, or as they ever could have been or have come to be. Self-interest is not, and could never have been, the mainspring of action; passion, duty, tradition, a sense of human or national solidarity; shame, conscience, awe, the sense of a divine presence, cannot be reduced to 'modifications' of the rational egoism of a 'nation of shop-keepers', 'hucksters' often deflected by irrational passions or frustrated by ignorance, which Vico declares to be Spinoza's caricature of men; and Locke is no better. The true route to the past is through 'the popular traditions which must have had public grounds of truth'. But these evidences have been inevitably distorted by the mere passage of

---

1 More than half a century later the German metaphysician F. H. Jacobi perceived in this the embryo of Kant's transcendental method; and indeed the analogy is not absurd.

2 N.S. 149, 150.

3 N.S. 338.

time, by the human tendency to forget and breed fictions, by the vanity
—*boria*—of nations and scholars, above all by changes in language
which cause words to mean something different in one age from what
they meant in another. Nevertheless, there are laws of social development on which the *New Science* rests; moreover group memories
persist, something lingers, and if we set about it in the right way
(because we are men, and there is a spiritual affinity between us all, so
that what one generation did or suffered, another can 'enter into', and
comprehend as part of its own autobiography) and make that immense
effort of imagination of which Vico never tires of talking—we can get
a glimpse of what the world looked like to remote barbarian, or even
remoter savage eyes. He thinks that what survives of the earliest age of
men clearly shows that the origins of men were crude and barbarous.
These monuments of the past have been falsely interpreted by the
scholars of our own 'cultivated and magnificent times', who talk nonsense about the 'matchless wisdom of the ancients',[1] ascribe their own
knowledge to the past, suffer from cultural and national arrogance
and self-centredness, and, above all, like to think that what interests
them, and what they know, must have existed and been known from
the beginning of time.

VII

The nature of men, as of everything, can be discovered by asking
the question 'What comes into being, at what time, in what fashion?'[2]
Men began not in Rousseau's state of innocence unspoilt by institutions,
but as 'semi-bestial giants'[3]—stupid, insensate, horrible brutes—filled
with fears, lusts and frightful (*spaventose*) superstitions. A peal of
thunder from the heavens was a voice that spoke to them, raging at
them, or warning them, or thundering commands. They were shocked
by such natural terrors into seeking hiding-places; shame and fear of
some super-human power caused them to drag their women with them
into the caves to which they fled, and so out of *pudore* and lust, privacy
and matrimony began. What Vico calls their forms of early prowess
(*virtù*) were disfigured (*mascolate*) by horrible rites and bestial cruelty.
He conceives these men as being like the Cyclops Polyphemus in the
Odyssey, fathers of primitive families, despotic, savage, violent, ferocious,
able to survive only by means of the most terrifying discipline, by
enforcing absolute obedience. Nature for these men was filled with

[1] N.S. 384.　　[2] N.S. 147.　　[3] N.S. 243, 338, 547, 644.

frightening powers; ritual and rigid forms of institutional behaviour—self-protective devices—were there from the start: they slaughtered their children to appease the unseen rulers (the Phoenician Moloch is Vico's example), a practice of which, among the 'gentiles', Ennius had spoken with horror.[1] Brutal as the exercise by the fathers of their absolute power might be, it was, nevertheless, modified by an embryonic sense of shame and awe: this is the root of religious feeling, the means used by Providence to raise men from their wild beginnings; not self-interest, which could never have sufficiently checked their savage egotism. Without such feeling, they would not have been human: without shame and awe there can be no self-control or self-direction, and without these not even the minimum of civilization, still less liberty under the law of a later day, could ever have arisen.[2] These men knew nothing of beauty; even now, Vico remarks, peasants are remote from any such concept.

These owners of the original homesteads were subject to attack by the still lawless, 'natural' men—savage vagabonds roaming the earth. To resist these marauders, they joined with each other, and the first organized groups created the first embryonic common settlements. Some among the nomads themselves, in terror of stronger creatures, sought protection in these primitive stockades against the violent vagabonds with their 'infamous promiscuity'[3] and so arose the first class of servants and slaves, and with it a class structure, and, in due course, class war. It is not true (as, for instance, Bodin had supposed a century earlier) that the earliest form of political life was kingship—that is a typical blunder, Vico declares, probably based on an unhistorical etymology—the word 'kings' used by Homer and the early writers in their time plainly meant not individuals but ruling groups. The earliest societies were small oligarchic 'republics', groups of fathers living together, chained by iron laws—the necessary condition of survival—ruling over women-folk, children, clients and slaves. This is the Age of the Gods: of the 'mute' signs and hieroglyphs. At first the rulers were prudent and temperate,[4] then the laws were abused by them,

---

[1] *Et Poenei solitei sos sacruficare puellos.* N.S. 517.

[2] 'In this way the first theological poets created the first divine fable, the greatest they ever created, that of Jove'. Jupiter Optimus Maximus, the strongest and greatest, terrible but also *Soter*—saviour, for he did not destroy them, and *Stator*—stabilizer, for he provided them with ritual, institutions, social structure. (N.S. 379).

[3] N.S. 1099.   [4] *Ibid.*

the slaves revolted, demanded recognition, and forced a compromise.[1] This marked the creation of the first civil order with defined rights for both classes, patricians and plebeians, noblemen and their clients (Vico's imagination is throughout obsessed by the history of Rome). This is the heroic age.

The beliefs of an age—what, before Herder had invented the *Volksseele*, Vico had called the 'common sense' of a society, 'the judgment without reflection felt in common by the whole of a people, order, nation, or the whole human race'[2] is embodied most vividly in its literary monuments. The 'heroic' age is faithfully reflected in the early poetry with its pride, avarice, cruelty',[3] qualities typical of every ruling aristocracy, and of the culture which it generates. The laws were cruel, because men cannot be governed in any other fashion at this 'heroic' stage of their development (the Homeric age, and the beginnings of feudalism in the West, are, for him, parallel cases of this phase). These rules, and the social order which embodied them, came into being because men cannot at this stage survive without them. But they would have lacked the absolute authority—the power to cause unruly savages to prostrate themselves before them—if they had been conceived as issuing from mere individual human wills.

Primitive men are bound by rules more rigid than those of advanced societies, and can advance only if the rules seem to them made not by themselves, but to be objective and absolute, carrying the authority of some vast external sanction—nature, God, or something too mysterious and terrible to mention. These unconscious creations of men's minds, which are inevitable at a certain stage of social growth, must, no less inevitably, at this level of mental development, present themselves as external entities, demanding absolute obedience —issuing rules on pain of terrible penalties. This is the first formulation of the celebrated theory of reification, one of the forms of alienation, *Entfremdung*, a cornerstone of Hegel's philosophy of history and of Marx's sociology, whereby men are for long ages governed by rigid beliefs, unseen divinities, laws and institutions, created indeed by men, but deriving their authority from the delusion that they are objective, timeless and unalterable like the laws of physical Nature. Vico's notion of history makes use of this concept long before Feuerbach. Men fear death, and collectively invent gods stronger than death. They crave for laws, and so invent objective entities called laws, justice, the divine will, to

[1] N.S. 1100. [2] N.S. 142. [3] N.S. 38.

61

maintain and protect their form of life. Rites that inspire terror are created, albeit unconsciously, to preserve the tribe against dangers and enemies, external and internal. Yet all this is man's own creation, and man can come to understand it, however imperfectly, because (fulfilling though he is a plan not of his but of God's devising) he alone made it. That is what makes history penetrable to him in the very sense in which nature remains for ever opaque.

The institutions of the heroic age—the framework of 'divine', imprescriptible laws, a cruel discipline imposed within it by the rulers on their subjects—dominate the second phase of social evolution. Nor must words mislead us. The liberties for which these men fought were liberties for themselves against usurpers and despots, not liberty for their servants or dependants, whom they ruthlessly punished and exterminated. It is later ages, Vico points out, which have grossly misinterpreted such words as 'liberty' and 'people' as they occur in 'heroic' writings, and have given them a democratic meaning, thereby showing a lack of the sense of history. In due course the plebeians became dissatisfied with their inferior status, founded upon the metaphysical assumption of the inherent inequality of their natures, which debarred them from such rights of their masters as inheritance, land-ownership, legal marriage, legal succession, and the like. Once again there arose mounting social pressure, sometimes erupting into violent battles for civil or religious rights. Plutocracy and rewards for merit succeeded oligarchy, and this in its turn broke down before demands for popular sovereignty by the majority of the unprivileged. The rich grew too secure, and were defeated by the populace. The rule of democratic justice set in, with its accompaniment of free discussion, legal arguments, prose, rationalism, science. Freedom of speech inevitably breeds unrestricted questioning of accepted values, that is, philosophy and criticism, and in the end undermines the accepted structure of society. Individualism grows to excess, dissolves the ties that unite the mass of the people, now no longer clamped together by the terror of inexorable, supernatural laws. This leads to scepticism, destruction of piety and unifying faith, and the disintegration of the tightly knit 'organic' state. The process ends either in anarchy, or (Vico is a deeply anti-democratic thinker) in 'the unchecked liberty of the people that is the worst of tyrannies'.[1] Civic virtue melts away, and is replaced by *anomie* and arbitrary violence. This disease duly breeds its own drastic

[1] N.S. 1102.

remedy: it is repressed either by a strong individual who dominates his society, and restores order and morality (as Augustus did in Rome), or by conquest at the hands of a fresher and more vigorous society, at an earlier, more primitive stage of its development. But sometimes the rot has gone too deep, and the members of the decadent society collapse into a kind of second barbarism, the 'barbarism' not of youth or of 'the senses', but of 'reflection'—a kind of senility and impotence, when each man lives in his own egotistic, anxiety-ridden world, unable to communicate or co-operate with his fellows. This is the situation in which men, although 'they still physically throng together, live like wild beasts in a deep solitude of spirit and will, scarcely any two of them able to agree, since each follows his own pleasure or caprice'.[1] The human beings dehumanized by what, in a remarkable phrase, he calls this 'second barbarism of reflection' (*la barbarie della reflessione*)—'base savages under soft words and embraces'[2]—finally succumb to their own weakness and corruption. Society falls to pieces; frightful wars, both internecine and with foreign foes, destroy its members, civilization collapses, men scatter, cities fall; over their ruins forests rise again. Thereby one cycle completes itself, and a new one begins.

Once again there is the reign of simplicity, brutality, and the Cyclopean 'fathers'. Among the relics of a dead culture, now overgrown with new virgin woods, 'men once more become pious, truthful and faithful'.[3] Religion once more takes its proper place as the sole truly cohesive force of society. It was so in Rome after barbarians overran it, and the new cycle opened, with its inevitable succession of the three stages of civilization: first came the Cyclopean Frankish 'kings' with primitive forts built against wandering barbarians, blind authority, protection sought by the weak from the strong, the beginnings of feudalism. Then came the second 'heroic' period, symbolized by crests and coats of arms, heraldic emblems that are the natural symbolism of this phase of culture, wrongly interpreted by later generations as conscious artifice. The second cycle is not a precise replica of the first, if only because it contains memories of its predecessor. Besides, it is Christian.[4] The movement is, as it were, a spiral rather than circular. Nevertheless, the correspondences are striking. Mediaeval society, like the heroic age of the classical

---

[1] N.S. 1106. [2] *Ibid.* [3] *Ibid.*

[4] Yet even so, they seem, unlike pre-Christian Jews, doomed to traverse the stages of the *storia ideale eterna* of the gentiles. Vico seems to offer no explanation of this anomaly, strange in a Christian writer.

world, was dominated by priests, and in due course generated its own great poet, the wielder of the new 'heroic' Italian language—Dante, the Homer of the second lap of human culture. The place of the gods of Olympus is now taken by the Christian saints. Even the public ritual repeats itself: in Homeric times, when a city was besieged, the gods of the city were solemnly adjured to leave it before it was finally sacked and destroyed; so now the saints were invited to leave the doomed towns by conquering Christian armies. This oligarchical order in its turn has been (by Vico's time) succeeded by a plutocracy, and will, no doubt, be succeeded by democracy, individualism, scepticism, atheism, and in due course, dictatorship or conquest. Once again a period of high civilization will be followed by a decline and fall, and, after that, the inevitable primeval forest. These are the famous *corsi e ricorsi*, that are Vico's form of the cyclical pattern of the succession of civilizations, perhaps the most celebrated of all his doctrines. It is not the least among the misfortunes of this singularly unlucky writer that he should be best known to posterity for the least interesting, plausible, and original of his views.

VIII

The notion that human history moves in cycles was an old and, in Vico's day, widely discussed one. Plato, Aristotle, Polybius, and their followers, particularly during the Renaissance,[1] had advanced similar hypotheses. What is novel is Vico's notion of what later came to be called the phenomenology of the human spirit. He sees the history of mankind as 'an ideal, eternal history traversed in time by every nation in its rise, growth, decline and fall'.[2] This is the *idée maîtresse* of his whole thought. He means by it a pattern of development which human society, wherever it is found, must obey. Indeed this pattern, like a Platonic Idea, is what makes human nature human: it is not a necessity imposed on men's souls or bodies from outside—from above by a deity, or from below by material nature. It is the principle of growth, in terms of which nature herself, *Natura* as *nascimento*—birth and growth—is defined. Human nature is to be defined dynamically, in terms of the ascent of man from 'crude beginnings' to our own 'magnificent age',

---

1 Machiavelli is the best known among them.

2 N.S. 349, cp. 245, 393—*La storia ideale eterna, sopra la quale corron in tempo le storie di tutte le nazioni, ne' loro sorgimenti, progressi, stati, decadenze e fini.* At other times he speaks of *un diritto eterno che corre in tempo.*

and, who knows, to what sublimer heights as yet unscaled. For Vico, human beings are not Cartesian substances, or static entities definable in terms of their Aristotelian entelechies or essences, whose development consists in the emergence, one by one, of properties which have lain hidden within them eternally, from the beginning, and then gradually come into being, become 'unfolded' and revealed, like the leaves of a book or the feathers of a peacock's tail. In Vico's conception man is not distinguishable from the actual process of his development— at once physical, moral, intellectual, spiritual, and, equally, social, political, artistic. For him the nature of men is intelligible solely in terms of men's relations with the external world and with other men, interaction with whom in the realization of ends which they cannot but strive to fulfil (and which can be realized only by society as a whole, and not by individuals alone) is the history of mankind. This 'ideal eternal history' is the single, universal pattern which all societies, in their rise and fall, are bound sooner or later to fulfil. Particular societies traverse this path in different ways and varying *tempi*. The advance of one may be observed at the same date as, and be affected by, the collapse of another. But the stages of the journey are set in an unalterable order, for each arises out of the needs created by the completion of the potentialities of its predecessor. The potentialities to be realized do not coexist from all eternity, for each possibility of development is literally conditioned only by the fulfilment of its predecessor. There is an objective order among them; one faculty, capacity, outlook, way of feeling, acting, cannot arise until and unless it has been called into existence by needs created by the changes which its antecedent has brought about. This growth of mental life of men is for Vico the growth of the institutional life of society. When a society is young, vigorous, disciplined, it is 'poetical', then 'heroic' and governed by myths and blind dogma. When it has been undermined by critical rationalism, then philosophy, democracy and the sciences transform social organization too. The path is fixed by the structure of 'the mind',[1] and is the same for all men and all societies (at any rate

---

[1] *Mente* is not a clear concept in the *New Science*: it is most often the mind of individuals, but sometimes seems to be a collective entity, not unlike the similarly ambiguous *Geist* in German Idealist thought. This, as might be expected, has generated conflicting interpretations of Vico's metaphysical views—Hegelian, Catholic, Marxist, existentialist, empiricist, and combinations of these; nor is the end in sight.

'gentile' societies), for it alone is what makes them human. Before Hegel and Saint-Simon, Vico defined human nature as an activity, and necessarily a social one.

This progression is not conceived as a causal process, in mechanistic terms. Vico is a Christian teleologist, no less than Augustine or Bossuet. He believes that mankind pursues purposes which God has once and for all set before it. But, unlike Bossuet, Vico believes that this purpose has not been directly disclosed to all men, only to the 'philosophical' Jews to whom the goals of man had been revealed by Moses and the prophets. They alone do not seem subjected to the cosmic wheel. The 'ideal, eternal history', the unalterable pattern, is the history of the 'gentiles'. Its content as opposed to its general structure—its temporal order—cannot, although it is metaphysically necessitated, be known in advance of the facts. But neither is it an empirical hypothesis, or mere conjecture. It is eternally true, events cannot falsify it: in Leibniz's language it is a *vérité*, not *de fait* but *de la raison*. How do we grasp it? Vico never clearly tells us: but there is little doubt that he supposed that once we had immersed ourselves in the concrete historical evidence, we should perceive the pattern as an *a priori* truth, scientifically *per caussas*, as the thinkers of Vico's time in general supposed the central principles of the sciences to be known, as Descartes or Spinoza, or Leibniz or Newton, conceived of the laws of nature; save that Vico believed the laws of social development to be more certain than those of the external world, indeed the most certain form of knowledge of the world that was open to men. Indeed he blames Grotius, for example (and could have criticized Bodin), for offering principles which are not 'necessary', but merely probable and 'veri-similar',[1] whereas the true constituents or 'elements of history'[2] can be established with absolute certainty—in the manner of Plato rather than Bacon. Are these 'elements' the categories, the basic relationships, presupposed by historical thinking—an application of Kant's transcendental logic *avant la lettre*—as Jacobi thought?[3] Whether his certainty is of a metaphysical-Leibnizian or a critical-Kantian sort, it seems to be this that permits him to call his discoveries a new 'science': something which has been discovered once and for all beyond corrigibility: the preordained timetable of human history: it is

[1] 'Probabiles verisimilesque' (see the opening of *De Uno, Opere*, II, 32).

[2] *Veri elementi della storia.*

[3] This, if I do not misunderstand him, is also Dr Leon Pompa's view, *op. cit.*

what it is and not otherwise: *è tale e non altro*.[1] Even so, man cannot attain to the perfect knowledge which only the Author of the entire cosmic drama can possess. But although it is, of necessity, finite, such historical knowledge is yet superior to all other human knowledge; since the comprehension by the actors of the parts that, in some sense, their own acting creates, will, if they understand the regular and recurrent structure of the ends and methods of social activity, be superior in kind to the knowledge possessed by spectators, however perceptive they may be. In history we are the actors; in the natural sciences mere spectators.[2] This is the doctrine, above others, on which Vico's claim to immortality must rest. For upon it rests the crucial distinction between *Geisteswissenschaft* and *Naturwissenschaft*. The battle over this distinction has continued unabated until well into our own day.

IX

In reading Vico it is constantly necessary to sift the chaff from the grain. This is not an easy task. All his philosophical works, and the *Scienza Nuova* in particular, are an amalgam of sense and nonsense, an ill-assorted mass of ideas, some lucid and arresting, others shapeless or obscure, bold and novel thoughts cluttered with trivial fragments of a dead scholastic tradition, all jostling each other in the chaos of his astonishingly fertile, but badly ordered and overburdened mind. He is at once obsessed by a single vision of mankind and its history, strictly obeying laws of social development which he is the first to discover, and overwhelmed by too much detail, too many implications of the central thesis, large and small, clamouring for expression at the same time. He seeks desperately to fit everything into the framework of his central pattern, but the new ideas prove too heterogeneous, too rich and too self-contained to fall into the scheme provided for them; they fly apart and pursue their own paths through the mass of superfluous and, at times, wildly irrelevant matter with which their author's digressive and intuitive mind is at all times clogged; nevertheless their intrinsic force and uniqueness somehow break through. Add to this Vico's lack of literary talent, his struggle and frequent failure to create adequate terms to convey so much that was novel and wholly out of tune with the spirit of his times, an ill disciplined imagination which

---

[1] *Opere*, V, 62-3.

[2] For a sixteenth-century anticipation of this (in Baudouin's *De Institutione Historiae Universae*) see Part Two, p. 137, n. 1.

has tempted so many later writers to read their own very different thoughts into the luxuriant jungle of his mind, the haste and clumsiness with which his masterpiece was knocked together (or rather, painfully extracted out of the larger, unpublished work) in the intervals from ill-health and menial hackwork, then endlessly corrected and recorrected, added to and altered, under an incessant pressure of an inexhaustible supply of examples, allusions, parallels, associations, which he could not organize, circling round the same central notions by which he was obsessed; if all this is taken into account some of the shortcomings of the *New Science* and its lack of readers are not difficult to account for. Nevertheless it remains a work of genius.

I shall not attempt to assess the plausibility of Vico's specific schema of human history. His obsession with triads, which influenced later thinkers; his parallels between the patterns of rise, apogee, and fall of civilizations, the first in a series of fanciful constructions which culminate in the morphologies of history of Saint-Simon, Fourier, Comte, Ballanche, Spengler, Sorokin, Toynbee; his peculiar interpretations of Greek, and especially Roman, history and philology (which is his paradigm), and much else of this kind, seem of remote interest now. Indeed, his more specific reconstructions of the past carry little conviction in the light of subsequent research. Vico's merit lies not in the discovery of new facts, but in asking new questions, throwing out new suggestions, and establishing new categories the grasp of which has altered our ideas of what kind of facts are important for the understanding of history, and why. That the vocabulary of savages was poorer in nouns than ours may be false; that language changes or evolves may have become, by Vico's day, a truism; but that to each type of society belongs its own peculiar structure of myth (or language, or artistic creation, or economic habits) expressive of its own unique outlook, is an idea of major importance. That every society must inevitably pass through the same stages of oligarchy, slavery, serfdom, tenancy and 'Quiritarian' ownership, as in Rome, is not true. But the notion that social institutions evolve under the pressure of conflicts between classes which arise out of property relationships, is one of the great transforming hypotheses of our age. Vico perceived a revolutionary truth when he asserted, before Herder or Hegel or Marx, that to each stage of social change there correspond its own types of law, government, religion, art, myth, language, manners; that fables, epic poems, legal codes, histories, express institutional processes and structures which are parts of the structure, and not of the 'superstructure' (in Marxist terms); that together they form a single pattern of which each element conditions and reflects the others; and that this pattern is the life of a society.[1] He said something scarcely less important when he asserted that social history was in large measure (not wholly—that is a later, Marxist dogma) the struggle of the 'have nots' for rights and powers—economic rights of possessing the soil, moral rights in the form of claims to legal status, particularly marriage and inheritance, originally confined to the patricians and gradually won by the plebeians after a series of bloody insurrections, political rights to a share in the government of the state, e.g. the right of taking auspices, which give the right to guide its destinies. Moreover, he looked for the evidences and reflections of such social struggles in new places, in what had hitherto been the preserve of antiquaries remote from political or social problems, for example in the story of the successful pressure of the 'under-privileged' minor divinities, *Di minorum gentium*, for full citizen-ship of Olympus where the *Di majorum*, the gods of the major Roman *gentes*, had hitherto enjoyed undisputed supremacy.

The 'organic' interconnection of these, not *prima facie* connected, spheres of human action (which today few would question) is due to the fact, so Vico tells us, that men's lives are governed not by chance, as Epicurus and his disciples Hobbes and Machiavelli held, nor by fate, as the Stoics, Zeno and Spinoza, believed[2]—for this would make history incapable of rational explication—but by the divine spark in man, his effort to get away from brute nature, towards 'humanity' or 'civilization'. Conscience, shame, a sense of the numinous or divine authority, of law, of responsibility, whence spring their sense of rights, of the minimum that they need to lead a life in which their faculties can obtain adequate scope; these are the universal human goals to which (under the concealed impulsion of Providence) men's 'divine' craving to realize themselves urges them. Laws and customs are the social products which respond to changing social needs. They are not

---

[1] He is, however, careful to point out that customs change slowly (N.S. 249), and consequently the new forms of life tend to retain for some time the impress of their previous customs (N.S. 1004).

[2] N.S. 342. 'It was therefore with good reason that Cicero refused to discuss laws with Atticus unless the latter would give up his Epicureanism and first concede that Providence governed human affairs.' N.S. 335. Grotius and Pufendorf ignored it in their hypotheses, Selden took it for granted; but the Roman jurists really established it. See N.S. 310, 350, 394-7.

the embodiment of infallible rules which individual sages, lifted above the stream of history, conceive in the fullness of their perfection, and lay down as immutable codes for all men, at all times, in all places. For men evolve: there can be no timeless minds or timeless laws of this kind.

Civilizations start from 'crude beginnings', 'gross imaginings', 'frightful superstitions'. Out of its dark, confused origins (of which Schelling was later to make so much), humanity moves forward slowly and painfully, and reaches maturity, usually after turmoil, struggle, cruel oppression and bitter conflict. Must this price always be paid? Vico's entire doctrine rests on the affirmation that it must. He cites those who think otherwise. Lucretius, the greatest disciple of Epicurus, held the influence of religion responsible for most of the crimes and miseries of mankind. Earlier still, Polybius had declared that 'if philosophers had existed then [in the early ages of man] there would have been no need for religion'.[1] This implies that if wise and rational teachers had existed, they could, at any time, have saved humanity from its follies and sins and agonies, so that it was simply a piece of bad luck for the human race that at critical junctures no sages arose, or made themselves heard—a view strongly implied by Voltaire and other thinkers of the Enlightenment who rejected appeals to the inscrutable will of God made by theists who gloried in the blindness of their faith. Vico had read Lucretius' magnificent poem with veneration, and borrowed from it (especially from the Fifth Book, even if he concealed this later), and he owed still more to Polybius. Moreover, he admired Stoicism, especially the Roman Stoics. And he was a pious if peculiar Christian. But these views he rejected totally and with passion. The notion that men could have been rational, virtuous, wise, from the beginning—that savagery and barbarism could, but for the intervention of forces beyond human control, have been avoided; that religious obscurantism and the fear and ignorance which led to it were either disastrous accidents, which need never have occurred, or unintelligible mysteries—this seemed to him blindness to man's nature as a historically evolving entity, failure to understand what it is to be a man. For Vico, men are what they are in virtue of their development according to an intelligible sequence through stages which explain each other. Man cannot spring fully armed like Athena from the head of Zeus. Rationality is painfully acquired. Just as individuals cannot be conceived of

---

[1] N.S. 1043.

as fully rational until they have attained to a certain level of maturity—until they have gone through, and, in due course, grown out of, earlier modes of experience, the outlook of infants, children, savages, the worlds of immediate sense and imagination; so a society of men for Vico, as for Pascal (who described mankind as being like a single centuries-old man), cannot attain to, for example, civil equality or monotheism or republican virtue, until it has gone through the phases which must necessarily precede this culmination, until it has exhausted these simpler forms of life, authoritarian, magical, animistic, polytheistic, of which the full flowering of a culture is at once the fulfilment and the destruction. Polybius' error thus consists, for Vico, in the neglect of history as an essential category, which underlies his fallacious assumption that philosophic wisdom could have occurred in any social *milieu* at any time, that it was a mere accident that it took so long to arrive, leaving the field open to its calamitous rival—religion; and no less fortuitous that when philosophy (or science) did finally speak its truths, they should have been so little followed, and become so soon forgotten in the long, sterile night of the Middle Ages. Vico attributes this lack of the true sense of history to Polybius; but he could equally well have cited Descartes[1] or Grotius or Spinoza or Voltaire.

The analogy between the individual and society, microcosm and macrocosm, is at least as old as Plato. But the notion of movement towards *humanitas* owes more to stoicism and the Renaissance humanists. So Marsilio Ficino says that boys are more cruel than men, the dull than the intelligent, madmen than the sane, because they have less *humanitas*, are less fully human: brutality is a form of immaturity. This doctrine is common to Vico and the Enlightenment. But whereas for the *philosophes* the stages represent merely imperfections to be transcended, for Vico they also possess marvellous 'poetic' properties which are lost in the process of civilization. No *Iliad*, no *Divine Comedy*, can be created in 'our own magnificent times', but only during the 'heroic' phase to which the avarice, cruelty, arrogance of the rulers are intrinsic. This is Vico's phenomenology: there is no real bridge between his

---

[1] 'Sparta's greatness' was attributed by Descartes to 'circumstances there originated by a single individual, so that its laws tended to a single goal'. (*Discourse on Method*, Everyman Edition, p. 11.) A century earlier, Machiavelli paid a similar tribute to Lycurgus. Vico, for whom Lycurgus is a social myth, regards such individualism as being characteristic of Descartes' blindness to the nature of man and history.

thought and that of the progressive intelligentsia of his time. What was for them the beginning of liberation by reason, was for him the beginning of the disintegration of the social texture.

The doctrine that he attacked lay at the heart of the teaching of the Enlightenment both in Vico's own day and in the two centuries that followed. What Descartes cautiously implied, the radicals of the eighteenth century proclaimed boldly and clearly: that every form of belief and practice that was not founded on a rational basis, such as religious or non-rational or subjective thought or feeling, is so much gratuitous deviation from the one, eternal, timeless truth. The follies, vices, crimes and miseries of mankind are, in this view, principally due to the (largely unexplained) failure to appear, when they were most needed, of teachers of sufficient knowledge, virtue and authority over men, to set humanity on the right path and break, once and for all, the sway of the fools and impostors who have hitherto wrought havoc with men's lives. In so far as Vico, with his doctrine of the *storia ideale eterna* in which human nature transforms both itself and its environment, denied precisely this possibility, such optimistic reformers as Helvétius, Holbach, Condorcet (and their followers in the nineteenth and twentieth centuries) would, if they had read them, have found in Vico's writings all that they most passionately rejected: historicism—that is, belief in the unique character and indispensability, and above all, validity at its own stage of development, of each of the phases through which mankind has passed and will pass; belief in an immaterial soul, with its own immanent laws of growth, modified by external factors but not subject to mechanical causation; belief that men understand themselves and their own works in a different, and superior, sense to that in which they know the external world; the view that history is a humane study in some sense in which physics is not; finally, that the goals of men are set by Providence, and that their past and future are strictly governed by it, and much else of the same sort that they would have found wholly repugnant. In this sense Vico was a reactionary, a counter-revolutionary figure, opposed to the central stream of the Enlightenment. His hostility to Descartes, Spinoza, Locke, and to all attempts to apply the concepts and methods of the natural sciences to what is human in human affairs—which seemed to him tantamount to dehumanizing men—anticipated the positions of Hamann and Herder and Burke, and the romantic movement. 'The listener to his lectures should have been a Francesco de

Sanctis, or a Georg Hegel, or a Barthold Niebuhr, who would continue the renewal (*rinnovamento*) of criticism, philosophy, history, that he had begun.'[1] This may account to some extent for the neglect to which his work was instinctively consigned by generations dominated by the advance of the natural sciences.

X

Nevertheless there is another and profounder sense in which Vico (like Montesquieu) was more of an empiricist than his materialist and utilitarian adversaries. For while it is true that he believed that man's nature and potentialities, and the laws which govern him, had been bestowed on him by his Creator to enable him to fulfil goals chosen for, and not by, him, he also believed that we could not know the Creator's ultimate purpose as He knew it; and moreover he believed that only one way was open to us of discovering what this nature and these potentialities and laws were—that of historical reconstruction. We must pay minute attention to historical facts—to the story of men's daily lives and activities on earth, which alone revealed the pattern which determined what men were, had been and might have been, could and would be. Unlike Leibniz (whose doctrine of development his own at times seems to resemble), Vico says nothing to imply that an intellect of sufficient penetration could, by mere insight into the structure (the 'essence') of any given human soul, or any 'spirit of the age', deduce *a priori* what it is bound to be and do—and so be enabled in principle to calculate the entire past, present and future of all men without recourse to empirical evidence. Nor, like the majority of the jurists of the seventeenth, and the *philosophes* of the eighteenth century, did he hold that a relatively simple set of psychological laws was sufficient for the analysis of the characters and acts of men. Vico worked on the opposite assumption—that only empirical knowledge, at times abstruse and peculiar, of what actually occurred, and exceptional imaginative power brought to bear upon it, reveals the working of the 'eternal' pattern that shapes the characteristics of human beings, the laws that are responsible for those parallels and correspondences of psychological and social structure that are found between societies or individuals remote from one another in space and time, race and outlook— correspondences in virtue of which, despite their differences, these

[1] F. Nicolini, preface to Vico's *Opere* (Ricciardi, Milan-Naples, 1953), pp. ix-x.

societies nevertheless constitute links in one great, winding, rising and falling stair. Each step in this spiral or cyclical structure leads to the next in an intelligible fashion—for they are all necessitated by the development of one and the same entity—the creative human *mente* guided by Providence. This 'mind', which for Vico appears to be, at times, simply men interacting in pursuing their needs and utilities, guided by Providence, can by memory, imagination, intelligence, the new method based on Vico's conception of a science of history, understand its own past states as stages towards its single ultimate, never fully realized goal—the realization of its capacities, as they come into being, each in its own due season, each in response to the demands created by the operation of its predecessor, each generating outlooks, institutions, forms of life, cultures, an 'organic' interweaving of diverse activities and states of mind or feeling—physical and spiritual, religious and legal, political and economic, spontaneous and self-conscious, stimulated by fear or interest, love or shame, awe and the sense of right, by desire for order or knowledge or freedom or fame or power or pleasure. The totality of these activities and states is the history of mankind.

For this reason to condemn an activity because it offends against our present-day morality is for him an approach both arrogant and shallow. The savage religions with all their horrors fulfilled an indispensable function in their own day, of binding (Vico suggests that the very word 'religion' stems from this) a chaotic multitude into a disciplined whole. Moreover (to this he returns again and again), many human acts have unintended consequences of vast utility and importance. Like many thinkers before and after him, Vico interprets this as evidence for a supreme purpose concealed from human eyes, transcending individual purposes—the hidden hand of a divine Providence without which the movement of history cannot be grasped, and which resembles Hegel's 'Cunning of Reason'. 'There are forms of order which, without human discernment of intent, and often against the designs of men, Providence has given to this great city of the human race.'[1] Legislation out of 'ferocity, arrogance and ambition' creates 'soldiers, merchants, rulers' and by this means arise 'strength, riches and wisdom of commonwealths'; and so 'out of the three great vices which could certainly destroy all mankind on the face of the earth, legislation makes civil happiness'.[2] Something of this kind had been said by Hobbes and Mandeville, and

---

[1] N.S. 342.   [2] N.S. 132.

would be said again by Helvétius and Adam Smith and Bentham. Legislation can turn private vices into public virtues by dangling rewards and punishments judiciously before men. Their egoistic instincts can be canalized by education and laws into doing public good. But this is not what Vico means. When he explains how lust and fear lead to marriage and the family, or the violence of patrons to their clients leads to revolt and so to the establishment of cities; how the oppression of the plebeians ends in its opposite—laws and liberty; how the risings of the people bring about monarchy; while the corruption of peoples by their rulers leads to the opposite of the rulers' purpose, namely conquest by stronger and purer peoples from without; how self-destructive decadence leads to solitude and savagery,[1] and then, by a miracle, to the resurrection of the phoenix out of its ashes and the new cycle of human history, what Vico means is something closer to the ideas of Herder and after him Schelling and Hegel; he believes, like them, that there exists a cosmic, purposive tendency which moulds men's passions and desires into institutions and forms of social life in an intelligible pattern, and consequently that this cannot be done, as the utilitarians thought, by the conscious control of intelligent experts who know how to canalize human weaknesses either for the society's advantage, or for their own selfish ends.[2]

---

[1] The primary cause of this is the destruction of religion, which, for Vico, is the social cement without which there is no 'shield of princes ... no shield of defence ... nor basis of support, nor even a form by which [peoples] may exist in the world at all'. N.S. 1109.

[2] This is asserted in the magnificent peroration with which the *Scienza Nuova Seconda* virtually ends: 'It is true that men have themselves made this world of nations (and we took this as the first incontestable principle of our Science since we despaired of finding it from philosophers and philologists), but this world without doubt has issued from a mind often diverse, at times quite contrary, and always superior, to the particular ends that men had proposed to themselves; which narrow ends, made means to serve wider ends, it has always employed to preserve the human race upon this earth. Men mean to gratify their bestial lust and abandon their offspring, and they inaugurate the chastity of marriage from which the families arise. The fathers mean to exercise without restraint their paternal power over their clients, and they subject them to the civil powers from which the cities arise. The reigning orders of nobles mean to abuse their lordly freedom over the plebeians, and they are obliged to submit to the laws which establish popular liberty. The free people mean to shake off the yokes of their laws, and they become subject to monarchs. The monarchs mean to strengthen their own positions by debasing their subjects with all the vices of dissoluteness, and they dispose them to endure

Providence disposes; man is free but severely limited; he can make virtues of his passions, but only those virtues which the particular stage that he has reached makes him psychologically and socially capable of conceiving. To this extent he is not free, since he is determined by the cosmic design of rise and fall, the *corsi e ricorsi* which he cannot control. Cultures are not insulated from one another; one culture can influence another, but only to the degree made possible by the particular step in the ladder or cycle it happens to have reached; a culture may be destroyed by an invasion or some other disaster, before completing its cycle—the *storia ideale eterna* of the gentiles will complete itself only if there is no interference: this depends on Providence, whose ways are ultimately inscrutable. Men cannot help being, in the long run, self-destructive, but, in the still longer run, Vico seems certain, human society will not perish utterly: always, in Schiller's phrase, 'new life will spring from the ruins'.[1] This is not the result of deliberate human design, but is the work of the human spirit (*mente*) obeying its own essential nature, created by a transcendent God who so made it, and provided for it in ways intelligible after the event, but often unforeseeable before it. The notion that man can break out of this circle, control his own destiny, make his own laws as he pleases, build on indestructible foundations, and be free and wise and rational for ever

---

slavery at the hands of stronger nations. The nations mean to dissolve themselves, and their remnants flee for safety to the wilderness, whence, like the phoenix, they rise again. That which did all this was mind, for men did it with intelligence; it was not fate, for they did it by choice; not chance, for the results of their always so acting are perpetually the same.' N.S. 1108.

It is difficult to believe that neither Hamann, nor his far more influential disciple Herder, did more than glance at Vico's philosophy of history, and that they did even this well after they had composed their own; or that the sole link between Vico and the early Herder (whose central views possess an uncanny resemblance to those of the *New Science*) is Vico's disciple Cesarotti, with whose commentaries on Homer Herder was acquainted, with, perhaps, a memory of a vague mention by Thomasius. Yet it may well be the case; there is as yet little evidence worthy of the name for any other conclusion. The effect of one thinker upon others is, at times, anything but direct; and the origins and rise of the new conception of society and social evolution, which reached its apogee in the German Historical School, despite the devoted labours of Meinecke and his disciples, still await their historian.

1 There is a story that Albert Einstein, not long before his death, was asked what, in his opinion, would follow the 'nuclear' technology of our day, and that he replied 'bows and arrows'.

—the faith of Condorcet or Saint-Simon or Comte or Marx—is not Vico's creed.

Vico is in obvious ways a relativist, but in spite of this, and without attempting to reconcile the two, a devout Christian. His orthodoxy shows itself in many ways. He speaks of man's fallen state, and clearly assumes it in his account of the inevitable collapse of all civilizations. He venerates the work of Grotius, but says that he will not annotate it because it was written by a Protestant and a heretic. He avoids all but a very few references to the Old Testament, and largely confines himself to the anthropological evidence provided by the classical authors of Greece and Rome, together with the fragmentary, and often fanciful, stories which, in his time, passed for the antiquities of primitive Scythians, Germans or Celts, as well as accounts of American Indians, who still live in the age of the Gods, and Siamese and other remote pagan societies. He insists throughout that his pattern works only for 'the gentile nations', for to the Jews God has revealed himself directly through their sacred scriptures; if they ignored the moral or spiritual truths vouchsafed to them, it was from wilfulness, or vicious blindness, and not because, like the gentiles, they had no choice but to wait until awareness of the truth became historically due. It is true that 'men have themselves made this world of nations', but not alone, not, as Marx was to say, 'out of the whole cloth.' Finite minds have not invented the laws that they obey, for then they would have had to exist before these laws in order to invent them; and what laws could their minds have obeyed in the course of inventing laws? Providence did it all, as he never tires of repeating. Yet his heterodoxy is, as has often been remarked, equally obvious. His insistence on the natural origins of language is not Christian doctrine. Nor is the cyclical theory which seems to preclude the entire Judaeo-Christian teleology, in particular, the culmination of the whole of history in a unique event —the Second Coming towards which all Creation moves. Moreover, the *ricorsi*, though Vico specifically confines them to 'the gentile peoples', evidently embrace the Christian ages also, for is not the attitude to the local saints shown to be parallel to that towards the local gods of antiquity, and is not Dante the Homer of his age? His attack on Grotius' doctrine of natural law is no less subversive than if he had directly assailed its Catholic version, e.g. that of Aquinas and his predecessors and the Spanish Thomists, in which Grotius' principles are rooted. The *New Science* in effect rejects the notion of absolute,

77

timeless values, and its historicism is as fatal to the Christian as to any other doctrine of natural law. His doctrine of the evolution of mankind from the *ferini*—the bestial creatures who wandered over the earth, at any rate after the Flood—is, as has been noted by all the commentators, taken from Epicurus and Lucretius: it is to be met in Euripides, Cicero, Horace, Diodorus Siculus, and again in the most notorious naturalists and atheists of the eighteenth century and later; but it has no point of contact with Catholic orthodoxy. The attack upon it of the learned Dominican Francesco Finetti in 1768[1] was perfectly justified, and, as Croce ultimately came to concede, Duni's attempts to defend Vico's self-proclaimed orthodoxy are totally unconvincing. His modern editor, Fausto Nicolini, has little difficulty in disposing of most modern writers (the most learned and interesting is F. Amerio), who wished to annex Vico to the ranks of orthodox Catholic theorists.[2] Although Vico makes a point of distinguishing *bestioni* from the *semplicioni* or *scempioni di Grozio, i destituti ed abbandonati di Puffendorfio* and *i violenti e licenziosi di Obbes*, there is no relevant difference between them; Vico protests too much about this, as indeed he does his piety and devotion to the precepts of the Church. Perhaps, as Corsano thinks, he was afraid of the Roman Inquisition in Naples, which, although not as savage as that of Spain which it replaced, did punish some of his free-thinking friends and silenced others, so that Vico would, for all his genuine piety, have had reason to be as frightened as Descartes had been in 1619 by the terrible fate of Vanini. Nicolini thinks that this is exaggerated, for the victims of the Neapolitan inquisition were few, obscure and not deprived of their lives. Croce's image of a poverty-stricken schoolmaster nervously genuflecting to avoid disgrace or censorship, anxious to be counted a devout member of his Church even though his views were suspiciously

---

1 In his *Apologia del genere umano accusato di essere stato una volta una bestia* (Venice, 1768). Reprinted by Croce in 1936 as *Difesa dell'autorita della Sacra Scrittura contro G. Vico* (Laterza, Bari). There were attacks on similar lines by Damiano Romano in 1736, Cosimo Mei in 1754, Donato Rogadeo in 1780, etc. (For the bibliography of anti-Vichismo, see B. Croce and F. Nicolini's magnificent *Bibliografia Vichiana* [Ricciardi, Napoli, 1947-8, 2 vv.] and Paolo Rossi, 'Lineamenti di Storia della Critica Vichiana' [in *I Classici Italiana nella Storia della Critica*, vol. II, *a cura di* Walter Bini, La Nuova Italia, Florence, 1962]).

2 See the first essay in Nicolini's *La Religiosità di Giambattista Vico* (Laterza, Bari, 1949), particularly the introduction and second chapter.

non-conformist, is probably correct. '*Vico fait d'étonnants efforts pour croire qu'il est encore croyant*', wrote Michelet in 1854,[1] and this echoes his remark in 1831 that Vico's thought '*est plus hardie, que l'auteur lui même l'a soupçonné. Heureusement le livre était dédié à Clément XII*'.[2] Moreover, Vico's use of critical methods first applied by Spinoza and Père Simon, the fathers of Higher Criticism, is obvious enough. Vico loathed Spinoza, but did not escape the influence of his method; he applies it only to pagan antiquities, but he applies it. Stranger psychological contradictions could be found. There is no reason, for example, to think that Machiavelli, who had moved further in an obviously anti-Christian direction, was insincere when he wrote his canticles of penitence[3] or when he made his last confession when he was dying. Hobbes, too, probably regarded himself as a Christian. The attempt to defend Vico after his death on Averroist lines—on the ground that his philosophical views belonged to a different realm from his religious or theological convictions, and that therefore there was no possibility of collision between them—whether or not it is philosophically defensible, undoubtedly reflects what has been psychologically true of men who remain fervently orthodox in their own minds, and passionately desire to remain loyal members of their Church or party or nation, while professing dissident views. There is no doubt that during the entire second part of his life—his most creative years—Vico lived in the most intimate intercourse with priests and monks, and looked to them for sympathy, help, advice, protection. His dislike of materialism, atheism, natural science, and his ignorance of the major scientific advances of his own century, are patent. He was a faithful and fervent ally of 'spiritualism' and religion as such. Indeed, the cornerstone of his reconstruction of the life of primitive men is the belief that religion alone, however primitive and delusive, alone creates and preserves the

---

[1] See *Jules Michelet* by G. Monod, Paris, 1905, pp. 15-16 (quoted by Oscar A. Haac in his article 'Michelet and Vico' in *Giambattista Vico, an International Symposium, op. cit*).

[2] *Histoire Romaine*, p. 13, quoted by O. A. Haac, *op. cit*. Or again: "Vico shows us how gods are made and unmade . . . it is man who is their creator. He ceaselessly moulds his own self, he manufactures his own earth and his own heaven. This revelation is so bold and shocking, that Vico is himself afraid of it, and endeavours to convince himself that he is still a believer"—from a largely unpublished note in 1854 by Michelet (quoted by Alain Pons in his article 'Vico and French Thought' in *Giambattista Vico, op. cit.*, p. 182).

[3] Although their authenticity has lately been questioned.

social bond, alone humanizes and disciplines savage men; without Providence there is no progress; it may work through the human faculties (hence we can, to a limited degree, discover its methods), but without the divine plan we should still be wandering in the 'great forests' of the early world; religion alone—shame before the thundering God in Heaven, a feeling of awe implanted by the true God—is the first and most powerful of the ways used by Providence to turn our vices into means of our preservation and improvement. The weakening of the feeling of awe, of piety, of religious authority, spells the doom of the entire social texture and leads to that second barbarism described in a famous passage of the *New Science* (remarkable enough to be quoted more than once) when men 'though physically thronging together, shall live like wild beasts in a solitude of spirit and will, scarcely any two able to agree, since each follows his own pleasure and caprice'[1]. Religion is not for him, as for Comte or even Saint-Simon, simply a social cement whose value lies in its utility: it is what makes men men: its loss degrades and dehumanizes. Unorthodox Vico plainly was: heretical perhaps; but unswervingly religious.

Despite these deviations and contradictions, Vico's central schema is not obscured. It remains, in its essentials, a theory of history founded on a metaphysical conception of men's nature as driven on by its own inner purposes, with a vitalistic sociology which can be held as fervently by an atheist as by a Christian. 'The world of human society has certainly been made by men, and its principles are therefore to be found within the modifications of our own human mind.'[2] This is what counts. It is this humanist doctrine, neither mechanistic nor determinist, but also not transcendental, that made the doctrine of this 'reactionary', less than a century after his death, acceptable to the secular defenders of French or Italian nationalism, who could not have held an uncompromisingly theocratic and authoritarian doctrine like those, for example, of Bossuet or de Maistre (or even Burke). This is so because Vico's arguments for the finger of God in history are, in the end, no more than contentions that attitudes, purposes and forces are never wholly man-made or planned, and in particular that some of the most beneficent, permanent and universal human institutions are not the results of men's conscious intentions. But all that this shows is that even if men largely create their own history, they do not do so alone,

1 N.S. 1106.   2 N.S. 331.

and do not create themselves. An atheist is left free to assume that the co-author of men's lives is an impersonal, and indeed purposeless and inanimate, nature, the laws of which are wholly discoverable by the material sciences. Vico would doubtless have rejected this; it is Providence that shapes our lives, and it is therefore presumptuous for men to claim wholly to understand its ways, but they are its instruments and of one spiritual substance with it, and therefore able to understand what they themselves create.

'The ideal eternal history', 'the laws that govern the history of every nation in its rise, development, maturity, decadence and fall', seem based on a polyphonic simile, in which each group of instruments (each nation, each culture) plays its own tune, the structure of which corresponds to the identical, or at least similar, tunes played in other keys and *tempi* by other groups of instruments—other nations and cultures, elsewhere, at other times.[1] Obscurities and problems remain. In Vico men can retrace the cycles of *sorgimenti, progressi, stati, decadenze, fini*, because men have 'made' them; consequently, they can recover them by sufficiently powerful intellectual-imaginative effort. How is this done? Can men do this because they are in communion with, live in, the *mente eterna ed infinita che penetra tutti e presentisce tutto*;[2] because they are a part of a universal spirit which entitles Croce to speak of Vico if not as a pantheist at least as an Absolute Idealist? But then, what are we to make of his insistence on a personal God, the transcendent deity of orthodox Catholic Christianity? Or can men do this because 'the world of civil society has certainly been made by men, and its principles are therefore to be found in the modifications of our own human mind'[3] by the *verum/factum* principle, and, therefore, not in the modifications of the Divine Mind, to claim to 'penetrate' which would be absurd and blasphemous? Again, if the criterion of truth is 'to have made it', and we claim to know our past, what becomes of divine intervention? When Vico speaks of 'our human mind', 'our

[1] It is a Leibnizian image, not a harmonic one which could have been intelligible only some decades later, like that which dominates, for example, Hegel's organicism, where the significance of individual sounds—particular ingredients in the development of world history—may not be intelligible save in conjunction with the other 'sounds', which, taken by themselves, at times may seem ugly, or meaningless, and acquire meaning and value only when 'heard' as elements in, and from the standpoint of, the organic whole.

[2] *Opere*, ed. Ferrari, IV, 39.

[3] N.S. 331.

intentions', 'the human mind of nations', 'our human thought', 'our spirit',[1] and so on, do such phrases refer to what is common to all individual minds, or some 'collective' mind, like Jung's Collective Unconscious, but with pantheistic implications? Or is the use of the term *nostro* merely metaphorical or distributive? Or again, when Vico says 'For natural reason is that whereby the gentiles are a law unto themselves'?[2] Do the *gentes* create 'law'? Are they rational precisely to the degree to which, and because, they have created it themselves and understand it, as they would not if it had been imposed upon them by an inscrutable Providence? Vico is a rich, suggestive and original, but scarcely a clear or coherent, thinker. One is tempted once again to quote Heine's celebrated comment on Berlioz that 'he has not enough talent for his genius'. The tension between Vico's theism and his humanistic historicism, between his conception of the cunning of Providence, and his constant emphasis on the creative and self-transforming labours of men, is not resolved in the *New Science*; to call it dialectical is only to conceal this fact by the use of a portentous term; Vico's Catholic interpreters lay stress on the former, Michelet and humanist thinkers on the latter, strain in his thought. It is certainly the humanist vision that seems to evoke his most ardent words. 'There is (for human beings) a divine pleasure in seeing the great cosmic ideas working themselves out';[3] divine because we see our own creative activity. 'History cannot be made more certain than when he who created the things described them'.[4] And then, in a curious, obscure, but arresting and characteristic passage, he adds: 'By logic men invent language, by morals they create heroes, by economics they found families, by politics they create cities, by physics, in a certain sense, they create themselves'.[5] What is this 'certain sense'? Vico does not explain. What men are and believe, they have themselves made: if not individually, then collectively. If the whole human race could speak as one man, it could perhaps remember all and understand all, and say all there is to be said. Because men have not each individually

---

[1] *Nostra mente umana, nostro intendere, mente umana delle nazioni, nostro umano pensiere, nostri animi* (see the terms from the First New Science of 1725 listed in the *Historical Theory of Giambattista Vico* by Thomas Berry, *passim*, [The Catholic University of America Press, Washington, D.C., 1949]).

[2] *Ratio enim naturalis ea qua gentes ipsae sibi sunt lex* (*De Constantia Jurisprudentis*, ed. Ferrari, p. 21).

[3] N.S. 345.　　[4] N.S. 349.　　[5] N.S. 367.

created the whole of human history, they cannot know the truth as the mathematician knows it about his invented entities; but because the subject matter of history is not fictional but real, the *New Science*, even if it is less translucent than mathematics, tells the truth about the real world, as geometry, or arithmetic, or algebra, cannot.

History, mythology, literature, law, these are among the studies that teach men what they are and what they were, why they must be what they are, what they could be, how 'the nature of peoples is first crude, then severe, then benign, then delicate, finally dissolute';[1] which stage in this cycle they have reached, where they are on the great stair of history, and what courses it is therefore best for them to pursue. Hegelianism, Marxism, Comtian positivism, the Catholic theories of 'palingenesis', to some degree social psychology influenced by Freud and his disciples, are attempts to elaborate and apply in very differing fashions the phenomenology of the *New Science*, whereby men seek, as it were, to psychoanalyse their own childhood and adolescence, and found predictions upon this evidence.

So caught was Vico by the novelty and the power of his new ideas, that he troubled too little to collect adequate evidence for his conclusions. By the end of the seventeenth century there came into being a plethora of travellers' tales and accounts of exotic peoples, upon which Montesquieu and many social and moral theorists in the eighteenth century drew avidly. Vico touched upon them, and mentioned them here and there, but on the whole made little use of them. Those whose minds are dominated by a powerful and revolutionary vision, which has transformed their view of the world, are sometimes averse from careful attention to empirical facts. Vico's outlook and his methods were unlike those of the inductive sciences; he was a philosopher and a jurist, he thought in terms of general ideas buttressed by occasional examples, but not of detailed evidence for carefully tested hypotheses.[2] He seems blind to the decisive impact of the natural sciences on Western culture. Perhaps this, too, helped to bring about the oblivion into which

[1] N.S. 242. Professor Paci (see his *Ingens Sylva, op. cit.,*) thinks that Vico conceived man's ascent as a struggle of the 'bestial' with the 'heroic'. Certainly Vico does not idealize the remote past—or, indeed, any other period.

[2] The reader should be warned that Professor M. H. Fisch does not agree with this, and regards the *New Science* as proceeding by induction and by hypothesis (*Giambattista Vico, op. cit.*, p. 423). I must own that I see little sign of this in the texts; moreover, it would contradict one of Vico's central theses—the unbridgeable gulf between the methods of natural science and historical disciplines.

his work sank after his death. In an age in which the physical sciences achieved unparalleled progress, Vico's audacious claim in the *De Antiquissima* that 'physics cannot define things *ex vero*', whereas history comes closer to this and his fierce opposition to atomism, 'epicureanism', utilitarianism—all the mechanical models which dominated the social and political thought of this time—stand out as a monument of (at times perverse) originality and independence.

XI

Vico had no doubt that he had discovered the central truth about philosophy and history; nevertheless he thought of himself primarily as a jurist, and his own greatest effort is directed against the application of the fallacies of Descartes and Grotius to the domain of law. The doctrine which he attacks with all his might is that of the great schools of natural law. His main charge against the famous masters of the seventeenth century—Grotius, Selden, Pufendorf (and, for that matter, the mediaeval Christian theorists too, although he tactfully does not say so)—is that they all assume a fixed, universal human nature, from the needs of which it is possible to deduce a single set of principles of conduct, identical everywhere, for everyone, at all times, and constituting therefore the perennial basis of all human laws, whatever special modifications and adjustments might be required by changing times and circumstances. For Vico there is no static nucleus, no unalterable minimum of this kind. 'Nature is the *nascimento*—the coming to birth of a thing at certain times and in certain fashions'.[1] Nature is change, growth, the interplay of forces that perpetually transform one another; only the pattern of this flow is constant, not its substance, only the most general form of the laws which it obeys, not their content. True natural law is not 'the Natural Law of the philosophers', not a set of universal rules, however general, however few, however old, but the emergence of new laws as expressions, in the social sphere, of each new way of life as it arises. Thus, for example, 'civil equity' is not a timeless and universal principle, latent in the souls of all men as such, but established by those whom Ulpian calls 'the few who have come to know what is needed to preserve society'.[2] No doubt each society is governed by some one set of rules, about which all, or at least most, of its members must be in broad agreement; but

1 N.S. 147.   2 N.S. 320.

these are not objective truths waiting to be discovered by a lawgiver of genius, and then 'received' by lesser men, or entire nations, bound by his vision of reality; they are produced by the fact that in a given set of circumstances human beings are liable to believe, express themselves, live, think, and act in common ways. 'The common sense' (by which Vico means something like the collective social outlook) 'of each people harmonizes various laws' without 'one nation following the example of another'.[1] 'The common sense of each people or nation so regulates social life and human acts that they accord in whatever the whole of a people or nation feels in common.' This is Vico's concept of true natural law, the 'Natural Law of the Nations', not of the philosophers.[2] There are, no doubt, some institutions which all men have in common—for instance, some form of religion; some form of marriage; some form of burial; these, Vico notes, are to be found in all societies. But he evidently does not think these a sufficient basis for a static universal law, since these forms vary widely from people to people, from age to age. It is impossible to abstract what is common to all the phases of a continuous dynamic process of change, as it is impossible to abstract what is common to all shapes, or all colours, or all human faces or lives, and pronounce that to be the basic or natural shape, or colour, the basic or natural human face or life. That is why it is idle to seek to abstract common unaltering beliefs and call them natural law.

What then is the natural law of the nations, *ius naturale gentium*? Vico characteristically explains that if by Nature is meant the monotonous repetition of causes and effects, that is precisely what men resist and transcend. The generations of birds learn nothing new, but merely do again and again what their ancestors have done before them, eternally. This is the mechanical 'nature' from which men can free themselves, which they must shun. '*Naturale*' for men means not fixed, but (again from *nascimento*) 'growing into society', and '*gentium*' means whatever is generated by the societies of human beings themselves (each generation bearing its successor on its shoulders), not by an élite of sages dictating from above, or speaking in the name of objective order—'*ipsis rebus dictantibus*', as the older theorists liked to say. Each society has its own 'civil law' appropriate to its stage of culture. But the nations, in their 'poetical' or 'heroic' phase, incapable as yet

---

[1] N.S. 311.   [2] N.S. 332, cp. N.S. 135.

of general ideas, unable to conceive their own slow evolution, tend to embody their sense of their own past in a myth—the god or the legendary legislator who gave them all their laws in one great creative act—Lycurgus, Draco, Solon, the great founders and fathers of their peoples, symbols of an entire society. But to see a myth for what it is, one must penetrate to the truth behind it.[1] Laws are the embodiment of a gradual and collective response on the part of an entire society. So, too, ancient poetry (Vico's principal example is the Homeric poems) is the 'greatest repository' of the laws and customs of the Greeks, of their view of life, in which the Hellenic nation, whatever origin it attributed to them, rightly saw an incarnation of its traditional values, the historical reasons for which, having as yet little self-consciousness, it could not know; and, since only God is omniscient, could never know completely. Such traditional wisdom tends to be questioned as self-consciousness and self-criticism grow. Thus their lowly status is accepted by plebeians so long as they do not question its metaphysical basis—the objective inferiority of their natures to that of the 'superior' patricians. Once critical reason causes them to question this dogma, then doubt it, and finally reject it, the path is open to rebellion, which in its turn is symbolized by the Roman myth of the Secession and by the institution of the Tribunate. Myths give way to metaphor, metaphor to conventional use of language which coincides with philosophy, democracy, the growing use of prose and the growing self-consciousness and artificiality of poetry as a deliberate aesthetic exercise. Natural law and positive law alike cease to be expressed in the 'grave poems' of ancient Roman jurisprudence. The evolution of law (and the entire story of the progress of humanity) can be traced best of all 'philologically', by looking at the transformation of the language in which the successive legal codes are expressed.

Vico's intellectual courage—even if it is the only kind of courage he possessed—was very great. It was a very bold undertaking to attack the ancient conception of natural law as being something universal, absolute, objective, a set of eternal truths in the light of which Europe had lived for two millennia. It was especially audacious to do so in the century the greatest jurists of which had laid it down that these laws

---

1 Yet, if Homer or Lycurgus could be explained away in this fashion, could not, his Catholic critics asked with justified suspicion, Moses, the Prophets, the Founder of the Church Himself, be dissolved in similar fashion? (cp. p. 79, n. 2, above, and Vico, *Autobiography, op. cit.*, Great Seal edition, p. 63 and p. 213, n. 65).

were as certain as those of mathematics and could not be altered even by God himself; and to substitute for this the notion of natural law as a set of rules covering all the vast variety of social experience, organized not by its deducibility from a single set of timeless axioms, but by its relation to the fundamental—not perhaps wholly immutable—categories in which human beings in fact think and act. Right and wrong, property and justice, equality and liberty, the relations of master and servant, authority and punishment—these are evolving notions between each successive phase of which there will be a kind of family resemblance, as in a row of portraits of the ancestors of modern society, from which it is senseless to attempt, by subtracting all the differences, to discover a central nucleus—the original family as it were, and declare that this featureless entity is the eternal face of mankind.

XII

Where the natural law theorists are abstract, Vico is concrete; where they invented fictions, the natural man, or the state of nature, he remained uncompromisingly committed to what he called history, a history which may not have been accurate, but which was time-bound through and through. Where they distinguished morals from politics, he regarded these as one organic evolutionary process, connected with every other self-expression of human beings in society. Where the natural lawyers were individualists, he grasped the social nature of man —in the sense that he thought that the majority of human activities would not be intelligible if one attempted to describe them as the acts of solitary Robinson Crusoes. For Vico, men acted as they did because their membership in social groups, and their sense of this relationship, was as basic and as decisive as their desire for food, or shelter, or procreation, as their lusts and sense of shame, their search for authority and truth, and everything else that makes men what they are. Where the lawyers were exact, clear, formal, rationalistic, utilitarian, he remained religious, vague, intuitive, disordered, and painfully obscure.

His theory of truth and certainty is equally *sui generis*.[1] He attacked the mathematical model of Descartes as leaving out the richest and most important part of human experience—everything that is not in the realm of natural science—daily life, history, human laws and institutions, the modes of human self-expression. Two hundred years before our time he conceived of mathematics as the invention of

---

[1] On this entire topic see Part Two.

fictions, as an art or game like chess, not as a descriptive procedure, or system of tautologies. He conceived of aesthetics, which he called 'poetics', as being concerned with a basic activity of men seeking not to give pleasure or embellish truths,[1] but to express a vision of the world, an activity that could be studied on a level with law or politics. He saw language and mythology as a free creation of the human spirit, and one providing more dependable data for human history than conscious records, and conceived history itself not as almost everyone else did in his time, and had done during two millennia since Herodotus, either as 'philosophy teaching by examples', or as a recital of past glories, or as the discovery of mechanical, recurrent causes and effects, or of what actually happened at specific moments, or as rendering justice to the dead, or as providing entertainment—but as the story and explanation of successive stages of social organization and consciousness. He exposed the inadequacy of utilitarianism before Kant, and of the atomistic view of society before Rousseau and Hegel. He distinguished the canons of certainty and judgment from those of both validity and demonstrable truth, discovery from invention, making from recording, the nature of principles, rules, laws, from that of propositions, the categories of cognition from those of the will, and anticipated ideas developed in the nineteenth century, and still more in the twentieth, by legal and moral philosophers and philosophical sociologists. He is the true founder of the German Historical school in his rejection of natural law and emphasis on human plasticity and the interpretation of all the aspects of social life. He preceded Hegel and the social psychologists in pointing out that the direction of a society may be very different from the sum of the conscious intentions of its members, so that one can speak of a society seeking this or that goal even if its members, or a majority of them, are, as individuals, consciously striving for something else. He perceived the formative part played by myths, archetypal images and symbolic structures before Hamann or Schelling, Nietzsche or Durkheim, or the founders of psychoanalysis. He, if any man, is the creator of the great realm that comprises the comparative studies of mythology, anthropology, histori-

---

1 Horace's almost universally accepted maxim—*aut prodesse volunt aut delectare poetae*—is precisely what he denies. He anticipated Herder's conception of artistic creation as self-expression, not the purveying of beautiful objects the value of which is independent of their creators, that is, as communication, not as manufacture; he is in this respect a direct forerunner of the romantic critics.

cal archaeology, philology, as well as linguistics, historical criticism of the arts, above all history itself conceived as the development of cultures. He spoke of the central historical role played by class war before Saint-Simon, his doctrine of the new barbarism that must succeed civilization anticipates those of Herzen and Sorel, his notion of heroic values foreshadows that of Nietzsche. Above all he traced the frontier, disputed ever since, between the natural sciences and the human—between *Naturwissenschaft* and *Geisteswissenschaft*, the first proceeding by hypothesis and confirmation, inductively and deductively, arguing for and from generalizations and idealized models derived from the uniformities of the compresences and successions of phenomena; the second seeking to describe human experience as concretely as possible, and therefore to emphasize variety, differences, change, motives and goals, individuality rather than uniformity or indifference to time or unaltering repetitive patterns. He was, that is, the first modern thinker to grasp the fundamental difference between scientific and historical analysis—the X-ray and the portrait—between the method which consists in perceiving and abstracting what is identical or similar in a large number of different cases, in order to establish some law or model from which new knowledge can be obtained by applying it to the unknown future or past; and, as distinct from this, the method whose task it is to uncover not the common kernel of dissimilar cases, but, on the contrary, the individual character of each—that which makes each action or event or person, or society or school of art or work of literature what it is, uniquely; and does so by placing the human beings with whom it deals in their own specific time and environment, their own moral, intellectual, historical and social 'context', by means, and by reference to standards, more refined than, but not necessarily different in principle from, those used in the normal processes of life by men in their intercourse with one another. He described only those historians as useful who present facts in all their individual concreteness, and not those who deal in wholesale generalizations, as philosophers are bound to do. There is something of this in Bacon, but Vico takes it further.[1] He was the first thinker to ask himself about—and deny— the possibility of assimilating the methods of history (and life) to those of the natural sciences; and vice versa. The controversy over this issue is, if anything, more alive in our day than in his own.

---

[1] See the second epigraph at the head of this study.

XIII

Did anyone read Vico? Does anyone do so now? Eminent *dilettanti* like the Abbé Conti and Count Porcía in Venice, who commissioned his autobiography (then a relatively new *genre*, which he called 'periheautography'), realized that he was something more than a locally well-known polymath. His patron, Cardinal Corsini, when he was elected to the Papacy, did not altogether forget him. But he remained, on the whole, out of account. He was at best looked upon as an eccentric writer with flashes of talent, but of interest only to specialists. Conti recommended his *New Science* to Montesquieu when the latter visited Venice, but despite Croce's assertion to the contrary, there is no solid evidence that Montesquieu ever read it, or even that he had acquired it for his library.[1] Vico's reputation, despite Leclerc's encouragement, remained largely Neapolitan, that of a remarkable local scholar, the friend of Gravina and Muratori, of interest to students of Italian learning. After his death, portions of his work were made accessible at various dates by Pagano, Cesarotti, Genovesi and Galiani. The *abbate* Galiani, a nephew of one of Vico's ecclesiastical patrons, was a brilliant and original talker and writer, a diplomat, an economist, and a friend and ally of Holbach and Helvétius, who evidently thought he could pay his queer compatriot no higher compliment than to describe him as a forerunner of Montesquieu. 'Vico', he wrote, 'tried to ford the marsh of metaphysics, and although he sank in the morass, he gave footing to a more fortunate thinker about the spirit of the laws of the nations'.[2] In 1787 the Neapolitan lawyer Filangieri gave a copy of the *New Science* to Goethe, who glanced at it and sent it to Jacobi. 'Filangieri introduced me to the work of an older writer', Goethe wrote later, 'whose profound wisdom is so refreshing and edifying to all Italians of this generation who are friends of justice. His name is Giambattista Vico, and they rank him above Montesquieu. From a cursory reading of the book, which was presented to me as if it were a sacred writ, it

---

[1] On Montesquieu and Vico, see the account given by Robert Shackleton in *Montesquieu* (Clarendon Press, Oxford, 1961).

[2] Quoted in *Galiani, ses amis et son temps*, by P. Maugras, Paris, 1881, p. xxxvi. Galiani claimed, however, that at least one French writer had used Vico's ideas without acknowledgment. Predari, who edited the *Scienza Nuova*, a century later, says in his introduction (pp. xxx-xxxi) that Hume, Boulanger, de Brosses, d'Alembert, Helvétius, and Bentham all borrowed from Vico. This appears to be pure fantasy.

seems to me to contain a sibylline vision of the good and the just, which will or should come true in the future, prophecies based on a profound study of life and tradition. It is wonderful for a people to have such a spiritual patriarch (*Aeltervater*). One day Hamann will be a similar bible for the Germans.'[1] As anyone can tell who has the smallest acquaintance with the doctrines of the *New Science*, Goethe's remarks bear little relation to the text. He evidently did not bother to read the 'sibylline' book.[2] In this respect, however, he does not seem to have differed much from other Germans whose acquaintance with Vico's work is usually cited by the scholars. J. G. Hamann (the *Aeltervater* referred to by Goethe), who had ordered the book in 1773 evidently under the illusion that it dealt with the new economics—for what other new science was there?—in a letter to his young friend Herder said that the introduction to the *New Science* seemed to him a 'very long-winded' explanation of the allegorical frontispiece, 'whereon Metaphysics and a pillar of Hermes are the main figures, the rest being hieroglyphs'.[3] Twenty years later Herder looked at the *New Science* himself, and after comparing Vico with 'Bakon [in his spelling] Montesquieu, Milton, Harrington, Sidney, Locke, Adam Smith, Ferguson, Millar' decided that Vico was looking 'for the basic social principles (*Gemeinschaftliche Grundsätze*) of physics, ethics, law, the Law of nations—*dell'umanità delle nazioni*—and found it in Providence and Wisdom'.[4] This was certainly an advance on Goethe, but a somewhat modest one.

Yet the parallels with Herder's ideas are very striking; indeed, it is difficult to think that Herder is not, at times, consciously echoing Vico's theses. Yet Herder is not known to have seen the *New Science* before 1797, long after his own major ideas had been given to the world. Even if Hamann had told him something about Vico twenty years before (of which, so far as is known, there is no evidence), this still, at the earliest, came a few years after the publication of his most Vichian views. Five years after receiving it from Goethe, Jacobi read

[1] *Die Italienische Reise*, March 5, 1787 (quoted from the translation by W. H. Auden and Elisabeth Mayer, Pantheon Books, Random House, New York, 1962, pp. 182-3; also published by Penguin Books, Harmondsworth, 1970).

[2] Friedrich Meinecke in his *Die Enstehung des Historismus* (trs. by J. G. Anderson as *Historism*, Routledge, 1921) slides over this somewhat disingenuously, evidently out of piety towards the venerated figure of Goethe.

[3] Letter of 22nd December 1773 (ed. Roth, vol. V, p. 267).

[4] *Werke*, ed. B. Suphan, letter 115, vol. 18 (pp. 245-6, 1797).

the book, and both he and Baader thought that it anticipated Kant's transcendental method, a judgment which tells us more about the historicist interpretation of Kant than about the central ideas common to him and Vico. The famous classical scholar F. A. Wolf, whose own revolutionary 'dissolution' of Homer into a succession of multiple storytellers had been published in 1795, some ten years later had his attention drawn to the fact of Vico's formulation of a similar hypothesis almost a century before. He was not pleased; and in 1807 mentioned Vico's theory casually and irritably in an attempt to minimize the fact of its existence. Nor did the great Niebuhr welcome the suggestion that his own epoch-making transformation of Roman history could be found in a developed and articulate form in the pages of a forgotten Italian jurist, either when Orelli tactlessly pointed this out to him, or, some years later, when the poet Leopardi (so we are told by Ranieri) insisted quite spontaneously on bringing this to his attention in Rome in 1816.

Savigny, the greatest figure in the Historical School of Jurisprudence, was somewhat more generous, even while he felt it necessary to defend his great compatriot and friend from suspicion of plagiarism: 'Vico, with his profound genius', he wrote, 'stood alone among his contemporaries, a stranger to his own country, overlooked or derided, although now the attempt is made to claim him as a national possession. In such unfavourable circumstances his spirit could not come to full fruition. It is true that one finds in him scattered thoughts on Roman history resembling Niebuhr's. But these ideas are like flashes of lightning in a dark night, by which the traveller is led further astray, rather than brought back to his path. No one could profit from them who had not already found the truth in his own way. Niebuhr in particular learned to know him only late and through others.'[1]

The real rise in Vico's fortunes began when the Neapolitan patriot Vincenzo Cuoco, seeking to defend the abortive liberal revolution of 1799 which had been made in his native city against French invasion, went to Vico as an original source of anti-Jacobin, gradualist, moderate nationalism, and used him as a text for his own homilies to the French on the difficulty of translating institutions from one society to another,

---

1 *Vermischte Schriften*, vol. 4, 217. This historical account owes a great deal to the discussion of this topic by Professor M. H. Fisch in his most valuable introduction in his edition and translation of Vico's autobiography. Savigny's remarks will be found on p. 70 of the Great Seal edition.

inasmuch as each obeys its own specific 'organic' laws. Cuoco's propaganda had a good deal of success: Chateaubriand, Joseph de Maistre, Ballanche, and other counter-revolutionary writers duly discovered in Vico a kind of Italian Burke. Sixty years after his death Vico was resurrected and celebrated by the publicists of the Restoration as a major link in the great chain of secular Italian political thought which began with Marsilio and Machiavelli. Gioberti and Manzoni carried his fame abroad. Gianelli wrote about him very intelligently, but remained unread.[1] Lomonaco, Salfi, Prati tried to establish a reputation for him in France, and Pietro de Angelis persuaded the omnivorous philosophical *vulgarisateur* Victor Cousin of his importance. Cousin sent de Angelis to his colleague the historian Jules Michelet, who realized, the first man to do so, that he had come upon a work of genius. He was immensely excited by the *New Science*, and felt, he wrote in 1824, like Dante led by Virgil into an unearthly world: 'Vico. Efforts. Infernal shades. Grandeur. The golden bough.' He declared that Vico had totally transformed his ideas—for the first time he understood that history was the account of the spiritual and self-creation of peoples in the unending struggle of men against nature. Michelet became a fervent, effective and lifelong apostle of Vico in the artistic and intellectual circles of Paris. His translation of selected texts from Vico, romanticized but exceedingly readable, appeared in Paris in 1824-5. He induced his friend Edgar Quinet, who at that time was preparing a French translation of Herder, to read Vico too. A more ponderous but somewhat more accurate French version appeared under the name of the celebrated Princess Belgiojoso ten years later; it may well be the work of Quinet. Michelet was the true rediscoverer of Vico, and himself the only man of genius among his disciples. In 1869 he could still write, 'I had no master but Vico; his principles of the living force of humanity creating itself, made both my book and my teaching.'[2] His ardent advocacy created a new image of Vico as a forerunner of romanticism and humanist nationalism, and, for a while, his name enjoyed celebrity in Paris and its intellectual dependencies: Balzac and Flaubert, for example, both mention him as a famous thinker. The more sober estimates of him by earlier French writers, such as Chastellux, Degérando, Fauriel, were swept away by the torrent of Michelet's eloquence: 'In the vast system of the

---

[1] See the account by Paolo Rossi, *op. cit.*
[2] Michelet's preface to his celebrated history of France.

founder of the metaphysics of history, there already exist, at least in germ, all the labours of modern scholarship. Like Wolf he said that the *Iliad* was the work of a people, its learned work and last expression, after many centuries of inspired poetry. Like Creuzer and Görres he interpreted the heroic and divine figures of primitive history as ideas and symbols. Before Montesquieu and Gans he showed how law springs from the customs of a people and represents faithfully every step of its history. What Niebuhr was to find by vast research, Vico divined: he restored patrician Rome and made its *curiae* and *gentes* live again. Certainly, if Pythagoras recalled that in a previous life he had fought beneath the walls of Troy, these illustrious Germans might have remembered that they had all formerly lived in Vico. All the giants of criticism are already contained, with room to spare, in the little pandemonium of the *New Science*.'[1] Yet, despite this and Comte's cooler, but equally firm, admiration, interest in Vico declined; the book, even in Michelet's version, was no longer read. Taine took some interest in him, to no avail. Vico remained a name in encyclopaedias and the more comprehensive histories of philosophy.

In England his fame was spread by the Italian exiles, the greatest of whom, Ugo Foscolo and Mazzini, were his devoted admirers. Coleridge quoted him with enthusiasm in 1816. But in spite of the interest taken in him by Thomas Arnold (who understood him and paid him a tremendous tribute) and by F. D. Maurice; despite the fact that he had secured a place beside Herder in the Positivist Calendar, and was duly celebrated by Bridges and Grote and the English Comtians; despite Robert Flint's admirable Victorian monograph, his influence remained negligible. He was shown to be the founder of the philosophy of history, but like other intellectual pioneers he remained in England a figure of interest only to specialists. In Germany he was taken a little more seriously: the *Scienza Nuova* was translated in 1822 and edited in 1854. The Hegelian radical Eduard Gans in 1837 pronounced him to be one of Hegel's forerunners. Marx recommended him to Lassalle and saw him as the father of the history of human technology. A German monograph—greatly inferior to Flint's book—appeared in 1881. Windelband and representatives of other philosophical schools showed some faint interest in him. But it was not until the devoted editorial labours of Fausto Nicolini in Vico's native

---

1 Preface to his Roman History, repeated in the preface to *Oeuvres Choisies* quoted by M. H. Fisch, *op. cit.* p. 79.

city, which sprang from the passionate advocacy and brilliant monograph of his compatriot Benedetto Croce, and the interest which this
stimulated in England and especially America,[1] that he began to come
into his own. Yet the formidable difficulties presented by the tangled
forest of Vico's thought and style have not been diminished by the
mere passage of time. Gentile and Collingwood developed his doctrines. Pareto and Georges Sorel, Joyce and Yeats and Edmund Wilson,
testified to his genius. It has made little difference. He is constantly
rediscovered and as constantly laid aside. He remains unreadable and
unread.

XIV

There is a particular danger that attends the fate of rich and profound
but inexact and obscure thinkers, namely that their admirers tend to
read too much into them, and turn them insensibly in the direction of
their own thoughts. Michelet took from Vico what he needed for his
own vision of history, but there is more of Michelet than of Vico in
his magnificent version. If Flint cannot be accused of imposing his
own personality on Vico, that is only because he had no philosophical
personality to impose. Among his modern disciples neither Croce nor
Collingwood escaped, or wished to escape, this temptation. Not only
his book on Vico but much of Croce's own philosophy is a development of Vico in a Hegelian direction, which the latter could scarcely
have understood. Croce paid his debt to Vico almost too generously:
for he put into Vico's thought more than he derived from it. Vico's
authentic features are at times concealed by the metamorphosis which
Croce, like all original thinkers, inevitably produces; he built a noble
monument to Vico, but transformed him into an Absolute Idealist.
Sorel (and perhaps Trotsky and Gramsci) saw him as a proto-Marxist.
He has been represented as a pragmatist, a Catholic apologist,
a Neapolitan patriot, a forerunner of fascism, an existentialist, and much
else. Gentile carried Vico's doctrine to extravagant lengths, intelligible
only in the light of the speculative flights of late neo-Hegelianism. As
for Collingwood, his most gifted English disciple, his fruitful notion
of the 'absolute presuppositions' of every culture, those basic categories
and concepts of an age or culture which determine the shape of its

---

[1] The labours of Messrs Bergin and Fisch, and especially the introductions to
the *New Science* and the *Autobiography*, to which this study owes a great deal,
are examples of philosophical scholarship at its most illuminating.

mental activity and render its problems uniquely different from those of all other cultures, that does indeed derive from Vico, and perhaps from him alone. But when Collingwood adds to this notion the far more questionable one of a capacity to transport ourselves into the minds of persons or periods historically remote from us, a transcendental, timeless flight across the barrier of time, culminating in the metaphysical act of penetrating into the mind of Julius Caesar, or, let us say, the Puritan movement, or the Gothic Revival, he goes beyond his master. Vico speaks of the need to make the appalling effort of trying to adjust one's vision to the archaic world—the need to see it through deeply unfamiliar spectacles—but this is very different from the quasi-mystical act of literal self-identification with another mind and age of which Collingwood evidently thought himself capable.

It may be that, finding in Vico so much that became fully articulate only in the nineteenth or twentieth century, I, too, am guilty of precisely the same fault. Yet I find it hard to persuade myself that this is so. Premature anticipations of the ideas of one age in another happen seldom, but they happen. A thinker whose most original ideas are misunderstood or ignored by his contemporaries is not a mere romantic myth. In the heyday of the age of science, when the last feeble defenders of the old scholasticism were finally routed by the new enlightenment, Vico preached distinctions fully intelligible to neither side. He distinguished between, on the one hand, observation, measurement, deductive reasoning, the construction of idealized models, fictional entities, and their application to the opaque outlines of the real world —the 'external' knowledge systematized by the natural sciences—and, on the other, the perception of the relations of elements in man-made patterns to each other and to the wholes to which they belong, of means to ends, of the purposes and outlooks of individuals to the activities of groups and generations. Above all he casts light on what it is for a wide variety of gestures, words, acts, ceremonies, rules, to be an expression of one and the same style, characteristic of a class, a nation, an age, a civilization. Furthermore, he identified what it is to understand this, to detect it, to trace it in detail, with the aid of the scientific methods of scholarship, and the way in which such human self-investigation must affect one's fundamental beliefs. In the course of explaining this, Vico distinguished differences of quality from those of quantity, of nuance from measurable forms, and, above all, between knowledge of factors at work in the continuous growth in time of persons, groups, institutions, and knowledge of the causal, repetitive uniformities of co-existence or succession. He discriminated, in effect, between the sense of understanding in which a scholar may be said to understand a text when, for example, he emends it successfully, or as a man may understand a friend, an artistic movement, or a political atmosphere, a sense not capable of precise analysis, and related to skills which can be trained and sharpened and make use of rules and laws, but which cannot be systematized or taught to the competent but insensitive or ungifted; and the techniques involved in inductive or experimental or deductive procedures—something which can be communicated and taught to any rational being. He did not, like Dilthey, categorize this contrast, but he used it in contrasting knowledge of man with knowledge of objects. He believed that a man could understand himself, and therefore others, and therefore what they were at, and how the world looked or felt to himself or them, and why, as he could not understand things or plants or animals of which he could only perceive the behaviour. Above all he had a sense of how various elements were blended in social existence—the pattern which Burke and Herder, Schelling and Hegel, Tocqueville and Burckhardt, Dilthey and Max Weber attempted to convey—a capacity for perceiving the way in which the 'senseless factor' in history interacts with conscious motives and purposes to produce unintended consequences, a quasi-aesthetic capacity for discrimination, integration and association, needed by historians, critics, novelists, more than the capacity for abstraction, generalization and dissociation of ideas indispensable to original discoveries in the natural sciences. The discovery and proclamation of this great dividing line seemed to Vico's critics and commentators during the last hundred years to be his major achievement.

No doubt Vico exaggerated. Pioneers are apt to do this in moments of creative excitement, particularly when, like Vico, they are largely self-taught and live in self-constructed private worlds. Moreover, few new truths have ever won their way against the resistance of established ideas save by being overstated. Plato, the Stoics, Descartes, Spinoza, Hume, Kant, Hegel all overstated their case, and might not have obtained a hearing if they had not. Vico belongs in this company (even if he is not a major figure in it) for his ideas are those of a man of original genius. He may well have hoped to be clear: his four intellectual heroes, Plato and Tacitus, Bacon and Grotius possessed this enviable gift. He did not succeed, and his ideas often remain tantalizingly dark. Nor did he invent, as he supposed, a new science based on the discovery of inescapable cycles in the life of societies; this idea proved a will-o'-the-wisp as it has to other imaginative thinkers before and after him. Like Columbus, like his own *grossi bestioni* whose desires lead to unsought for consequences, he came upon an unknown country: the study of the human past as a form of collective self-understanding.

It may be that, as with other original thinkers, future generations will think our verdict unduly limited by the experience of our own time, and (like James Joyce, whose later work was filled with allusions to Vico) will single out other aspects of his writings for the attention of the students of ideas.

PART TWO

Vico's Theory of Knowledge and Its Sources

I

ONE of the central theses of the *New Science*, which goes back to *De Nostri* of 1708 and *De Antiquissima* of 1710, is the distinction between truth and certainty, *verum* and *certum*. Yet neither in these works, nor anywhere else, does Vico make this radical distinction thoroughly clear. As so often in his writings, too many novel and inchoate ideas are simultaneously and feverishly struggling for expression, in language painfully ill-adapted for this purpose. This flood of clear and confused insights, antiquarian memories and constant diversions, gives his style, especially in the *New Science*, a rhapsodic, sometimes volcanic, force, but does not make for lucid exposition. Nevertheless an arresting new doctrine does emerge. This has not always been conceded by those who minimized its originality, either from lack of understanding, or out of national pride, or ideological antipathy, or jealous concern for the reputation of some other thinker[1]. Yet his contribution to philosophical thought is of the first order, if only because he distinguished and cast new light on the notion of historical understanding.

According to Vico we begin with *certum*—acquaintance with and beliefs about particular matters of fact—a pre-condition of all thought and action; and are capable of attaining to *verum*—knowledge of universal truths. He does not make clear whether a transition from one to the other can, even in principle, ever be achieved, or indeed

[1] See p. 90. The latest example of this is the assertion by Professor George Huppert in his *The Idea of Perfect History* (University of Illinois Press, 1970) that Vico was a mere 'straggler in the history of ideas, echoing Bodin, not announcing Hegel' (p. 166). This argues a degree of blindness both to Vico's positive achievement, and to crucial differences of his ideas on history from those of Bodin. (On this see p. 131 below.) Fortunately this glancing gibe is a mere footnote to Professor Huppert's main thesis, and does not significantly diminish the value of his interesting and informative book.

how it is to be attempted. Yet without general truths there cannot be a science, so that if the *New Science* is to justify its title, it must consist of a logically connected system of true general propositions about facts and events in time. How is this to be achieved? *Verum* for Vico is *a priori* truth, the truth such as is reached, for example, in mathematical reasoning, where, starting from axioms, every step is demonstrably and irrefutably proved; but this is accomplished (in the case of human thought) only at the cost of being left with artificial constructions, logical figments with no necessary relation to the outside world. By the *verum ipsum factum* criterion of 1710 we can logically guarantee only what we ourselves make: this alone is *verum*: of that alone there can, in the strict sense, exist a *scienza*. But if the structure of this *verum* is designed by us, how can it claim to reflect or describe 'scientifically', that is, demonstratively and irrefutably, anything outside itself—the character of the external world?

Vico accepts this startling conclusion. 'The truth is what is made': mathematics is a science because *Mathesis est scientia operatrix*. We do not create things in space, hence physics is not, for us, *verum*; it is so, he says (following Augustine), only for God, *quia Deus primus Factor*. The notion that there can be such a thing as creation out of nothing is, of course, a Judaeo-Christian idea; it is not Greek.[1] For Pythagoras the cosmos, the symmetries of nature, its mathematical structure, are built into the nature of things. This is equally objective for Plato: the demiurge in the *Timaeus* creates the world according to a plan of which he is not, however, the author: the plan is given from eternity. The notion of cosmic harmony had at least in part been known to the thinkers and artists of the golden age of Greece; it could be rediscovered, and the world be made beautiful and rational in its light—this is the central vision of the Renaissance. In a less mystical form it inspired the Enlightenment, too, in particular the physiocrats and the believers in the 'hidden hand' or the Cunning of Reason, which will always prevail in the end. Löwith[2] rightly points out that this was not so for Vico, who believed in divine creation *ex nihilo*.

Since physics deals with objects in nature which men do not create, Vico's first move, in 1708-10, was to degrade physics from the emin-

---

[1] On this, see Karl Löwith: *Geschichte und Natur in Vico's 'Scienza Nuova'*, Quaderni Contemporanei 2, 1968 (Istituto Universitario di Salerno; Libreria Scientifica editrice, Napoli, pp. 137-9).

[2] *Ibid.*

ence on which Descartes had placed it, to the level of other studies of that which men find but have not made; it now ranks above, but is classified with, history, literature, and so on, of which we can have no *scientia*, only *conscientia*—where we cannot attain to more than *certum*, that is, *de facto* truths, the kind of knowledge on which ordinary rational action rests. The reason for this is clear. Once you demand that your thought should correspond with something outside itself and independent of it—with reality—you can no longer guarantee *verum*, which must be wholly in your own control; you can speak at best of certainty, self-evidence, what later came to be called a sense of reality, which Vico correctly regards as something different from logically demonstrated truths. He does not use these terms, but the distinction is one between the truths of metaphysics or logic on the one hand, and those of ordinary observation or perception (including introspection) on the other. Certainty (which Vico at times also calls 'authority') is the light by which in fact we live our lives. It is not primarily inductive knowledge (in Bacon's sense, with which Vico at times mistakenly identifies it), but is rather our grasp of the basic data of direct experience, from which scientific hypotheses start, and to which they return for confirmation. Vico's illustrations of 'certainty' come not from the external world of sense perception, but from a sphere in which his chief interest lies, namely social relationships—'human necessities or the utilities of social life'.[1] We are born into a culture (which for him is a social process)—a network of institutions which springs from the claims of such necessities and utilities, forms of communal life which evolve in time, in which we live and think and have our being; language is such an institution: 'languages create minds (*ingenium*), not minds language' he said in *De Nostri*, and although the context suggests that this passage probably refers to his preference for the tradition of Italian imaginative writing over the drier, more cerebral and anti-metaphorical French style, the phrase is characteristic of what today would be called his socio-linguistic approach. We are able to conceive or express only that which our particular culture makes possible, and only by the means provided by the social structure of that culture because it has the properties it has, and represents the particular stage of social growth in an identifiable process or pattern of development. Thus we move from the culture of 'mute signs'—the ideograms and hieroglyphs of

---

[1] N.S. 347.

the 'Age of the Gods'—to the 'heroic' language of poetic metaphor and simile, and so, step by step, to the more literal and precise prose utterances of the law courts and philosophical criticism that belong to democratic life. One cannot generate a timeless universal symbolism, any more than one can invent a timeless, universal way of life which a rational being could pursue whenever and wherever he happened to be. One is what one is, in a specific historical context; no one can escape the particular categories, social and psychological, mental and emotional, that obtain in given times and places, and are subject to the laws of development. Nature is growth (*nascimento*). This is the world of the (evolving) *sensus communis* of a society, the 'judgment without reflection, shared by an entire class, an entire people, an entire nation, or the whole of the human race'.[1]

Such judgments embody not demonstrable truths, but (presumably) contingent ones. The fact that we cannot do without them is, for us at any rate, a contingent fact. If we would know the world as God, its Creator, knows it, then the *certum*, which is contingent, would be transformed into *verum*, which is *a priori*.[2]

Yet our knowledge of our own ideas and volitions, individual and social, including past experience—both that which men have individually and that which they share with others—is not simply given us as a brute fact: we can understand ourselves as we cannot understand sticks and stones. Men are finite and fallible creatures and so cannot understand even their own mental processes wholly. To understand other men, and what they were and the worlds they 'created', is to recognize—imaginatively grasp—their experience within the potentialities of our own human consciousness: *dentro le modificazioni della medesima nostra mente umana*.[3] What is wholly unlike ourselves we cannot hope to understand. We can understand only that which is potentially our own, which men can be or become without ceasing to be men. This is why it is not utterly impossible, although agonizingly difficult, to enter into the outlook—the thoughts, feelings, fears,

---

[1] N.S. 142.

[2] Leibniz formulated a similar doctrine about the relation of necessary (rational) truths to contingent (factual) truths. For God alone all truths are necessary. But this dichotomy leaves no room for what is peculiar to Vico—understanding of institutions, relationships, purposes, outlooks, which shape human behaviour and are neither wholly contingent nor deducible *a priori*.

[3] N.S. 331.

hopes, ambitions, imaginative experience—of beings very different and remote from us, like our first ancestors, the 'horrible' *grossi bestioni*, Polyphemus in his cave. To grasp motives, intentions, to understand, however imperfectly, why men act and live as they do, is to have knowledge *per caussas*, and therefore, however incomplete, is superior to, 'more godlike' than, mere 'knowing that'—the awareness 'from without' which provides the data of the natural sciences, or of the ordinary knowledge of the external world, and is equally superior to 'knowledge how'—the acquisition or possession of a skill or method. Experiment does, no doubt, help to understand nature, as Hobbes pointed out. But merely to take a thing apart and put it together again is not to understand it through and through, as Vico holds that we understand the 'inner' movements of our own spirit, since the ultimate constituents of matter which in experiments we rearrange at will are still not ours—are *extra nos*.[1] Knowledge *per caussas* is that of a creator when he understands his own creatures, as an artist understands his work of art, and, at times, his own creative activity. Even the neo-Platonists of the Renaissance—Marsilio Ficino, Pico, Landino—did not suppose that the poet did more than create a world of his own parallel to that of God, and, in this, were followed by Tasso (misquoted by Shelley in *The Defence of Poetry*), Philip Sidney, Donne, Dennis, Shaftesbury, and the eighteenth-century forerunners of Romanticism. Vico goes further. He supposes not merely that the poets create artificial worlds, but that all men during the early 'poetical' stage of culture can conceive of the real world only 'in this fashion', that the creative imagination plays a dominant role in the normal consciousness of this stage of development, so that song is the natural mode of expression before speech, poetry before prose, written symbols before spoken; and this, he holds, constitutes a vision of reality which is more primitive than, but not necessarily superior or inferior to, that which follows it, more barbarous, but not less valuable (if not spiritually, then at least aesthetically), and superior, perhaps, in sheer power and spontaneous vitality to its more civilized successors. This was, indeed, to swim against

[1] 'Since God combines all the elements, both external and internal, of things, because he contains and disposes of them; while the human mind, because it is limited and is outside all the things that are not itself . . . can indeed think about, but cannot understand things', quoted from *De Antiquissima*, 1.4, by A. Child, *Making and Knowing in Hobbes, Vico and Dewey* (University of California Publications in Philosophy, vol. XVI, Berkeley, 1953).

the current. The seventeenth century is a time in which the very use of metaphor was widely suspect, especially in the centres of progressive thought, in France, in England, in Holland, inasmuch as this kind of luxuriant imagery was associated with a pre-scientific or anti-scientific frame of mind. Metaphor, we are informed by an eminent authority, was connected with 'the false world of ancient superstition, dreams, myths, terrors with which the lurid, barbarous imaginations peopled the world, causing error and irrationalism and persecution'.[1] Thomas Sprat, one of the founders of the Royal Society, declared that 'specious tropes and figures' should be banished 'out of all Civill societies as a thing fatal to peace and good Manners'; the Royal Society should avoid 'myths and uncertainties', and return to 'a close, naked, natural way of speaking . . . as near the Mathematical plainness as they can'.[2] So, too, Hobbes banished metaphor from all writings aimed at 'the rigorous search for truth'.[3] Locke, Hume and Adam Smith say much the same, although Hume allows that rigid adherence to 'geometrical truth' . . . 'might have a disagreeable effect upon the reader'.[4] It enters into the celebrated controversy between the champions of the French and Italian styles which broke out towards the end of the seventeenth century, played a dominant role in France in the eighteenth century (particularly between the champions of the French and Italian styles in opera) and was almost as violent as the battle between the Ancients and the Moderns. Among the merits for which the great French masters—Racine, Molière, Boileau—are most highly praised is their freedom from metaphor, hyperbole, the vagaries of fancy. One of the best known leaders of the French school of criticism in the *grand siècle*, the Abbé de Bouhours, thinks that fiction, metaphor, similes, and the like, can only be permitted when, like transparent veils, 'they do not really hide what they purport to cover'; that the only possible reason for 'tropes' is the pleasure which such 'permissible lies' may give. But for Vico metaphor and the like is a fundamental category through which at a given stage of development men cannot help viewing reality—which is for them reality itself, neither mere em-

---

1 M. H. Abrams, *The Mirror and the Lamp*, p. 285.
2 *Ibid.*, quoted from 'The History of the Royal Society', in *Critical Essays of the Seventeenth Century*, vol. 2, ed. Spingarn.
3 *Leviathan* (Cambridge, 1904), pp. 14-15.
4 M. H. Abrams (*op. cit.*) gives a great many other examples of, and references to, this highly prevalent 'Cartesian' attitude.

bellishment, nor a repository of secret wisdom, nor the creation of a world parallel to the real world, nor an addition to, or distortion of, reality, harmless or dangerous, deliberate or involuntary: but is the natural, inevitably transient, but, at the time of its birth or growth, the only possible, way of perceiving, interpreting, explaining, that is open to men of that particular place and time, at that particular stage of their culture. Such ways of speech, he supposes, only later become artificial or decorative because men have by then forgotten how they came into being and the purposes for which they were originally used. Such myths and their modes of expression, however faulty they may seem to the theologians or philosophers of our own sophisticated times (and to those of earlier 'classical' periods too), were, in their own day, appropriate and coherent. To understand the metaphors of the 'heroic' age—the world of ballads, lays, epics—one must transport oneself by the imagination, and therefore reconstruct, with learned care and insight, the vision of which they formed an organic, inalienable part.

The times were not propitious for this conception of man, society, history; less so, perhaps, than even the preceding century. Even though the roots of this doctrine are far older, it was not until Herder that this kind of historicism began to bind its spell on European thought in general. In spite of his habit of presenting his works to as many of the learned and influential critics of his day in Italy and abroad as he could reach, Vico failed to elicit the recognition which he felt that the originality of his discovery deserved. The tide was flowing too strongly against him.

II

In this connection, it may be useful to attempt to indicate the main features of Vico's epistemology. He seems to distinguish four types of knowledge: (a) *Scienza*: knowledge which yields *verum*, truth *a priori*; which one can have only of one's own artefacts or fictions: logical, mathematical, poetical, artistic; it is in this sense that God alone fully knows the world which he has created. (b) *Coscienza*: the 'external' knowledge of matters of fact common to all men, the *certum* that one has of the 'outer' behaviour of whatever entities compose the external world of events, men, things. (c) The kind of knowledge which Vico's admired master Plato claimed to possess: of patterns, eternal truths and principles (Vico throughout takes for granted revelation as a source of knowledge, e.g. for the Jews and, *a fortiori*, to the Fathers of the Church)—presumably this is how we can discern the unaltering pattern of the *storia ideale eterna*, which is the history of the 'gentile' nations. But how, without grace or revelation, men can acquire this kind of profane metaphysical insight Vico does not make clear; it is certainly not inductive or merely probable in Bodin's or Bacon's sense: Grotius is blamed precisely for supposing that it was. Perhaps it is connected with (*d*) the 'inner' or historical knowledge to which Vico gives no special name, the 'intentional' awareness which human beings have as actors, not mere observers from outside, of their own activities, of their own efforts, purposes, direction, outlook, values, attitudes, both present and past, familiar and exceedingly remote, and of the institutions which embody and, in their turn, determine them. This is certainly what he calls knowledge *per caussas*—obtained by attending to the *modificazioni* of our *mente*, and leads to knowledge of what men or societies or cultures are *at*, that is, not merely of what happens to them, or of how they react or behave as causal agents or 'patients', but of those internal relationships and interconnections between thought and action, observation, theory, motivation, practice, which is precisely what observation of the external world, of mere compresences and successions, fails to give us. In the world of things, we see only similarities, conjunctions, regularities, successions or their absence; these can be summarized under laws and necessities in a Cartesian or Newtonian system; but this yields no knowledge of why things and events are as they are; for no one but the Creator of this world knows what it is *at* or for. This distinction between the 'inside' and 'outside' views, between mechanical cause and purpose; between understanding and knowledge, the human and the natural sciences, was to be made much of by later thinkers like Herder, Maine de Biran, Fichte, Schelling, Dilthey, Croce, and, to some degree, Max Weber, and duly exposed them to the criticism of those who detected in this distinction anti-empirical, anti-scientific, obscurantist implications.

Vico was a deeply metaphysical thinker, but in this instance, what he meant was, I think, no more than the difference between active participation in something and passive observation of it. To know what it is to do something—what Vico called *operatio*—is to understand human motives, purposes, ideals in their relations with the environment and the material on which men are at work, as well as the relationships that individuals have with other goal-pursuing, motivated, active beings—which seemed to him to be different from the mere contemplation of a succession of mental and/or physical states, and the systematic classification of them and their behaviour in uniform patterns that enable men to predict and manipulate. When Vico speaks of knowledge 'through causes', he means by 'cause' not a mere correlation of the uniformities of either characteristics or events, but the active and deliberate making or doing of something by someone (individual or collective: the life of institutions is for him a collective activity).[1] His sense of causing and making is that in which we speak of a man or a class or a movement or an idea as causing a change of mind in a man (or a group), or as causing or making a revolution. The emphasis upon this distinction—between activity and the passive registration of experience, between the 'senseless' factors of history versus the 'motivated'—has played a major role in philosophical theories of action, of history, of mind and of moral and social life.

Nature, events in time, do not, for Vico, depend on what men make of them. He explicitly acknowledges the role of inductive and deductive techniques in the researches of scholars, above all in the sifting by scientific historians of fact from fiction. But this is not for him the same as the use of imaginative understanding, *fantasia*. A capacity for such critical scholarship, as practised, for example, by his friend the great Muratori, indispensable as it is, is only the most refined and solid establishing of *certum*, not in principle different from the natural sciences. But selection, classification, above all, interpretation, of the material—these (as Erich Auerbach points out in one of his excellent studies of Vico) are our own: ultimately subjective, dependent on our own experience, our own investigation of the *modificazioni* of our own minds. The sounds may be independent of the hearer, but different cultures will listen to, and select, different patterns from the self-same sounds; and all the melodies, harmonies and rhythms are equally genuine and real.

Vico virtually invented the concept of the understanding—of what Dilthey and others call '*verstehen*'. Others before him, philologists or historians or jurists, may have had inklings of it; Vico brings it to light. No one after reading him will suppose that the sense in which we are said to understand a feeling, a gesture, a work of art, a man's character; an entire civilization or a single joke; the sense in which a man can

---

[1] He does not distinguish, as Aristotle did, between 'doing' and 'making'; nor, for his purposes, was this necessary.

be said to know what it is to be poor, to be jealous, to be a lover, a convert, a traitor, a banker, a revolutionary, an exile, is (to say the least) the same sense as that in which we know that one tree is taller than another, or that Hitler wrote *Mein Kampf*, or how one text differs from another, or what neutrons are; nor is it like knowing the differential calculus, or how to spell, or play the violin, or get to Mars, or what an imaginary number is, or what prevents us from moving faster than light. It is much more like the kind of awareness that is fed and developed by varied activities and experience of how things look in different situations, how the world appears, through what concepts and categories, to individuals or groups in different social or emotional conditions. It is this kind of knowledge that is spoken of in such terms as plausible or absurd, realistic or idealistic, perceptive or blind; that makes it intelligible to describe the works of historians and social theorists, artists and men of action, not merely as well-informed, or skilful, or lucid, or misled, or ignorant, but also as wise or stupid, interesting or dull, shallow or profound—concepts which cannot be applied to knowledge in either of the two senses discussed in our time by Gilbert Ryle: of 'knowing that' and 'knowing how'. This is what Vico called *fantasia*: man's unique capacity for imaginative insight and reconstruction.

There is another way of approaching this distinction. *Certum* presides over the realm of facts as we perceive and deal with them. *Verum*—for human beings—presides over the realm of what men make: for example, rules, norms, standards, laws, including those which shape 'the facts' themselves. These are categories of the will, of action, of creative imagination; what they generate individually or collectively is not discovered *a posteriori*—by, for example, psychologists or anthropologists—as so many objects leading an existence independent of their creators, but can be known in advance, at any rate to those who make them, like (to take only the products of conscious purpose) decisions, or agreed conventions, or codes of law, or anything else that men invent and live by, which therefore have no logical claim to 'correspond' to any 'outer' structure of things. It is only when such human arrangements are mistakenly assimilated to objects or laws of nature, that hypostatization—what Hegelians and Marxists call 'reification'—arises, and with it 'false consciousness' and the self-alienation of men from the world they have themselves had a hand in creating. The distinction is, of course, not absolute: 'facts' are not hard pellets of experience, independent of concepts and categories by which they are discriminated, classified, perceived, interpreted, indeed shaped. Nevertheless, the distinction made by Kant or James or their modern followers, or thinkers influenced by Hegel or Marx or the psychologists or anthropologists or linguists of our own century, still stands. We perceive and act in terms of responses to our questionings, which themselves are conditioned by our institutional life, but we do not generate the answers freely, 'out of whole cloth'. The answers to our questions are not arbitrarily invented by us, but their shape is determined by the nature of the questions: selection is a creative art. In this respect Vico is the ancestor of those romantic voluntarists, idealists, pragmatists and existentialists who stress the role played in men's experience by their own transforming acts, individual or collective; or indeed, of those who, if they are metaphysically inclined, go beyond him and virtually identify the world with such activities; and *per contra*, he is opposed to the claims of rigorous determinists, positivists, philosophical realists and materialists, or psychologists, sociologists and philosophers of science with a mechanistic bias, and the like.

As early as 1700 Vico declared in his third Inaugural Lecture that *homo est quod vult, fit quod lubet*. This overweening belief in the individual's freedom to take on any shape or semblance (which is substantially modified in the *New Science*) is in line with Renaissance voluntarism, of which the most famous expression is Pico della Mirandola's great discourse on the Dignity of Man. Nevertheless, Vico came to think than an objective science of the cultural development of men is possible, based on the uniformity of the *voci mentali*—the basic symbols or notions that are common to all nations, that embody the great 'natural', non-arbitrary, institutional human regularities—the analogous responses of human groups, remote in time and space, to similar conditions, inasmuch as they spring from similar needs. His examples are the ideas of Gods, marriage and burial rites, as well as family, auspices, sacrifices, paternal authority, and so on. It is the ubiquity and uniformity of the 'maxims of vulgar wisdom' that embody these responses that make generalizations about the growth of a single human culture possible. But before one can generalize and use abstract terms for such notions or institutions, recognition of them, acquaintance with them—as particular, concrete phenomena at particular times and in particular places—is indispensable. The history of culture is, for Vico, the development of human creatures from unorganized, savage, 'ferine' sensations to the beginnings of critical self-consciousness and organization—from 'sensuous' perceptions of objects to experience 'with a troubled mind'—and so to calm thought, by way of images, myths, and symbols appropriate to each stage. This conception can be criticized as too exclusively anthropocentric and too social, ignoring as it does irreducibly natural—physical and biological—causal factors, not to speak of psychological ones as well. This bias may well spring from Vico's over-violent reaction against Cartesian mechanistic and atomistic notions. His desire to move from *certum* towards something which, if not fully *verum*, is an approach towards it—from brute fact to intelligible purposive conduct, clearly dominates his thought.

Can the gap between *certum* and *verum* be bridged, at any rate for finite creatures? Can we ascend from knowledge of what we do not make, to the *a priori* knowledge that we have of mathematics, and God has of all there is and could be? Is this possible, even in principle? Vico does not make this clear. He holds that we rise above mere external observation, as in physics, to the degree to which we can reproduce natural processes and objects artificially, as in the laboratory. Hobbes and, indeed, Bacon had supposed as much.[1]

But then is everything in our own historical development created by ourselves? Are there no *elementa rerum naturalium extra nos*—our

---

[1] Professor C. F. R. von Weizsäcker, in his comments on *De Nostri* (see Giambattista Vico, *De Nostri Temporis Studiorum Ratione*, Lateinisch-Deutsche Ausgabe, Wissenschaftliche Buchgesellschaft, Darmstadt, 1963), anxiously wonders whether the distinction, crucial in Vico, between observation from outside and knowledge of our own artefacts, is not approaching vanishing point with the achievements of modern technology, and the startling increase in the rate at which man's capacity for modifying, reproducing and creating new entities is growing at present. This leads him to gloomy reflections about our misuse of our newly found powers. While the scientific and technological picture has radically altered since Vico's day, and one can sympathize with and, indeed, share Professor von Weizsäcker's social and moral concern, his theoretical point seems to me to rest on a plain mistake. So long as we remain unable to create *ex nihilo*, and are limited by uniformities of nature that we appear unable to alter and upon the continued existence of which the very possibility of technology rests, Vico's distinction stands. To identify it with the diminishing differences between various kinds and degrees of empirical knowledge of 'the given', or of growing skill in operating on it, is a mere confusion. So long as we merely transform the 'given' which we cannot make, knowledge remains, to that degree, in Vico's sense, *ab extra*, that is, what he calls *cogitatio*, and not 'internal', not his *intelligentia*. Miss Hannah Arendt's similar reflections seem to me to rest on no better ground (see *Between Past and Future*, N.Y., 1961, pp. 57-8).

bodies—indeed the whole of physical and biological nature—which play as essential a part in human activities as ideas, relations, feelings? If we cannot 'make' all these—nor all our mental states either— (not to speak of the unintended consequences of our actions on which Vico lays such stress, inasmuch as they are for him evidences of the 'providential' nature of history) why is Vico's new discipline dignified with the name of *scienza*—a term originally annexed only to *verum*, to *a priori* knowledge, the free creation of a *scientia operatrix*? The answer is, I think, twofold: it lies in the interplay of what Vico symbolized as the 'Platonic' and the 'Tacitean'—the general and the particular, the eternal and the temporal, the necessary and the contingent, the ideal and the actual. Some would call this relationship 'dialectical'. Whether Vico could have begun to understand this term in its Hegelian or post-Hegelian sense, I do not know. However this may be, the empirical or Tacitean aspect emerges in Vico's conception of historical knowledge as consisting in the understanding by *fantasia* of particular men's particular activities—e.g. of what specific groups of human beings in the past intended, wanted, felt, of how they reacted to the world, much of which, of course, they had not made; acting not only deliberately in pursuit of conscious purposes and according to ideas formulated in their heads, but also unconsciously or instinctively, or out of habit, or in ways which they did not themselves fully (or at all) comprehend, no matter how they might have explained their behaviour to themselves (or others) when reflecting upon it.

Vico (influenced perhaps by 'magical' theories of becoming one with the object, widespread in the Renaissance) is one of the true fathers of the doctrine of the unity of theory and practice which was afterwards developed so richly in various directions by Hegel and his disciples and, in various new directions, by Marx, Nietzsche and Freud. He believed that in principle we could re-enact in our minds—'enter' by sympathetic imagination—into what a class, a society, perhaps (though he gives no example) individuals were at; what such beings wanted, worked for, were after; what forwarded, what frustrated them in their search to satisfy their needs—the demands of social necessities and utilities in this or that situation; how they were affected by their own creations—cultural and historical. He supposes that we can, by a species of imaginative insight, turn every *an sich* (to use Hegelian language)—an entity observed from outside by the agent (even if it is his own state of mind or body)—into a *für sich*, an element in, assimilated to, his purposive, 'spiritual' activity. If we fail to effect this transformation, even after Vico has pointed the way, this can (for him) only be for lack of sufficient imaginative power—reconstructive *fantasia* undistorted by anachronistic analogies fed by reading into the past the writer's own nationalistic or philosophical ideas—a faculty with which some men (Lucretius, Tacitus, Bacon) were more generously endowed than others; and of which, evidently, no mortals have enough. But such deficiencies are not obstacles of principle, i.e. logical or metaphysical, but empirical—of 'brute' fact. How many men have enough reconstructive genius to recapture the light of perennial human needs in their systematic evolution, the entire past of their society or class? In principle, given adequate powers of *fantasia*, plus the 'laws' which Vico supposes himself to have discovered—the laws of his 'ideal, eternal history of the nations'—any stage of human history can be mentally resurrected. Men 'make themselves', and men can therefore re-experience the process in imagination. The *fantasia*, which creates myths and rites in which primitive conceptions of the world are acted out, is the faculty that generates our sense of the past. Vico comes perilously close to implying—if he does not actually state —that our historical consciousness, even in our sophisticated, self-conscious, civilized condition, may be no more than the vision which belongs to the particular stage that we have reached: itself a kind of myth, the myth of the civilized; in other words, the view that all history is mythological—not an account required to correspond to a structure of fact independent of it, but something which human imagination creates as a pattern demanded by the needs of practice, by men's needs to domesticate themselves in the world. This, if pushed to its logical culmination, would destroy, at least in principle, all distinction between history as a rational discipline and mythical thinking. But Vico, unlike some modern irrationalist thinkers,[1] does not make this move. This implication of the *storia ideale eterna*, developed by Schelling and Nietzsche, does an injustice to Vico's sense of the realities of human development in contrast with patriotic and other fantasies about it. Yet the danger always remains. It is not this kind of synthesis of Plato's vision of man as he should be, and Tacitus' view of the imperfect creature that he is, that is to be found in the *New Science*. The relations of *verum* and *certum* are somewhat differently treated. Vico does

1 E.g. the use made of Vico's ideas by Professor N. O. Brown in his later works; and by James Joyce, especially in *Finnegans Wake*.

undoubtedly hold that there exists a fixed pattern or order in the growth of human societies—of, in theory, only the 'gentile' peoples, although he sometimes forgets to add this proviso, and speaks as if the *corsi* and *ricorsi* govern the whole of mankind. This story—the succession of dark, rude beginnings through youth, maturity, decline, collapse, which characterizes every cycle (apparently without end)—is, in its structure a *storia ideale eterna*, a Platonic pattern, *verum*, in principle knowable *a priori*. It is not a hypothesis which could be falsified or weakened, or an inductive generalization, resting on empirical evidence which is never perfectly known and could be interpreted in different ways. The structure of the *storia ideale*, fashioned and guided by Providence, is an eternal truth, a major discovery and Vico's claim to immortality as the founder of a new science based on the uncovering of the true theodicy. How do we come to know it? Not, it is clear, because we have made it. We do, in some sense, make our own cultures, but not the laws which they—that is, we—obey; these are the work of God. They may be rules for their divine inventor, but they are inexorable laws for us. We did not, even in some half-conscious or 'poetical' way, plan them: they are a *verum*, and no more a *factum* made by us than the laws of physics. Their operation is due to divine Providence but for which we should never have risen above the beasts. Indeed the original sense of awe, the primeval terror inspired by thunder which caused the *bestioni* to feel shame about promiscuity beneath the open sky and drove them into caves, was created by Providence, working through man but not originated by him. Nor did man create the mysterious machinery which transforms human vices into forces making for social solidarity, morality and civilization. The doctrine of the universal, unalterable, eternal, cyclical character of the stages of man's history—its Ideal Form—has Pythagorean, Platonic, neo-Platonic, and Renaissance roots; it is wholly *verum*; but it is difficult to see, since it is not the content of an identifiable human purpose, however occult, how it can be grasped as such by men. Yet Vico knows it: and knows that he knows it, and claims it as a major discovery. This is the Platonic strain in his thought and a link with Hegelian and pantheist doctrines. The relationship between what men 'make' and the laws and categories which govern their operations, like the related tension between value and fact, human purpose and the nature of things, freedom and determinism, action and 'the given', seems (to me at least) to have been made no clearer by Vico than by the post-Kantian idealists and Marxists who also struggled with this problem. I envy those more fortunate thinkers who have found in one of the great metaphysical systems final solutions to these ancient puzzles.

Providence is the author of the cosmic drama; but, according to Vico, the actors can understand their parts—*are* their parts; and can, in principle, achieve self-understanding. As for the nature of the relation between God's creation and men's self-creation: between what is given or determined by powers beyond human control or under-standing, and what men can mould—this our author, either from excess of prudence, or because of sheer failure to think it through, does not tell us. What is clear is that he believed that men and societies grow and alter in response not only to natural factors but also to their own goal-pursuing activities and goal-understanding capacities, and that consequently there is no unaltering and unalterable human nature, nor has it any fixed, timeless goals. In the excellent words of Professor M. H. Fisch 'Vico shares with the Marxists and the Existentialists the negative view that there is no human essence to be found in individuals as such, and with the Marxists the positive view that the essence of humanity is the ensemble of social relations, or the developing system of institutions'.[1] Whether, and if so, how far, Vico's thesis is tenable is another matter. But there can be little doubt of its remarkable originality.

III

THE SOURCES

When an idea of genuine audacity and power is met in the history of thought, the question of its sources is bound to present itself to historical scholars. There is always a peculiar danger that attends any such enter-prise. The assumption that no idea can ever be wholly original—that it must always be traceable to earlier notions, of which, even if it is not a mechanical compound, it must at least be a development or peculiar synthesis analysable into its original ingredients—seems to entail the odd proposition that nothing can ever be said literally for the first time: that there can be no such thing as wholly novel invention in this world. This unacceptable paradox seems to spring from the crude application of something like a theory of the conservation of

---

[1] *The New Science of Giambattista Vico* (Anchor Books, 1961, Doubleday, New York. Introduction, J4, p. xiv).

matter—a kind of vulgar atomism—to the realms of art and thought; as if all thinking begins with a collection of Cartesian or Lockean 'simple ideas', uncreated units present from the beginning, out of the combinations or modifications or, at best, 'development' of which, all other ideas arise. It is true that the very notion of historical scholarship, and particularly of the history of culture, seems to imply the notion of the continuity of civilization, of a developing, complex interplay of personal and impersonal factors, of which men's lives consist. From this it is, at times, held to follow that no matter how audacious a leap of genius a given work of art or thought may seem to embody, it is what it is wholly because of its antecedents, and is intelligible only in terms of its context, its roots, its *milieu*—the 'trends' and 'currents' which bring it into being and shape its path. This method, applied rigorously, threatens to melt the individuality of any human achievement into impersonal factors, and so lead to a kind of historicist depersonalization. In a sense no one did more for this doctrine than Vico himself, who virtually dissolved the 'essences' of men and their natures into the historical process of their generation. Even if one takes care to avoid either of two extremes—the Scylla of analysing a work away into its sources (or the process of its creation), or the Charybdis of insisting that only the end result matters, only the beauty of the flower or the pleasure given by the fruit, to which knowledge of its roots is irrelevant; even if one takes a middle course, and draws a distinction between the value of the flower and its coming to be, while at the same time maintaining that knowledge of its roots is indispensable to the full understanding of what it is (and that it is this, indeed, that constitutes the ultimate and only justification of learning as such), this principle will prove to have been more difficult to apply to Vico than to the majority of other thinkers of first importance. For his major discoveries have seemed to his interpreters to derive from no obvious sources, and have often been represented as a brilliant illustration of that very act of inspired creation out of nothing, so dear to the champions of extreme romanticism for whom even historicism seemed too much of a concession to the hated doctrines of classicism and Mimesis. But can this ever really be? Has Vico no intellectual parentage, no true anticipators? Are his most revolutionary ideas generated *ex nihilo*?

The late Erich Auerbach in his comparison of Herder with Vico[1]

---

[1] 'Vico and Aesthetic Historicism', in *Scenes from the Drama of European Literature* (New York, 1954).

says that whereas Herder's ideas were clearly influenced by Shaftesbury and Rousseau, by Ossian and German patriotism, by reaction against Voltaire and by the new biology, Vico cannot be so explained, and he leaves the matter there. Efforts have been made, of course, to trace the genesis of his views. Professor M. H. Fisch[1] lays emphasis on the vast impetus to historiography given by the Reformation both as a result of the coming into the open of books and manuscripts hitherto locked in monastic repositories, and the recognition on the part of the Roman Church of the need to fight historical attacks upon herself with historical weapons; and he speaks also of the stimulus given to historical writing by the national pride (Vico's *boria*) of the new nation states; and mentions the influence of Bacon's propaganda against abstraction and in favour of concrete data. While this is true and important and casts light on the rise of interest in history in the seventeenth century and the analysis of documents by Bollandists, Maurists and secular scholars, particularly in England, this is not, by itself, sufficient to account for the roots of Vico's most original theses. Nor does it do this even if we add the influence of the growing new literature of travel, stimulated by the discovery of new worlds, in the East and in the West. Vico mentions such sources a good deal less than might be expected. He does occasionally refer to the customs of exotic and barbarian people to illustrate his theses,[2] but their part in his work, even as illustrations, is comparatively minor. Much original and illuminating work has, of course, been done by historians of ideas, particularly Italian scholars, headed by Benedetto Croce (the true rediscoverer of Vico for our time) and the indefatigable Fausto Nicolini, to trace the origin of individual doctrines in Vico's work. Thus Karl Löwith[3] asserts, against Croce,[4] the dominant influence of Aquinas and Thomism on the *verum*/*factum* doctrine. This doctrine ultimately stems from the Augustinian dogma that God by knowing creates, that for Him knowing and creating are one, a doctrine that goes back to the conception of the Divine Logos; God alone knows all because He creates all;

---

[1] In his introduction to Vico's *Autobiography*, *op. cit.*, by far the best and most succinct account to date in English of Vico's intellectual genealogy.

[2] See G. Giarizzo, 'La Politica di Vico' (in *Quaderni Contemporanei*, No. 2, Istituto Universitario di Salerno, Libreria Scientifica editrice, Napoli, 1966, pp. 114-77) on Vico's references to the ancient Germans, Scythians, and modern Hungarians and Saxons, as examples of transition from 'heroic' to 'human' culture.

[3] *Op. cit.*   [4] *Op. cit.*

man, because he is made in God's image, has a limited power of creation, and therefore full knowledge only of what he himself creates and of nothing else. Whether one accepts the derivation of Vico's view from orthodox Catholic doctrine by Löwith (which seems to me convincing) or Croce's counter-argument against this (in support of which he cites the nineteenth-century Spanish theologian Jaime Balmes), it seems clear that the *verum/factum* doctrine is mediaeval and Christian and, by Vico's time, a theological commonplace. The application of this principle by him is another and far more interesting matter.

Again, the great edition of Vico's works to which Nicolini devoted his long life, and which he surrounded with a small flotilla of other works of interpretation of various aspects of Vico's life and work, remains a model of illuminating *Kulturgeschichte*; taken in conjunction with the monographs of Corsano and Fassò, Paolo Rossi and Paci, Badaloni and Gianturco, Amerio and Cantelli, Vaughan and Fisch, Whittaker and Adams (to mention only contemporary scholars), it gives us a great deal of information about the influence upon Vico of writers ancient and modern: Polybius and Lucretius, Campanella, Ficino and the neo-Platonist schools, Sanchez and Bodin, Bacon and Hobbes, Grotius, Pufendorf, Selden, Descartes, Bayle, Leclerc, and the scholars of his native city, Cornelio, Aulisio, di Capua and many others. All this is valuable: it does much to explain Vico's ideas about the ascent of man and his 'ferine' origins, and in particular his views of myth and ritual as practical tools in man's attempts to dominate his environment, as well as his notions of the relations of law to politics and morals, and a multitude of other conceptions, theories and allusions scattered in what Michelet called the 'little pandemonium of the *Nuova Scienza*'. But it does rather less towards the solution of the question of the sources, or at least anticipations, of Vico's two dominant doctrines: the conviction (which grew evidently during the 'silent' years in Naples between *De Antiquissima* of 1710 and the *Diritto Universale* of 1719-20) that the *verum/factum* formula could be applied to human history conceived in its widest sense—to all that men have done and made and suffered; and arising out of it, the very conception of culture as a category of historical thought, and indeed of thought in general. This transforming idea which links both these doctrines is surely Vico's greatest single claim to immortality. Whence did it originate? Where else do we find the notion of *verum/factum* as the master key to the understanding of history? Or the doctrine of the existence of a variety of autonomous cultures, entire ways of life, each with its own outlook and values flowing out of one another, but not a mere succession of efforts, attended by varying success, to achieve the same universal goals —indeed of the very notion of a culture as the central style of ways of life—of the entire range of feeling and thought and action of human communities? None of the writers for whom Vico expresses admiration, however deeply some of them were concerned with something wider than the mere sequence of important events or dominant personalities and their acts, conceived explicitly of a culture as a total expression of an individual society, a central style which pervades and connects the differing activities of its members—its literature and religion, its politics and its arts, its language and its legal, military, economic institutions, its class structure and its *mores*. None among them, neither Plato nor Polybius, neither Varro nor the *quattro autori* spoke of a unifying pattern, at once individual and developing (in Meinecke's words), which lies at the heart of a given society's peculiar structure (so that its constituents tend to reflect one another to some degree) and thus serves to distinguish it as an identifiable and, above all, intelligible whole among the many similar evolving structures or cultures of which human history consists. Is it possible to trace the origins of this view and method in the vast variety of texts, ancient and modern, which Vico consumed so voraciously? Or was his vision spontaneously generated in his own fervid imagination?

It is natural enough to look for the answer in Vico's own social and intellectual *milieu*—the kingdom of Naples in the seventeenth century. This is the path pursued by Nicolini[1] and Corsano[2], whose reconstructions of the social, political and religious life of the kingdom are models of lucid and imaginative learning. The most recent and perhaps the most ambitious attempt along these lines is that of Professor Nicola Badaloni.[3] He finds the answer in the history of scientific ideas in Naples, especially those of Bishop Caramuel and the Society of the *Investiganti*. He speaks of the neo-Pythagoreanism of the Renaissance; of the single dynamic principle, dear to it, that activates all things, as expounded by such men as Severino and Della Porta, who held that men

[1] Especially in *La Giovinezza di G. B. Vico* (Laterza, Bari, 1932), and *Uomini di spada, di chiesa, di toga, di studio a tempo di G. B. Vico* (Hoepli, Milan, 1942).
[2] In *Umanesimo e religione in G. Vico* (Laterza, Bari, 1935), and *G. B. Vico* (Laterza, Bari, 1956).
[3] Nicola Badaloni, *Introduzione a G. B. Vico* (Feltrinelli, Milan, 1961).

and animals ultimately differ only in degree; of Bartoli and Cornelio, who believed in the unity of mind and nature; of Porzio, who saw man as the ripest fruit of nature, of the single great indwelling *Spiritus*; of Borelli's and Caramuel's stress on the role of experiment and hypothesis, on the empirically probable as against the *a priori*, mathematically demonstrable, character attributed by the dominant Cartesianism to all scientific knowledge. Professor Badaloni lays particular stress on Borelli's theories of *vis percussionis* and of *conatus*, the heart of the vitalistic natural philosophy of his day. There is, of course, a good deal in Vico to which all this is relevant. Vico, too, formulated a physical theory. He believed in 'metaphysical points' of which *conatus* was the attribute—points which in some fashion 'mediate' between God and material bodies; and he attributes this theory to Zeno (it is not clear which of the two Greek philosophers of that name is meant: perhaps he did not distinguish between them). In *De Antiquissima* he speaks of *motus quo flamma ardet, planta adolescit, bestia per prata lascivit*—a *motus* and *conatus* which evidently make the world go round; and this may well derive from the thinkers whom Professor Badaloni's formidable learning resurrects. But this Renaissance metaphysics, neo-Platonic and vitalistic, which influenced Leibniz, too, is not what is most original or important in Vico. Whether, and how deeply, he read in the works cited by Professor Badaloni is less significant than the fact that all these *conatus* and *motus*, whether they came from Borelli or Leibniz or Della Porta, are not accessible to human insight; we do not understand their workings *per caussas*. All this is part of Vico's doctrine of the external world, of which we attain to *coscienza* which cannot get beyond the *certum*—an object of knowledge which is opaque to our intellect in the crucial and contrasting sense in which human volitions, thoughts, actions, are held by him not to be, in this respect, opaque. Vico does not, so far as I know, anywhere say that there is any continuity between the metaphysical points and their *conatus* on the one hand, and human activity on the other. Philosophers of nature before him, Paracelsus, perhaps, and Campanella, and after them Herder, Schelling, the Romantics, did believe, as against both Descartes and Kant, in precisely such continuity, and it forms the heart of their doctrines. So, in their own fashion, did Hamann and Goethe and Coleridge. Professor Badaloni's early Neapolitan scientists may well be among the ancestors of these writers. But Vico's claim to originality lies in the exact opposite: not in identifying, but in distinguishing between, on the one hand, natural processes which are more or less inscrutable, and, on the other, human activity which we can 'enter'. So far from deriving his ideas from these monistic forerunners of Schelling, Ravaisson, Bergson, Teilhard de Chardin and all the modern adherents of various kinds of *Naturphilosophie*, Vico opposed them. It is true that Caramuel and the other early scientific writers cited by Professor Badaloni were anti-Aristotelian and anti-Cartesian; that they were admirers of Bacon; that so, too, was Vico. And it may be that the emphasis of the *Investiganti* on experimentalism and the concrete, like Campanella's (and, of course, Bacon's) recourse to the senses and the imagination, and their antipathy to the abstract and the *a priori*, had their effect on him. Moreover, Vico's views on physics are not wholly without interest, as anything may be that relates to men of genius; but they remain peripheral to his thought, as Descartes' physics, or Kant's racial theories, are to theirs. When Signor Badaloni draws a parallel between Aulisio's theory of biblical mythology (e.g. his identification of Moses with Mercury, in the spirit of Spinoza and Père Simon) or Grimaldi's notions about *verum* and *certum* and Vico's corresponding doctrines, or draws our attention to Leonardo di Capua's theory of myths, or of the relation of theory to practice, he makes novel, useful and interesting additions to our knowledge of Vico. But his central thesis—that Vico's cardinal doctrines are traceable to Caramuel and the *Investiganti*—is not helped thereby.[1] Caramuel and his followers were concerned to show that the true path to natural, and perhaps all factual, knowledge (other than theology) lay through experience and not through *a priori* reasoning. Such knowledge could arrive at no more than high probability: *a priori* certainty was a snare and a delusion; in this respect

---

[1] All this quite apart from the question of how much Vico actually knew of the work of Bishop Caramuel and the *Investiganti*. Professor Paolo Rossi is surely right in speaking of Vico's cosmology as 'giuristico-cabbalistica', derived from the Hermetic and neo-Platonic mystical tradition stretching back to the *Timaeus*. To insist on a place for Vico, who seemed unaware of the great intellectual revolution of his century, in the history of natural science, seems misplaced piety. The more arresting fact, noted by H. P. Adams in *The Life and Writings of Giambattista Vico* (George Allen & Unwin, London, 1935), that for him myths are not so much imaginative reconstructions of nature, as of social life—are in fact a kind of mythologised politics—gives him an honoured place in the history of sociology, and makes him, with his emphasis on class war as a central factor in history, a genuine forerunner of Saint-Simon and Marx—a very different matter.

they stood close to Bacon. But Vico's central point—and his ultimate claim to genius—rests on the proposition that historical knowledge is, in fact, capable of much more than this: if not of greater truth, then of truth of another and superior character which the natural sciences cannot hope to reach. 'The whole of Vico's philosophy should be interpreted', says Professor Badaloni, 'as a transfer to the level of civil (that is social and political) philosophy of the experimental method of the *Investiganti*, and of the metaphysics of *mens*'[1], now no longer applied to the natural world, but (he goes on to say) 'taken as Socrates had already taken it, from Heaven to earth'. If this were so, then all that Vico would be saying is that history and social science should be satisfied with the probable—a commonplace which few before him questioned. To say that natural science was not an *a priori* discipline in method and conclusions, was, if not revolutionary, at any rate a bold rejection of the prevailing Cartesian doctrine and, at the same time, resistance to a powerful tradition of Aristotelian scholasticism, if not Aristotle himself. To say this of history was simply to reiterate what not only Descartes, but virtually all philosophy and, indeed, common sense had maintained since time immemorial; that real certainty was not attainable in human affairs. Whoever did not believe this? To reduce Vico to this platitude is indeed to relegate him to the level of a very minor empiricist. Vico, whatever else he was, was not a monist as Caramuel and his allies evidently were. He became a dualist: this, indeed, was his cardinal move. He did not draw a line at the point at which Descartes drew it—between mind and matter, or between *a priori* knowledge of the real world and *a posteriori* perception of the world of the senses, with its unreliable secondary qualities. Vico drew such a line, but he drew it elsewhere: between activity and passivity, between, on the one hand, *mens* in human affairs, incarnated in human beings, guided, indeed determined, by God and Providence, but themselves creative agents, who have constructed the civil or political-historical world; and, on the other, *mens* in nature, which God, whose instrument it is, can understand, but which to men, who have not made it, is opaque and inscrutable. This gulf is, in its own way, as wide as any that Descartes conceived—although it stretches across a different part of the metaphysical map. The development which is at

[1] *Op. cit.* p. 291. '*Nel suo complesso infatti la filosofia del Vico deve essere interpretata come un aggiornamento sul piano della filosofia civile del metodo sperimentale dagli investiganti e della metafisica della mens.*'

the centre of Vico's vision—his Phenomenology of the Spirit—does not bridge this gulf: it does not move from nature to mind, nor from the contingent to the logically necessary (as that of Leibniz does), nor (as in late Idealism) from the *an sich* of things to the *für sich* of persons. Professor Badaloni's interpretation of Vico's *verum/factum* formula is part of his general—to me unconvincing—thesis. It is, he says, intended to curtail the sole domination of *mens*: mind—the minds of men—must take account of nature, i.e. of *factum*: there must be interplay between them. There can presumably be no such interplay between *mens* and *verum*, because *verum* is intrinsic to *mens*: created by it indeed. But in that case neither can there be any 'interaction' between *mens* and *factum*, since Vico explicitly says that *factum* and *verum* are literally interchangeable; what God has made by men's agency is ours already; what he has made outside it is impenetrable to men. 'The rule and criterion of truth is to have made it', he said in 1710: this, and nothing else, is what *verum et factum convertuntur* means. The break is that between what men's minds 'make', and what they do not make but find or act upon: the former is, or can be, transparent to mind: the latter resists it. For Vico (it is necessary to say once again) nature remains opaque. He attacks the new scientific ideas precisely because they acclaim scientific method, which can deal only with 'externals,' as the open sesame to all problems. Professor Paolo Rossi[1] seems to me to come much nearer the mark in supposing that Vico was a conservative, not to say a reactionary, intellectually as well as personally close to the Jesuits,[2] e.g. in his anti-mechanism and, perhaps, his ambivalent attitude to freedom of the will. Despite his fascination with the growth of civilization, the whole of Vico's doctrine, in particular his emphasis upon the objective order—the eternal law which governs the cycles of the *storia ideale delle leggi eterne*—has a conservative tendency; for it seems to entail that one cannot force the pace, break with the past, create a lasting rational order rapidly, in the manner attempted by, for example, Vico's contemporary, Peter the Great. This is the spirit of Hooker, Matthew Hale, Montesquieu, Burke, Hegel, even Joseph de Maistre.[3] Whatever the correct interpretation of Vico's position, to turn the father of a profoundly theological historicism into a champion of scientific rationalism, a militant

---

[1] *Op. cit.*, p. 331. [2] *Ibid.*

[3] See Elio Gianturco, *Joseph de Maistre and Giambattista Vico* (Columbia University, Doctoral Dissertation, New York, 1937).

social progressive, an ally of the Royal Society, of Voltaire, the *philo-sophes*, ultimately of Engels and the Dialectics of Nature, is to run counter to the most obvious facts. Professor Enzo Paci[1] may go too far in representing Vico as looking on nature with existentialist eyes, as the wild, terrifying, primeval forest of the savage, panic-stricken *grossi bestioni*, a vision which, he suggests, irrupts even into Vico's elaborate, baroque world, in the form, for example, of the rough and barbarous soldier Antonio Caraffa whose biography he had written. But Paci is fundamentally right in stressing that at the heart of Vico's thought is the contrast between two worlds: the recalcitrant external world which we can manipulate only within limits set by Providence, and the world of men, which their creative spirit 'makes', with its recurrent images, mysteries and symbols that haunt men's collective consciousness, the man-made world of which we are true citizens, the stream of history in which alone we are at home. Professor Badaloni's book is an erudite and richly informative account of seventeenth-century Neapolitan science; but, whatever else it does, it does not provide a convincing answer to the question of the sources of the central doctrines of the only Vico who matters—the author of the *Scienza Nuova*. Are there no obvious bridges between its radical break with tradition and earlier thought? Did historicism come, fully fledged, without antecedents, out of the head of an isolated Italian antiquary into the world of Newton, Locke, Voltaire? Before conceding that this was indeed so, I should like to advance, somewhat tentatively, at least a partial answer to a problem to which men of far greater learning have thus far not succeeded in providing a satisfactory solution.

IV

Since Vico's main claim to fame rests on his views about the nature and methods of historical knowledge and its relations or absence of relations with the methods of the natural sciences, that is, in the field of theory and methodology, and not upon his achievements as a historian or a jurist, it is in the fields of philosophy, theology and scientific theory that scholars have tended to look for the sources of his ideas. Yet he was, above all, a legal scholar preoccupied with the history of jurisprudence, more especially the history of Roman Law, which is the central paradigm of his *storia ideale eterna*, and to which he

---

[1] In his most original study of Vico, *Ingens Sylva*, *op. cit.*

constantly returns. He was immersed in the study of legal antiquities far more deeply than in metaphysics or even theology; there is no branch of learning or disputation with which he was more familiar; it is in this field that he so desperately wished to make his name and obtain the coveted post that was so unjustly and dishonourably denied him. Yet this is a direction which has not perhaps been investigated sufficiently. What was it that first planted in his mind the notion of the diversity of cultures? Attention has often been drawn to the familiar fact that the discovery of new and strange societies in the New World provided new evidence for the well known contentions of Greek Sophists about the variety of customs and the relativity of values. Yet this commonplace needs to be treated with caution. Travellers' tales about American Indians or the peoples of the Far East were just as widely used to prop up the doctrine of the universality of Natural law, whether classical or Christian, Catholic or Protestant, since it was this universal human code that was believed to have survived in an uncorrupt form among these primitive and remote societies, uncontaminated by contact with (and untouched by the sources of) degenerate European morals. This was part of the Humanist tendency to look for the uniform and the universal, to rediscover the basic structure of moral and social, as of physical and metaphysical, reality that had been forgotten or perverted during the long night of the Middle Ages. Those who wished to stress the relativity of attitudes and values did not need these discoveries: examples from modern civilization had for a long time lain close at hand; Pascal did not need to go beyond Europe to point his celebrated moral that what was orthodox on this side of the Pyrenees was heretical on the other. Vico does indeed adduce examples from remote societies—Spanish America, Siam, the Celts; but C. E. Vaughan,[1] who has counted these examples, says that there are not more than a dozen of them; this contrasts sharply with, say, Montesquieu's, Lafitau's, Voltaire's, even Bodin's far richer use of such material. What engages Vico's thought is ancient Rome, and after Rome, Greece—the classical hunting ground of the theorists of Natural law; and he draws a moral that is precisely opposite to that of the Natural lawyers: that man's nature is to be conceived in social terms, not individual; those of movement and change, not fixity and rest; to be sought in history, not in a timeless metaphysics. Vico's con-

[1] *Op. cit.*

ception goes well beyond the rise, or rebirth, of historical consciousness whose roots are described by Professor Harold M. Fisch.[1] To say that historical knowledge differs from scientific is one thing: but Vico's thesis that historical knowledge is better founded than scientific is quite another and a much bolder one. The labours of pious Bollandists and Maurists, of Mabillon or Montfaucon, of Leibniz or Muratori, increased interest in origins, and in history as a repository of examples of virtue and vice, success or failure, useful for giving guidance to later generations; or as a witness to the truth of the Scriptures or of Revelation; or as a monument to the achievements of a nation, a Church, a movement; or of the validity or the corruption of a tradition, especially that of the Roman Church; it became, in this way, the favoured field on which Papalists and Reformers, Jesuits and Jansenists, fought their battles. These motives for the study of history during the Renaissance and the Reformation do much to account for the new fascination that historical studies had for humanists and churchmen, and the contempt for them on the part of the new, science-oriented, Cartesian positivists. But this is a far cry from *verum/factum*—the sharp contrast between our capacity to understand man-made artefacts as against nature, which God, who made it, can alone fully know.

The history of early modern jurisprudence lay closer to Vico's dominant interests. Here, it may be, the long-sought-for clue may at last be found.

v

One of the best known episodes in the later history of this subject is the great controversy among Roman lawyers and their critics which rose to a climax in the sixteenth century, stimulated by political, at least as much as by purely scholarly, considerations. One of the central motives behind the labours of the Renaissance jurists and their disciples, particularly in France, was the conviction that eternal and universal truths, of inestimable value for the conduct of men everywhere, had been known to the great Greek and Roman thinkers, and could, with sufficient effort, be recovered. They believed that this *restauratio* could be achieved once the distortions, confusions, interpolations and incrustations of Byzantine and mediaeval editors and interpreters, from Justinian's editor Tribonian to the mediaeval Accursians and Bartolists

---

[1] *Autobiography*, Introduction, *op. cit.*

and their successors (sadly affected as these last were held to be by the anti-pagan bias of the traditions of the Church), were identified and removed, and the original texts disinterred, reconstructed and understood. In part, the work of restoration was stimulated by sheer love of learning, by intellectual curiosity, by desire to rescue the truth from ignorance, error and deliberate perversion, and by pure admiration for the classical world, free from any utilitarian or ethical purpose. But together with such disinterested motives, there clearly were at work theological and political passions too: Protestant, anti-papal, anti-mediaeval, and, particularly in France, Gallican and nationalist. Nevertheless, it remains true that the dominant impulse was that of Platonic and Humanist faith that in the light of the newly discovered standards of ideal truth and ideal beauty, gifted and energetic men, unaffected by the condemnation of this world by the *tristes docteurs*, and liberated from the tyranny of a superstitious and obscurantist priesthood, could once again develop the rich potentialities of human nature, and build a life worthy of their new-found knowledge and creative genius. The timeless principles in the light of which Roman law was built— whether *jus naturale* or *jus gentium* or *jus civile*—once the ground was cleared of the accumulated rubbish of centuries, would be the basis of a new life, both social and individual, which rational men, from whose eyes the mediaeval scales had fallen, would establish in accordance with the unalterable laws of nature, which were identical with those of human reason as they were formulated by the great classical philosophers and jurists. Yet this very preoccupation with the restoring of classical texts led to two unexpected consequences, that were at once interesting and paradoxical.[1]

1 My main source of information on this subject is *The Ancient Constitution and the Feudal Law* by J. G. A. Pocock (Cambridge, 1957), especially the introductory chapter. This seems to me much the most original and illuminating, as well as the best written, treatment of this topic to be found anywhere at present. Professor Pocock mentions Vico in passing, but does not seek to connect his doctrines specifically with the startling implications of the controversies which he describes and analyses. Other discussions that I have found exceptionally valuable on the sources of the new historical consciousness in the sixteenth century, particularly in France, are to be found in (I cite them in alphabetical order): Arthur B. Ferguson, 'Bishop Pecock' (*Studies in the Renaissance*, vol. XIII, New York, 1966, pp. 147-66); Julian H. Franklin, *Jean Bodin and the Sixteenth Century Revolution in the Methodology of Law and History* (Columbia University Press, New York, 1963); Eugenio Garin, *Italian Humanism* (trs. P. Munz, Blackwell, Oxford, 1965); George Huppert, *The Idea of Perfect History* (University of Illinois Press, 1970); Donald R. Kelley:

In the first place, the very process of faithful reconstruction of any form of human communication requires a correct understanding of the meaning of what is said. This, in its turn, entails knowledge of the character and intentions of those whose language is being studied, and especially of the social structure within which such communication takes place—the *milieu*, the period, and above all the specific conventions which govern both words and lives within it, for it is only in the context of a particular society, at a particular period in its development, that the significance and use of the terms used—legal, moral, religious, literary—can be understood. Hence every investigation of any aspect of human civilization necessarily carries the student beyond the specific object examined—from legal formulae to the habits and purposes of the men whom the laws govern, from liturgical phrases to religious rites and beliefs and cosmology in terms of which alone the functions of the words, and of the documents that embody them, can be correctly interpreted. This in its turn may require an investigation of origins—of the genesis and evolution of customs, laws, ideas, institutions, and the role played by legal or theological language in them. Hence the work of resurrecting any monument of antiquity, however uninterested in wider aspects of the past, as such, the restorer may be, involves him, willy-nilly, in some social history, or historical sociology or anthropology. The need for reconstruction has, consequently, acted as a powerful stimulus, not only to historical studies,

---

(a) 'Historia Integra: François Baudouin and His Conception of History' (*Journal of the History of Ideas*, vol. 25, 1964, pp. 35-57); (b) 'Budé and The First Historical School of Law' (*American Historical Review*, vol. 72, 1967, pp. 807-34; (c) 'Fides Historiae: Charles Dumoulin and the Gallican View of History' (*Traditio*, New York, 1966, pp. 347-402); (d) 'Legal Humanism and the Sense of History' (*Studies in the Renaissance*, vol. XIII, New York, 1966); (e) and especially the important *Foundations of Modern Historical Scholarship* (Columbia University Press, New York, 1970) in which a good deal of the foregoing, but by no means all, is summarized, used and discussed, and which throws new light on the origins of historical and cultural history, to be found nowhere else; Frank E. Manuel, *Shapes of Philosophical History* (Stanford University Press, 1965, Chapter 3); A. Momigliano: (a) 'Ancient History and the Antiquarian' (*Journal of the Warburg and Courtauld Institutes*, 13, 1950, pp. 285-315); (b) 'La Nuova Storia Romana di G. B. Vico', *op. cit.*; (c) 'Vico's Scienza Nuova', *op. cit.*; Franco Simone: (a) 'Introduzione ad una Storia della Storiografia Letteraria Francese' (*Studi Francesi* 8, 1964, p. 455); (b) 'La Coscienza Storica del Rinascimento Francese e il Suo Significato Culturale' (*Convivium*, 22, 1954, pp. 156-67).

but to a historicist attitude: to looking for the answers to legal or theological or political questions in social growth, in the interplay of a variety of social factors in determining the part which this or that set of symbols, or enactment, or institution, played in the lives of a particular group of men—men whose ends and way of life were (to quote the *New Science*) 'of this rather than of that kind' and 'came to be what it was thus and not otherwise'.[1] The mounting enthusiasm for the study of monuments and institutions was perhaps not totally unconnected with the rise of profound scepticism about the reliability of narrative history itself.[2] Critics like Cornelius Agrippa in the beginning, and Patrizzi in the middle, of the sixteenth century, delivered the most vehement attacks on the reliability of narrative historians since Plutarch's onslaught on Herodotus. The historians and chroniclers were accused of inferiority of mind,[3] ignorance, irrational or corrupt motives such as vanity, fanaticism, personal, political and religious jealousies and hatreds, patriotic exaggeration, venality, lack of coherent purpose or method and the like, that from the very beginning had caused constant and violent disagreements among them which there was no possible means of resolving. The attack, at times, went a good deal further—some of the assailants maintained that history was, in principle, incapable of arriving at truth or even verisimilitude, for all history was, in the end, founded on the evidence of eye-witnesses, or at least contemporaries; these were either themselves involved in the events described, or they were not. In the former case they were liable to be partisan; in the latter they got their data at second-hand, and even then not the most secret, and sometimes most important, information;

[1] N.S. 147.

[2] One of the best accounts in English of 'Pyrrhonism' and of the 'historicist' reaction against it, and in particular of the political uses of the attacks on the notion of Natural law by the champions of custom-based, traditionalist and regionalist diversity, is to be found in the monograph on Bodin (*op. cit.*) by Julian H. Franklin. This valuable study of anti-universalism and anti-rationalism before Montesquieu and Burke casts a good deal of doubt on conventional accounts of political thought in the sixteenth century.

[3] This charge was revived three centuries later by Thomas Henry Buckle, who declared that history had not advanced as far as the sciences for the simple reason that historians were not as mentally well-endowed as scientists, since the best intellects in modern times had been attracted to the pursuit of the natural sciences. Once some really able people could be induced to occupy themselves with history, it would not be long before it was transformed into a properly organized natural science.

consequently, they could always know, and discount, the real springs of action of those involved, the crucial factors known only to participants, and liable to be used by them to feed historians with tendentious information, or to bribe them, in pursuit of personal ambition, or for the sake of a cause, or out of spite, or desire for glory, or for money, or from countless similar motives. Consequently, if historians were well-informed, they were likely to be biased, if impartial, to be ignorant or misled. The horns of this devastating dilemma have, in one form or another, loomed before serious historians ever since. Nor was this all. A century later such philosophical opponents as Descartes and his followers, attacking from another quarter, maintained that without axioms, definitions, deductive rules, intellectual rigour, history could not, in any case, be a source of systematic knowledge.[1]

Caught in this pincer movement, narrative history, indeed history itself, might have been hard put to it to maintain its claims, were it not for new weapons against such scepticism provided by the new masters of 'philology'. Gifted scholars and critics, literary, antiquarian and legal, began to arrive at their conclusions by careful scientific techniques, using neither the materials nor the methods of the older narrative historians, but basing themselves on monuments—literary documents, inscriptions, coins, medals, monuments of art and architecture,[2] laws, rites, continuing or remembered traditions—'objective' entities, *realia*, which, it was maintained, could not be corrupt or unscrupulous or tell lies. Thus the very desire to recover timeless verities, which had been forgotten or perverted, resulted in bringing into being a new dimension of historical understanding founded on a revival of antiquarian scholarship, accompanied by a new respect for a Varro or a Scaevola as against even the greatest narrative historians of the ancient world. The truths so reconstructed were perhaps more general than those which the narrative historians claimed to report, but also seemed more solidly based, and to possess wider significance. When Patrizzi maintained that monuments no less than stories could, in fact, be made to fit into almost any pattern, that out of such bricks any edifice could be built, what he was saying was not, indeed, absurd, but certainly exaggerated; the tests of internal coherence in the reconstruction, say, of the constitution of Periclean Athens, or of Private law in the Rome of Ulpian or Gaius, could in principle be made as

[1] See pp. 9-11, *esp.* p. 10, n. 1.
[2] See A. Momigliano, 'Ancient History and the Antiquarian', *op. cit.*

rigorous as the methods of medicine or geography. The emphasis laid by philologists and 'grammarians' on empirical evidence—concrete examples of the application of the general rules which Bacon and Campanella stressed so strongly, became the cornerstones of the new method. Thus the route to the genuine past, it was now believed, lay via 'philology'. Valla (and Dumoulin and Cusanus) demonstrated this in the course of exposing the forged Donation of Constantine; the great historical jurists, Budé, Cujas, Alciato, and their disciples, used the new method to clear away the mediaeval rubble and Byzantine carelessness which, in their view, concealed the authentic texts of the great Roman lawyers. One of the great battle fronts was that between the upholders and critics, both Gallican and Protestant, of the authority of the Vatican: all sides appealed to tradition. This itself, as Professor M. H. Fisch has pointed out,[1] gave a great fillip to historical studies. But what is more relevant to the formation of Vico's views is the fact that the appeals to the past largely took the form of examination of etymology and monuments, as well as documents and narrative history. The great Gallican controversialist, Charles Dumoulin, the disciple of Valla and the one-time friend of Calvin, appealed to linguistic usage in interpreting the true tradition in his defence of the claims of the French monarchy against Roman universalism. In the same spirit, the defender of Roman orthodoxy, Raymond Le Roux, takes Dumoulin to task for being over-literal: words change meanings: lawyers who deal with facts and not with mere words should not fall into the error of attaching static meanings to words: central terms change meanings at different times and in different states.[2] But the same principle could be used with equal effect by the opponents of Rome: language and monuments can be used not only to expose clerical anachronisms and forgeries, but to reconstruct the structure of past societies in terms of which alone the significance of this or that sentence in the Digest or Ulpian can be understood.[3] So François Baudouin demanded knowledge of universal history on the part of anyone claiming true mastery of the law; to understand the tradition of the Church one must understand the Commonwealth 'in whose bosom, as it were, the Church was nourished'; all history and all jurisprudence should ideally be united

---

[1] *Op. cit.*
[2] See Donald R. Kelley, '*Fides Historiae*'. Professor Kelley's works (listed on p. 126, n. 1) are an invaluable historical guide to this movement of thought.
[3] See Kelley, 'Legal Humanism and the Sense of History', *passim*.

in one single great volume.[1] Law and history are one and indivisible.[2] It is by adhering to this principle that Budé and Cujas, Alciato and Le Douaren and their disciples succeeded in purging the texts of Roman law from the distortions and blunders of mediaeval 'barbarians'— Bartolists and Accursians; indeed it was only by using such methods that the unhistorical lumping together of Roman texts of different dates by Justinian's editor Tribonian—the *bête noire* of the new school of French jurists—could be exposed, and the chronology and therefore significance and relationships of the texts properly established. Had not already Valla declared that it is *ab institutione, ab artifice* that the historical meaning of the crucial terms can be revealed?[3] This is equally the doctrine of François Hotman, and of his master Cujas. Even the papalist Le Roy declares that languages, like all things human, have 'their beginnings, progress, corruption, end'.[4]

This is the very language of the *storia ideale eterna*. The hunt for anachronisms in mediaeval or Byzantine compilations goes back to the fifteenth century,[5] but becomes more systematic in the course of the legal and religious controversies in the sixteenth, particularly in France. The heightened sense of changing styles, and consequently of the stream of history and the evolution of ways of life, in the Christian West, which these styles reflect, is certainly a new door to the past: the marriage of 'philology' and law is the contribution of the *Mos Gallicus* to historical understanding. Bodin, a century before Vico, looked on myths and popular legends as evidence for social beliefs and structures. Vico's conception is larger and profounder: he discriminated what was, from what was not, compatible with this or that stage in the evolution of an entire culture, not merely with this or that linguistic usage or legal or constitutional set of rules: these last were for him themselves aspects of a single unitary pattern that was exhibited in all the manifestations of a particular civilization. Nevertheless, there is a similarity of approach, both basic and in detail, between the historical jurists, especially Hotman and Baudouin, and Vico. Distrust of narrative

---

[1] Cited by Franklin from Baudouin's *De Institutione Historiae Universae* (*op. cit.* pp. 44-6).

[2] '*Unius corporis indivisae partes aut membra divelli neque possunt neque debent.* See Kelley, *op. cit.*, pp. 129-141. The very title of Baudouin's *De Institutione Historiae Universae et ejus cum Jurisprudentia Conjunctione* is telling enough.

[3] Kelley, *ibid.*

[4] Kelley, *ibid.*

[5] This is well described by Arthur B. Ferguson, 'Bishop Pecock', *op. cit.*

history, antipathy to timeless principles, whether those of Natural Law, or later, Cartesianism, faith in 'philology' as a kind of rudimentary anthropology and social psychology, is common to both: they are equally remote from Augustine and Aquinas, Sanchez and the other accepted forerunners of the Neapolitan philosopher.[1] Vico does not discuss Budé or Dumoulin or Hotman in this connection. But the names of 'Cujaccio', 'Bodino', 'Otmanno', 'Salmasio', occur not infrequently in his pages: the hypothesis that Vico, or indeed any other legal scholar whose life was spent on the study of historical jurisprudence, knew nothing of, or paid no attention to, these great quarrels, seems improbable. Vico, if anyone, must have had it borne in upon him that the doors to antiquity had been opened, not by historians, but by 'philologists', the masters of classical learning and especially of Roman law. It would not be absurd to say that the history, indeed the very concept of culture, began in the heat of argument, especially in

---

[1] There are other anticipations of Vico's doctrines: Budé and Le Roy had spoken of life cycles of civilization, from the poetry and primitive beliefs of its childhood to an adolescence of scholarship and eloquence, ending in decline and corruption. (See Kelley's excellent *Foundations of Modern Historical Scholarship*, pp. 64, 83.) The French sixteenth-century historiographer La Popelinière also said as much, and spoke of the poets as the first historians (*ibid.*, p. 140). The succession of fable-folklore-truth is to be found in Christophe Milieu, Le Roy, Polydore Vergil, Grynaeus, etc. (*ibid.*, p. 304), and Pasquier speaks of the interconnectedness of cultural phenomena (*ibid.*, p. 309, and Huppert, *The Idea of Perfect History*, pp. 65, 158). Professor Kelley, so far as I know, is the first scholar to perceive these important links. He tells us that 'Vico was not so much the creator of a "new science" as the preserver of an old science, the science of philology. In this sense he did not so much found historicism as inherit it' (*op cit.*, p. 8). This seems to me an underestimate of Vico's achievement. The programme of the complete re-creation of a strange and barbarous past by a great and painful effort of the imagination, which seeks to enter into *la vasta imaginativa di quei primi uomini*, the discovery of a path to an entire world of the *grossi bestioni* as they and their 'heroic' successors conveyed it in rites and poetry and laws, viewed not as a more primitive version of, or step towards, our own more civilized society, but as a cruel, frightening, but powerful and self-contained, civilization, with its own inner coherence and its own peculiar values and creations, e.g. the Homeric poems which we cannot hope to match—this is surely a conception far beyond the perspective of even the boldest Renaissance philologists, jurists and men of letters. Vico's originality seems to me to be one not of degree but of kind. Even his wildest flights of anthropological etymology—as when he seeks to connect the words for acorns, water, books and laws—as well as his far-reaching economic interpretations of cultural symbols, seem well outside the intellectual region of the kind of philological fancies or legal muddles which Valla or Budé exposed or put right.

France, about the credentials of texts or traditions, which, however academic in manner and method, sprang from social, political and economic conflicts. Vico's doctrine appears as a bold and transforming development of methods invented by and for the polemics about where true—valid—authority for political action by the contending parties could be found. At the same time, the case must not be overstated: there is, so far as is known, no positive mention in Vico's works of these great cont rsies; and this total silence does need some explanation. The anti-papalists were, of course, dissidents and heretics—and to acknowledge a direct debt to them or to mention them with too much fervour would not have been either altogether safe in the Neapolitan kingdom of Vico's day, or likely to commend itself to Vico's friends and patrons, especially the clerical circles with which he was closely bound up all his life, and which he evidently found congenial. He does, of course, speak with favour of Grotius, Selden, Pufendorf, Bacon— Protestants all—but he rejects the central doctrines of at least three among them; nor did any of them conduct political and theological warfare against the authority of the Vatican in the sense in which this was done during the wars of religion in sixteenth-century France. Moreover, like many another discoverer of original truths, he was not, perhaps, too anxious to acknowledge intellectual debts of so direct a kind. Nevertheless, we cannot say, in the present state of knowledge, that there is positive evidence that Vico derived some of his central notions from the historical jurists: only that it is exceedingly unlikely that he did not do so; for this is the world that he knew best.

The second paradox has been mentioned already. One of the original motives for labouring to restore the texts of Gaius or Papinian was the belief that they contained the clearest statement of those universal rules of conduct to which all men aspire by nature, no matter how barbarous or deeply perverted they may be, so that contemplation of the principles of Roman law should give any man a sense of home-coming, return out of the long night of the Middle Ages to the rule of reason and the light of day. But what was gradually discovered was a way of life that seemed remote or, at the very least, unfamiliar to these seekers for the single true tradition. The more faithfully the despised mediaeval accumulation was removed, the stranger the classical world appeared: if anything, it was the alleged monkish distortions that gave it such affinity to the ideas of later ages as it once seemed to have. This was not what had been expected by neo-Stoics, neo-Aristotelians, or Platonists and neo-Platonists of the Renaissance. But it was grist to the mills of those who wished to protect local or corporate liberties and privileges against the encroachment of the great centralizing powers—whether papal or royal. Legal historians have often remarked on François Hotman's unceasing effort, while ostensibly wholly engaged on learned labours intended to establish the true meaning of Roman law, to emphasize the unbridgeable differences between it, and, indeed, the rules of *jus naturale*, too—and the ancient customs of France, which followed an authentic, native, 'Franco-Gallic' tradition; from which it followed that Roman law, whether 'municipal' or international, was not relevant to the French State. Hotman's and his allies' insistence on the gulf that divided Roman law from the 'immemorial', native Franco-German traditions, was part of their defence of feudal, or local, or national rights against the champions of uniformity, centralization and all those who appealed to timeless and universal truths to support claims to overriding authority.

This great argument, stemming as it did from many sources—early consciousness of nationhood, the zeal of Reformers, Gallicans and other dissenters against the Roman hierarchy, the claims of estates and provincial *parlements* and corporations against the central executive—from every movement or outlook that found it advantageous to underline differences between places, times, ways of life—was eagerly seized upon by the defenders of local custom, ancient ways, individual traditions that varied from place to place with roots too remote and tangled to be rationalized and fitted into any universal system. This great political and theological conflict, one of the great ideological battles which has continued into our day, as often as not clothed itself in legal forms, appeals to precedents and historical institutions the path to which was built by embattled jurists and grammarians. In the effort to diminish the authority of Roman law, to undermine the notion that civil law, even if it was not always, at least always strove to be, the application of Natural law to particular situations, Hotman speaks of '*les saisons et mutations de moeurs et conditions d'un peuple*'[1] which divides it from other people's, and indeed even from its own past; the French have their own '*complexion* and *humour*'.[2] What have they to

---

[1] See Kelley, 'Legal Humanism', *op. cit.*, p. 195.

[2] Quoted by Kelley, *ibid.*, p. 194, who adduces the similar remarks of Le Caron, Dumoulin, Pierre Ayrault and other adherents of the doctrines of territorialism and national autonomy.

do with the laws of a society long dead and originating in another country? What have the lists of 'Natural law' maxims enunciated by Gratian, or his predecessors, obedient mouthpieces of the Vatican, or spokesmen for an ancient civilization born in far away Athens and flourishing in an only slightly less distant Rome, what have they to do with our own peculiar, unique, Frankish, that is, in the end, Germanic, or 'Francogallic' individuality or 'complexion'? In his *Anti-Tribonianus* (which Vico cites in another connection),[1] Hotman uses this appeal to historical continuity in resisting royal claims as against the customary law of the Frankish conquerors of Gaul, or against other codes which had developed out of the needs and traditions of the varied associations of men of whom the King's realm consists. The Romans had a *respublica*, not a monarchy: 'our administration has nothing in common with theirs' said Etienne Pasquier.[2] The argument from the 'irrelevance' of what the Romans did to modern situations became a powerful weapon in the hands of the defenders of the prerogatives of various estates—Montesquieu's later defence of such *corps inter-médiaires*, and his anti-centralist pluralism, drew sustenance from the sharp contrasts between the variety of systems, each valid for its own day. Hence flowed relativism, historicism, political pluralism, and, more particularly, suspicion of abstraction, of tidy general schemas, whether *a priori* or naturalistic, advocated by no matter whom— Aristotle, Seneca, Ulpian, the Digest, Aquinas, Descartes, Locke, the *philosophes*. Hence, above all, ever since Lorenzo Valla and the new 'philology', the appeal to the concrete and the particular in specific times and places.

Nor is the new path to the past confined to historical lawyers. The *Mos Gallicus* captured history proper as well. Etienne Pasquier looks on laws as custom recorded in writing, and since society and its language and habits alter, there is need of constant readjustment. One can reconstruct the past not by attending to narrative history, so much as by renewed study of acts of *parlements*, juridical records, papal bulls, poems, coins, statues; historians tend to be subjective, a *je ne sçay quoy*

---

[1] See *Bibliografia Vichiana* (ed. B. Croce e F. Nicolini, Ricciardi, Naples, 1948, vol. 1, p. 51) and, for the echoes of this controversy in Gibbon and Hume, *ibid.* pp. 377 and 789.

[2] See Huppert, *op. cit.*, for a good many instances of this kind of expression, and all that it implies, in Hotman, Pasquier, La Popelinière and others in France in the sixteenth century.

de passion is apt to affect them, especially if religion is at issue.[1] Pasquier's distaste for Roman law and architecture throws the dissimilarity between the Roman past and the French tradition into sharp relief: this is surely the direct result of the doctrines taught in the schools of Bourges, Valence, Toulouse, Turin. Vignier, who treats Homer and the Bible in the same detached fashion as he does coins and inscriptions, shows no respect for the 'immemorial wisdom of the ancients'. La Popelinière[2] is concerned to achieve an understanding of ancient ways of life, '*les moeurs, et la police des Grecs*', for example, by examining the '*coustumes et façons de faire*' of a people, their '*forme de vivre*'; the path to this lies through the songs, dances, sagas, linguistic usage—for '*le langage symbolize ordinairement nos moeurs*'. He is correspondingly sceptical about the credentials of ancient historians—these must be checked with what one knows of their country, religion, sources, their patrons, and what charges they are concerned to ward off, and what degree of consistency they display. Even so, like Bodin, he thinks that their conclusions can never be more than probable: the mere fact of disagreements between historians ensures this. Vico, of course, thinks he can do better, and attain to a degree of certainty beyond mere probability by the use of his reconstructive *fantasia*; for him humane studies—'philology'—can claim superiority over the natural sciences: understanding of a world men have created is not governed by laws of sciences concerned with the opaque external world. Whether or not he is mistaken in this, it is important to realize that in this important respect he differs in principle both from Bodin and from the Neapolitan 'probabilists' (to whom Professor Badaloni vainly seeks to attach him); *scienza* for him is of the eternally true; indeed he reproaches Grotius precisely for supposing that historical propositions of which the *New Science* is the *scienza* can never be more than probable. Nevertheless, it is difficult to believe that his historical method, and indeed his entire schema of development, is wholly independent of the doctrines of these French jurists, 'grammarians' and historians: the arm of coincidence can scarcely stretch quite so far. What is altogether his own is the notion of history as the continuous self-transformation of man and of human institutions in the course of man's struggle to overcome human and natural obstacles, which, because it is the activity of men, and the

1 See Huppert, *ibid.*, p. 62. This pioneering study of the rise of the new history contains valuable information on the alliance between jurists and historians in this respect. 2 See Huppert, *op. cit.*, pp. 135-51.

consequence of human structures, can be understood by men, under-stood as nature cannot be. This is his own:[1] it is this original doctrine that inspired Michelet and Croce and gained the admiration of both Marx and Dilthey.[2]

In England, this movement took the form of Coke's sense of the Common Law, and Matthew Hale's doctrine that law was born not made, and of those other forerunners (e.g. Hume and Bolingbroke) of Burke, who reacted against the cut and dried 'rigidity' of ordered reason 'towards the customary, the native, the feudal, the barbarous' . . . 'the primitive, the inarticulate, the immutable'.[3] In the seventeenth century this movement spread to Sweden, the Netherlands and Sicily as well as England, and, provided with an ideological defence by Burke and Herder, ultimately led to the legal romanticism of Savigny and the German Historical School.

If this account is anywhere near correct, it follows that the late Renaissance gave birth to two seminal ideas. The first is that history—the restoration of the past—consists not merely in reporting a string of events or deeds, or providing portraits of the great human actors and their lives, or even the social, economic, demographic and 'cultural' facts and connections, together with comments upon styles of art which Voltaire, for instance, was among the first to select, discuss and evaluate; but also in understanding the historical stream as a whole, in terms of which alone that which is studied—a law, a religion, a policy, or the acts or fortunes of individuals or nations—makes sense; and

[1] It is true that Baudouin in *De Institutione Historiae Universae*, pp. 599 and 742 (quoted by Kelley, *Foundations*, p. 303) pointed out that in history man has the advantage of being an actor as well as a *spectator, judex* or *interpres*, as he is of nature; and Professor Kelley acutely notes the parallel with Vico, and adds the names of Croce and Troeltsch. But this, although remarkable enough, is, at most, like Manetti's contrast (see p. 25) of what is man-made ('ours') and what is not, the merest embryo of Vico's bold new doctrine, as sketched above.

[2] Professor Huppert's blind spot about Vico causes him to say that Michelet and the Germans mistakenly pay homage to Vico only because they did not know his sources. Although my knowledge of fifteenth-century historiography is based on secondary sources, such as his own very informative book, I find it hard to believe that the revolutionary notion of the self-transforming nature of man, or of language, myth, and symbolic rites as modes of experience and interpretation of reality, have been lying quiet and unperceived in the pages of Pasquier or La Popelinière, or even Baudouin.

[3] J. G. A. Pocock, *op. cit.*, Introduction. So began what Maitland once called 'the Gothic revival' in jurisprudence.

that the surest path to such understanding lies through 'philology', if only because monuments and institutions—language, customs, laws, coinage, art, popular beliefs—unlike historians, may be misinterpreted, but cannot lie.

The second is that the high civilizations of the past are a good deal less like our own 'glorious age' than the proponents of Natural law assumed; that they were the expressions of societies sufficiently similar to ours not to be totally unintelligible, but different enough not to be authoritative for us, with their own independent structures and patterns of development; and have been found fascinating by later ages precisely because they are remote, and incorporate values different from, perhaps superior to, but at any rate not compatible with, our own. This seems to me the authentic beginning of the idea of culture as a complete pattern of living, which can be studied not merely as the arts and skills and ideas of a community can be investigated, each in separation from the others,[1] but as a central style, exhibited equally by law and poetry, myths and forms of family life, economic structure and spiritual activities—all the diverse provinces of the behaviour of a society, a tradition, an age, which form an interrelated unity, a single pattern of development which, even if it cannot be precisely defined or even described, is sufficiently individual to enable us to recognize certain possibilities as incompatible with it—as being unGreek, or unRoman, or unFrench, or unmediaeval; this is La Popelinière's *façons de faire* of a society, in virtue of which we attribute them to that society and no other. In short, we are in at the emergence of the concept of the uniqueness and individuality of an age, an outlook, a civilization.

In its extreme form belief in an inexorable *Zeitgeist* which shapes all the phenomena of an age or a culture led to the dogmatic imposition of *a priori* straitjackets, idealist or materialist, on accounts of the past: inconvenient facts were eliminated or glossed over if they did not fit the theory. Even such scrupulous writers as Max Weber and Huizinga are occasionally guilty of this, not to speak of fanatical schematizers like Spengler or Pokrovsky. Nevertheless, the notion of a single central style which permeates an epoch has, by providing pointers to connections and similarities between phenomena in disparate regions of human activity, transformed the art of attribution and created the discipline of cultural history.

[1] As, for example, despite his claims and the claims made for him by some of his interpreters, was done by Voltaire.

No doubt the discovery of the native cultures in Asia or America increased awareness of the diversity of customs and attitudes. But the revelation of Roman culture which was remoter than had been supposed before was, in one sense, more important still. The societies of American Indians or Siamese could be represented as primitive versions of our own civilization: admired by some as shaped by man's true nature before his corruption and decadence, dismissed by others as immature, rudimentary and barbarous. Even the admired Chinese were conceded by Voltaire to be an arrested development. Rome was a different matter: it was the very paradigm of a fully developed civilization: not merely a step towards our own, nor a falling away from it; some preferred the Republic, others the Augustan age or that of the Antonines: in either case these ages were represented as the acme of cultivation. Voltaire thought, and the Enlightenment followed him, that Periclean Athens or Augustan Rome or Florence during the Renaissance, or France under Louis XIV, were peaks of a single range of ascending human progress. Yet if Rome and Greece at their best were not at all like the modern — post-Renaissance — West, it followed that more than one equally authentic, equally developed culture was possible, and that such cultures could be widely heterogeneous, could, indeed, be incomparable and incommensurable. This entailed genuine pluralism, and an explicit refutation of the belief that man everywhere, at all times, possessed an identical nature, which, in its quest for self-fulfilment, sought after the same ends, and that this, indeed, was precisely what constituted man's human essence. Yet this could not be so if different cultures had their own ideals, their own irreducible peculiarities. 'Nothing', said Leonardo Bruni, a fourteenth-century humanist, in a celebrated sentence, 'is said in Greek that cannot be said in Latin.'[1] This is precisely what Vico denied[2] and sought to refute in his works: everything is uniquely what it is: there are similarities, echoes, parallels: but no central identity that makes translation from one *milieu* to another wholly possible (or, as Herder would later add, desirable). If the concepts of Natural law or of a permanent human nature were to be retained, they would have to become far more flexible and elastic. Such modification is compatible

[1] '*Nihil graece dictum est quod Latine dici non possit*'. (Quoted by Hans Baron in *Humanistisch-Philosophische Schriften*, Leipzig, 1928).

[2] So, but with a good deal less emphasis, did Leibniz (see *Ermahnung an die Teutsche, ihren Verstand und Sprache besser zu üben*, ed. P. Pietsch, pp. 307 ff; also *Nouveaux Essais*, III, 9).

neither with strict Thomism, nor with the doctrines of Descartes or
Spinoza or Voltaire. The notion that there exist eternal and unalterable
truths, laws, rules of conduct which entail ends of life which any man
might, in theory, have recognized in any time and in any place, and
the discovery and pursuit of which is the sole and sufficient goal of all
human behaviour, is the central principle of the Enlightenment. Its
rejection, with its appeal for a far wider psychological imagination,
marks a decisive turning-point in the history of Western thought.

My thesis, although I offer it tentatively, is that these two notions
—of understanding through 'philology' and of the succession (or simultaneous existence) of equally authentic, yet autonomous, cultures
which cannot be assimilated to one another—do more to explain the
origins of Vico's conception of what cultures are and how we can
come to know them, than the philosophical or theological or scientific
ideas more commonly investigated by those in search of his sources.
It seems to me *prima facie* more probable that legal, historical and
literary scholarship were the regions closest to his lifelong interests.[1]
Nothing, needless to say, is thereby taken away from his claim to
originality. The application of *verum/factum* to history remains
indefeasibly his own. It was the fusion of this far older Christian
doctrine with the Renaissance notion of the interrelation of different
aspects of the spiritual activities of different societies that underlies
Vico's distinction between nature and culture, between events and
acts. This, in its turn, distinguishes what is history from what is not:
what can and what cannot be 'entered' by the human mind. This mind
is, as often as not, incarnated in institutions and traditions and the
sensus communis of entire nations or all mankind, as, guided by divine
Providence, it seeks to understand itself and its past in the many guises
which it has assumed in its unceasing effort to explain and master itself
and the external world. It was this synthesis that transformed the
scattered insights of jurists or antiquaries, or the historians influenced
by them, into a powerful and fruitful historical method.[2] After everything that is absurd, ephemeral, confused, pedantic, trivial in Vico's

---

[1] For the extent of Vico's legal learning, see Giuseppe Giarizzo, *op. cit.*, who
assures us that it stretched 'from Vulteius to Godefroy, from Cujas to Hotman'
(p. 113). Moreover Huppert tells us that the French historical writers of the sixteenth century were widely read (*op. cit.*, p. 167).

[2] Why has this probability, even if it cannot be demonstrated by references in
Vico's works to actual names (as if ideas do not travel without labels, and men

work has been forgotten, what remains is the new conception of what men are. He dissolves the concept of a static human nature—the unaltering kernel—*quod ubique, quod semper, quod ab omnibus*, and replaces it with a pattern of systematic change. Historical insight for him is a form of men's awareness of themselves as purposive beings whose modes of thought, feeling and action alter in response to new needs and activities, which generate new institutions, entire new civilizations, that incarnate men's nature. Men are able to understand these civilizations, no matter how remote from their own, in a fashion different from that in which they can know the external world, because they are largely man-made. From this stems the notion of cultural style, which in its turn led to such notions as the *Zeitgeist* and the *Volksgeist* and groups of related ideas, vague and treacherous concepts much misused by metaphysicians who have treated them as a queer species of independent causal forces. Nevertheless, this notion points to an easily neglected truth: that all classification, selection, interpretation is in the end subjective,[1] that is, does not correspond with, or fit into, 'objective' grooves in the external world, as the great mathematically minded realists had supposed; and, therefore, (even though Vico himself claimed objective validity for his schema) that, in Burckhardt's famous words, 'the outlines of a cultural period and its mentality may present a different picture to every beholder'.[2] Over everything in Vico towers the *idée maîtresse* that what we call the nature of things is their history, and that 'the nature of things is nothing other than

---

cannot be influenced by Marx or Freud unless they mention them by name), found no echo in the Italian commentators—from Duni and Cuoco to Croce, Corsano, above all Nicolini, who devoted his long and honourable life to reconstructing every detail of Vico's life and thought and intellectual descent? Why is it assumed that Vico cannot have had forerunners outside Italy and the Roman Empire? Why should a host of minor schoolmen and provincial, not to say local, Neapolitan writers be (reasonably enough) thought worthy of mention as possible sources of his ideas, when the great luminaries in a field that was peculiarly close to Vico's interest, men of European fame and influence, are not once so much as referred to in this connection? Can this be because they are Frenchmen, and the war between the two great styles of thought and writing, in which Vico himself took part, is not over yet? Is this a case of that nationalistic *boria* against which Vico protests as an obstacle to the discovery of truth in history? Whatever the explanation, the fact itself remains exceedingly puzzling.

[1] This is well brought out by Erich Auerbach in his 'Vico and Aesthetic Historicism', *op. cit.*

[2] *The Civilization of the Renaissance in Italy*, opening paragraph.

their birth in certain times and in certain guises; when they are thus and thus, then things arise, and they are such as they are and not different'.[1] The world of primitives is literally a different world from that of the sophisticated, as the world of the rich differs from that of the poor, or the world of believers from that of unbelievers; it follows that no single language is ever wholly translatable without residue into any other, for each categorizes reality in different ways. These ideas, which broke with the tradition that began with the Greeks and ended with the Enlightenment, have profoundly altered men's outlook. It is this transformation, among others, that makes it difficult, if not impossible, for those whom it has affected to return to the conceptions of human nature and the real world held by Descartes or Spinoza or Voltaire or Gibbon, or, for that matter, Russell or Carnap in our own day; or to the conventional conception of the function of history (offered, for example, by Leibniz) as satisfying curiosity about origins, disclosing the uniformity of nature, doing justice to men of worth, offering support to Revelation, and teaching useful lessons by means of examples. Vico attacked this view all his life; with much obscurity and confusion, but always vehemently, and with scattered insights of widely varying value, but, at times, of arresting genius. The controversy in which he played a major role has not ended; but at least the lines are today more clearly drawn.

1 N.S. 147.

Footnote 1 to Page 21:

1 I have, since writing this, discovered that Vico had at least one notable forerunner in this respect: Nicholas of Cusa, who sometime in the mid-fifteenth century boldly departed from Platonic orthodoxy and declared that mathematics was a purely human creation, which we know because we alone have made it. Honour where honour is due, although Cusanus did not, of course, apply his insight to historical knowledge or other humane studies. (See on this *Early German Philosophy* by Lewis White Beck [The Belknap Press of Harvard University Press, Cambridge, Mass., 1969; pp. 67, 69-70], from the excellent pages of which I have gleaned this fact, not, in general, noticed by students of Vico. Professor Beck does not mention Vico, and sees a parallel with Kant. He refers, as his source, to Nicholas of Cusa, *De Coniecturis*, I, chap. *XIII*, Paris ed., folio XLVIII.[R])

HERDER

and the Enlightenment

'We live in a world we ourselves create.'[1]

[1] Unless otherwise indicated, all references are to J. G.
Herder, *Sämtliche Werke*, ed. B. Suphan (Berlin, 1877-1913).
The quotation is from *Uebers Erkennen und Empfinden in der
Menschlichen Seele*, VIII, 252.

I

HERDER'S fame rests on the fact that he is the father of the related notions of nationalism, historicism, and the *Volksgeist*, one of the leaders of the romantic revolt against classicism, rationalism, and faith in the omnipotence of scientific method—in short, the most formidable of the adversaries of the French *philosophes* and their German disciples. Whereas they—or at least the best known among them, d'Alembert, Helvétius, Holbach, and, with qualifications, Voltaire and Diderot, Wolff and Reimarus—believed that reality was ordered in terms of universal, timeless, objective, unalterable laws which rational investigation could discover, Herder maintained that every activity, situation, historical period, or civilization possessed a unique character of its own; so that the attempt to reduce such phenomena to combinations of uniform elements, and to describe or analyse them in terms of universal rules, tended to obliterate precisely those crucial differences which constituted the specific quality of the object under study, whether in nature or in history. To the notions of universal laws, absolute principles, final truths, eternal models and standards in ethics or aesthetics, physics or mathematics, he opposed a radical distinction between the method appropriate to the study of physical nature and that called for by the changing and developing spirit of man. He is credited with having put new life into the notion of social patterns, social growth, the vital importance of considering qualitative as well as quantitative factors— the impalpable and the imponderable, which the concepts of natural science ignore or deny. Preoccupied with the mysteries of the creative process, whether in individuals or groups, he launched (so we are told) a general attack on rationalism with its tendency to generalize, abstract, assimilate the dissimilar, unify the disparate, and, above all, on its avowed purpose to create a corpus of systematic knowledge which in principle would be capable of answering all intelligible questions—the idea of a unified science of all there is. And in the course of this propaganda against rationalism, scientific method, and the universal authority of intelligible laws, he is held to have stimulated the growth of particularism, nationalism and literary, religious and political irrationalism, and thereby to have played a major role in transforming human thought and action in the generation that followed.

This account, which is to be found in some of the best known monographs on Herder's thought, is broadly true, but oversimplified. His views did have a profound and revolutionary effect upon later thought and practice. He has been praised by some as the champion of faith against reason, poetical and historical imagination against the mechanical application of rules, insight against logic, life against death; by others he has been classed with confused, or retrograde, or irrationalist thinkers who misunderstood what they had learned from the Enlightenment, and fed the stream of German chauvinism and obscurantism; still others have sought to find common ground between him and Comte, or Darwin, or Wagner, or modern sociologists. It is not my purpose in this study to pronounce directly upon these questions, although I am inclined to think that the extent of his acquaintance with, and fidelity to, the natural sciences of his day has often been seriously underestimated. He was fascinated and influenced by the findings of the sciences no less than Goethe, and, like him, thought that false general inferences were often drawn from them. Herder was, all his life, a sharp and remorseless critic of the Encyclopaedists, but he accepted, indeed he acclaimed, the scientific theories on which they based their social and ethical doctrines; he merely thought that these conclusions could not follow from the newly established laws of physics or biology since they plainly contradicted what any sensitive observer, since the beginning of social self-consciousness, knew to be true of human experience and activity.[1] But it is not Herder's attitude to the natural science of his day that I propose to discuss. I wish to confine myself, so far as possible (and at times it is not), to what is truly original in Herder's views, and by no means to all of this: in particular I shall try to examine three cardinal ideas in the rich welter of his thought, ideas

[1] On this, see the excellent studies by H. B. Nisbet, *Herder and the Philosophy and History of Science* (Modern Humanities Research Association, Cambridge, England, 1970), and by G. A. Wells, *Herder and After* (The Hague, 1959).

which have had great influence for two centuries and are novel, important, and interesting in themselves. These ideas, which go against the main stream of thought of his time, I have called Populism, Expressionism, and Pluralism.[1]

Let me begin by conceding the most obvious of Herder's debts to other thinkers.[2]

Herder's thesis that the proper subject of the historical sciences is the life of communities and not the exploits of individuals—statesmen, soldiers, kings, dynasties, adventurers and other famous men—had been stated by Voltaire and Hume and Montesquieu, by Schlözer and Gatterer, and before them by French writers on history in the sixteenth and early seventeenth centuries, and with incomparable imagination and originality by Vico. There is, so far as I know, no conclusive evidence that Herder had read Vico's *La Scienza Nuova* until at least twenty years after his own theory of history had been formed; but if he had not read Vico he had heard of him, and probably read Wegelin, and Cesarotti's Homeric commentaries. Moreover, the idea that great poets expressed the mind and experience of their societies and were their truest spokesmen was widespread during Herder's formative years. Shaftesbury celebrated artists as the inspired voices of their times, von Muralt, Bodmer and Breitinger in Switzerland placed Shakespeare and Milton and the old German Minnesingers far above the idols of the French Enlightenment. Bodmer corresponded on these topics with

---

[1] I shall necessarily have to omit much else that is relevant and interesting; for example, Herder's dominant influence on romanticism, vitalism, existentialism, and, above all, on social psychology, which he all but founded; as well as the use made of his imprecise, often inconsistent, but always many-faceted and stimulating thought, by such writers as the Schlegels and Jakob Grimm (especially in their philological excursions), Savigny (who applied to law his notion of organic national growth), Görres (whose nationalism is rooted in, even if it distorts, Herder's vision), Hegel (whose concepts of becoming, and of the growth and personality of impersonal institutions, begin their lives in Herder's pages), as well as historical geographers, social anthropologists, philosophers of language and of history, and historical writers in the nineteenth and twentieth centuries. My principal reason for choosing the three ideas on which I intend to concentrate is that they are conceptions of the first order of originality and historical importance, the origins and properties of which have not received sufficient notice. My purpose is to do justice to Herder's originality rather than his influence.

[2] The best discussion of this topic known to me occurs in Professor Max Rouché's excellent introduction to his edition and French translation of Herder's *Auch Eine Philosophie der Geschichte* (Aubier, Editions Montaigne, Paris, n.d.).

Vico's devoted admirer, Count Pietro Calepio;[1] the battle between literary historicism and the neo-classicism of Paris and its German followers was in full swing in Herder's youth. This may perhaps be sufficient to account for the striking resemblance between the views of Vico and Herder, and obviate the long and desperate search for more direct lines. In any case the notion of cultural patterns was far from new in his day, as the ironical title of his early *Yet Another Philosophy of History* was meant to emphasize. The case for it has been presented effectively, if in somewhat general terms, by his arch-enemy Voltaire in the celebrated *Essai sur les moeurs* and elsewhere.

So, too, the notion that the variety of civilizations is, to a large degree, determined by differences of physical and geographical factors—referred to by the general name of 'climate'—had become, since Montesquieu, a commonplace. It occurs, before Montesquieu, in the thought of Bodin, Saint-Evremond, the Abbé Du Bos, and their followers.

As for the dangers of cultural arrogance—the tendency to judge ancient societies in terms of modern values—this had been made a central issue by his older contemporary Lessing (even though Lessing may well have been influenced by Herder). Nor had anyone written more pungently than Voltaire against the European habit of dismissing as inferior remote civilizations, such as that of China which he had extolled in order to expose the ridiculous vanity, exclusiveness, and fanaticism of the 'barbarous' Judaeo-Christian outlook that recognized no values besides its own. The fact that Herder turned this weapon against Voltaire himself, and accused him of a narrowly *dix-huitième* and Parisian point of view, does not alter that fact that the head and source of all opposition to Europocentrism was the Patriarch himself. Voltaire had praised ancient Egypt, and Winckelmann the Greeks; Boulainvilliers had spoken of the superiority of the Northern nations, and so had Mallet in his celebrated history of Denmark; Beat Ludwig von Muralt in his *Letters on the English and the French* had, as early as 1725, drawn a contrast between the independent spirit of the Swiss and English, particularly English writers, and the conventional mannerisms of the French; Hurd, Millar, and, after them, Justus Möser, sang the praises of mediaeval Europe at the very height of the con-

[1] There is an illuminating discussion of this in Carlo Antoni's *Lo storicismo* (Turin, 1957).

148

temptuous dismissal of the Dark Ages by Voltaire and the *Encyclopédie*. They were, it is true, a minority, and, while Möser's paeans to the free life of the ancient Saxons before they were so brutally civilized by Charlemagne may have been influenced by Herder, they were not created by him.

There was new emphasis on cultural differences and protest against the authority of timeless general laws and rules. The notorious lack of historical sense that made Racine and Corneille represent classical or exotic oriental personages in the clothes and with the manners of the courtiers of Louis XIV was adversely commented on by Du Bos and successfully satirized by Saint-Evremond. At the other end of the scale, some German pietists, Arnold and Zinzendorf among others, laid great stress on the proposition that every religion had a unique insight peculiar to itself, and Arnold based on this belief a bold and passionate plea for toleration of deviations from Lutheran orthodoxy and even of heresies and unbelief.

The notion of the spirit of a nation or a culture had been central not only to Vico and Montesquieu, but to the famous publicist Karl Friedrich von Moser, whom Herder read and knew, to Bodmer and Breitinger, to Hamann and to Zimmermann. Bolingbroke had spoken of the division of men into nationalities as being deeply rooted in Nature herself. By the middle of the century there were plenty of Celtomaniacs and Gothomaniacs—notably Irishmen and Scotsmen who, even without the aid of Ossian, praised the virtues of Gaelic or Germanic tribes and represented them as being morally and socially superior to ancient Greeks or Romans, still more to the decadent civilization of modern Latin and Mediterranean peoples. Rousseau's celebrated letter to the Poles, advising them to resist forcible assimilation by Russia by stubbornly clinging to their national customs and characteristics, unacceptable as this was to the cosmopolitanism of his time, exhibits the same spirit.

As for the notion of society as an organism, with which Burke and Herder made such play, it was by this time very old indeed. The use of organic metaphors is at least as old as Aristotle; nobody had used them more lavishly than mediaeval writers; they are the heart and centre of John of Salisbury's political tracts, and are a weapon consciously used by Hooker and Pascal against the new scientific-mechanical conceptions. There was certainly nothing novel in this notion; it represents, on the contrary, if anything, a deliberate return to older views of social life. This is no less true of Burke, who was equally prone to the use of analogies drawn from the new biological sciences; I know of no evidence that Burke had read or heard of Justus Möser's or Herder's ideas.

Differences of ideals—of what made men and societies happy—had been illustrated vividly by Adam Ferguson in his highly original essay on the 'History of Civil Society', which Herder had read.[1]

In his general explanation of events in naturalistic terms, whether geophysical or biological, Herder adopted the normal approach of the followers of Locke, Helvétius and the Encyclopaedists, and indeed of the entire Enlightenment. Unlike his teacher Hamann, Herder was decisively influenced by the findings of natural science; he gave them a vitalistic but not the mystical or theosophical interpretation favoured by Hemsterhuis, Lavater, and other 'intuitivists'.

The ancient notion of a single great cosmic force of Nature, embodied in finite, dynamic centres, had been given new life by Leibniz and was common to all his disciples.

So, too, the idea of a divine plan realized in human history had passed in uninterrupted succession from the Old Testament and its Jewish interpreters to the Christian Fathers and then to the classical formulation of Bossuet.

Parallels between primitive peoples remote from one another in time and space—Homeric Greeks and early Romans on the one hand, and Red Indians or Germanic tribes on the other—had been put forward by Fontenelle and by the French Jesuit, Père Lafitau; the protagonists of this approach in the early years of the century, especially English writers such as Blackwell and the Wartons, owed much to these speculations. It had become part and parcel of Homeric scholarship, which flourished both in England and, under the impulsion of Vico, in Italy. Certainly Cesarotti had perceived the wider implications of this kind of approach to literature for comparative philology and anthropology; and when the *Encyclopédie*, in the course of a general article devoted to the Greeks, dismissed Homer as 'a Greek philosopher, theologian and poet' unlikely to be read much in the future, this was a characteristically partisan *boutade*, in the spirit of Descartes and Pierre Bayle, against reverence for the past and dreary erudition, a belated echo of

1 Harold Laski's description of Ferguson as 'a pinchbeck Montesquieu' throws light only on the quality of Mr Laski's critical judgment, in this instance probably a mere echo of Leslie Stephen.

the Battle of the Ancients and the Moderns. Nor was the Bible itself, which Vico had not dared to touch, left unmolested. Philosophical and historical criticism of the text, which had begun with Spinoza and Père Simon in the previous century, had been carried on cautiously —despite some opposition from Christian orthodoxy, both Catholic and Protestant—with strict regard to the rules of secular scholarship. Astruc in France, Lowth in England, and after them Michaelis in Germany (and Denmark), treated the Bible as a monument of oriental literature composed at various dates. Everyone knows of Gibbon's debt to Mosheim's coldly secular treatment of early Christian ecclesiastical history. Herder, who was not a trained researcher, had plenty to lean upon.

The same is true of Herder's linguistic patriotism. The defence of the German language had been vigorously taken up by Martin Opitz in the early years of the seventeenth century, and had since then formed part of the conscious programme of theologians, men of letters, and philosophers. Mencke, Horneck, Moscherosch, Logau, and Uden are names that may not mean a great deal to English readers today; but in the two centuries that followed the Reformation they fought with stubbornness and success under Luther's banner against both Latin and French; and more famous men, Pufendorf and Leibniz, Thomasius and Wolff, Hamann and Lessing, were also engaged in this campaign that had begun long before. Once again, Herder began with something that had by that time become established as a traditional German attitude.

As for the famous reversal of values—the triumph of the concrete over the abstract; the sharp turn towards the immediate, the given, the experienced and, above all, away from abstractions, theories, generalizations, and stylized patterns; and the restoration of quality to its old status above quantity, and of the immediate data of the senses to their primacy over the primary qualities of physics—it is in this cause that Hamann made his name. It formed the basis of Lavater's 'physiognomical' researches; it was at least as old as Shaftesbury; it is pertinent to the works of the young Burke.

The reaction against the reorganization of knowledge and society by the application of rationalist and scientific principles was in full swing by the time Herder came upon the scene. Rousseau had struck against it in 1750 with his First Discourse. Seven years later his moralizing and reactionary letter to d'Alembert denouncing the stage had marked a total break with the party of the *philosophes*, as both sides swiftly recognized. In Germany this mood was strongly reinforced by the inward-looking tradition of the Pietist movement. The human solidarity and mutual respect of these small groups, inspired by their burning Protestant faith; their belief in the unadorned truth, in the power of goodness, in the inner light; their contempt for outward forms; their rigid sense of duty and discipline; their perpetual self-examination; their obsession with the presence of evil, which at times took hysterical or sadistic forms and generated a good deal of unctuous hypocrisy; and above all their preoccupation with the life of the spirit which alone liberated men from the bonds of the flesh and of nature—all these strains are very strong in those who were brought up in this stern atmosphere, and particularly in the East Prussians, Knutzen, Hamann, Herder, Kant. Although a great intellectual gulf divides Kant from Herder, they share a common element: a craving for spiritual self-determination as against half-conscious drifting along the streams of uncriticized dogma (whether theological or scientific), for moral independence (whether of individuals or groups), and above all for moral salvation.

If Herder had done no more than create a genuine synthesis out of these attitudes and doctrines, and built with them, if not a system, at any rate a coherent *Weltanschauung* destined to have a decisive influence on the literature and thought of his country, this alone would have been a high enough achievement to earn for him a unique place in the history of civilization. Invention is not everything. If one were called upon to show what is strictly original in the individual doctrines of Locke or Rousseau, Bentham or Marx, Aquinas, and even Hegel, one could, without much difficulty, trace virtually all their doctrines to antecedent 'sources'. Yet this does not derogate from the originality and genius of these thinkers. 'Small change for a *Napoléon d'or* is not a Napoleon'. It is not, however, my purpose to evaluate the work of Herder as a whole, but only to consider certain authentically *sui generis* doctrines which he originated; to discuss them not only for the sake of historical justice, but also as views that are peculiarly relevant and interesting in our own time. Herder's final claim need not rest upon what was, if I am right, most original in his thought. For his vast general influence has sometimes, paradoxically, served to overshadow that which he, virtually alone, launched upon the world.

II

To return to the three topics of this study, namely:

1. *Populism:* the belief in the value of belonging to a group or a culture, which, for Herder at least, is not political, and is indeed, to some degree, anti-political, different from, and even opposed to, nationalism.

2. *Expressionism:*[1] the doctrine that human activity in general, and art in particular, expresses the entire personality of the individual or the group, and are intelligible only to the degree to which they do so. Still more specifically, expressionism claims that all the works of men are above all voices speaking, are not objects detached from their makers, are part of a living process of communication between persons and not independently existing entities, beautiful or ugly, interesting or boring, upon which external observers may direct the cool and dispassionate gaze with which scientists—or anyone not given to pantheism or mysticism—look on objects in nature. This is connected with the further notions that every form of human self-expression is in some sense artistic, and that self-expression is part of the essence of human beings as such; which in turn entail such distinctions as those between integral and divided, or committed and uncommitted (that is, unfulfilled), lives; and thence lead to the concept of various hindrances, human and non-human, to the self-realization which is the richest and most harmonious form of self-expression that all creatures, whether or not they are aware of it, live for.

3. *Pluralism:* the belief not merely in the multiplicity, but in the incommensurability, of the values of different cultures and societies and, in addition, in the incompatibility of equally valid ideals, together with the implied revolutionary corollary that the classical notions of an ideal man and of an ideal society are intrinsically incoherent and meaningless.

Each of these three theses is relatively novel; all are incompatible with the central moral, historical, and aesthetic doctrines of the Enlightenment. They are not independent of each other. Everything in the illimitable, varied, and exceedingly rich panorama which Herder's works present is interwoven. Indeed, the notion of unity in difference,

---

[1] I use this term in its widest, most generic sense, with no specific reference to the Expressionist painters, writers, and composers of the early decades of the twentieth century.

still more that of differences in unity, the tension of the One and the Many, is his obsessive *idée maîtresse*. Hence the recurrence through all his discussions of a constant theme: the 'organic' oneness of personality with the form of life that it leads, the empirical and metaphysical unity of the physical and the mental, of intellect, will, feeling, imagination, language, action—distinctions and classifications that he regarded as, at best, superficial, at worst, as profoundly misleading; hence the stress on the unity of thought and feeling, of theory and practice, of the public and the private, and his single-minded, life-long and heroic effort to see the universe as a single process. The celebrated words with which he opens his most famous and ambitious work, *Ideas towards a Philosophy of History*—'the earth is a star among stars'—are very characteristic. There follow chapters on geology, climate, mineral, vegetable and animal life, and lessons in physical geography, until, at last, man is reached; there is a corresponding attempt to link all the arts and all the sciences, to represent religious, artistic, social, political, economic, biological, philosophical experience as facets of one activity. And since the pattern is one, fact and value are not divided (*pace* Hume and Kant, with whose works Herder was only too familiar). To understand a thing was, for him, to see how it could be viewed as it was viewed, assessed as it was assessed, valued as it was valued, in a given context, by a particular culture or tradition. To grasp what a belief, a piece of ritual, a myth, a poem, or a linguistic usage meant to a Homeric Greek, a Livonian peasant, an ancient Hebrew, an American Indian, what part it played in his life, was for Herder to be able not merely to give a scientific or common-sense explanation, but to give a reason or justification of the activity in question, or at least to go a long way towards this. For to explain human experiences or attitudes is to be able to transpose oneself by sympathetic imagination into the situation of the human beings who are to be 'explained'; and this amounts to understanding and communicating the coherence of a particular way of life, feeling, action: and thereby the validity of the given act or action, the part it plays in the life and outlook which is 'natural' in the situation. Explanation and justification, reference to causes and to purposes, to the visible and the invisible, statements of fact and their assessment in terms of the historical standards of value relevant to them, melt into one another, and seem to Herder to belong to a single type, and not several types, of thinking. Herder is one of the originators of the secular doctrine of the unity of fact and value, theory and practice, 'is' and 'ought', intellectual judgment and emotional commitment, thought and action.

The sharpest critics of Herder have always conceded the power and breadth of his imagination. He did have an astonishing capacity for conceiving a great variety of actual and possible societies in the past and the present, and an unexampled warmth of sympathy for them all. He was inspired by the possibility of reconstructing forms of life as such, and he delighted in bringing out their individual shape, the fullness of human experience embodied in them; the odder, the more extraordinary a culture or an individual, the better pleased he was. He can hardly condemn anything that displays colour or uniqueness; Indians, Americans and Persians, Greece and Palestine, Arminius and Machiavelli, Shakespeare and Savonarola, seem to him equally fascinating. He deeply hates the forces that make for uniformity, for the assimilation, whether in life or in the books of historians, of one culture or way of life to another. He conscientiously looks for uniformities, but what fascinates him is the exception. He condemns the erection of walls between one genus and another; but he seeks for the greatest possible number of distinctions of species within a genus, and of individuals within the species. Hamann had preached to him the need to preserve sensitiveness to specific historical and cultural phenomena, to avoid becoming deadened by the passion for classification and generalization demanded by networks of tidy concepts, a fatal tendency which he attributed to the natural sciences and their slaves, the Frenchmen who wished to transform everything by the application of scientific method. Like Hamann, Herder preserved his childlike impressionability—his capacity to react spontaneously to the jagged, irregular, not always describable data provided by the senses, by imagination, by religious revelation, by history, by art. He did not hasten to refer them to their appropriate cases in the museum of concepts; he was penetrated through and through by the new spirit of empiricism, of the sacredness of facts. Not so much as Hamann, but more than even Lessing and Diderot, and incomparably more than such official materialists and 'sensualists' as Condillac or Helvétius, Herder avoided the temptation to reduce the heterogeneous flow of experience to homogeneous units, to label them and fit them into theoretical frameworks in order to be able to predict and control them. The notorious luxuriance and formlessness of his ideas is due at least as much to his sense of the complexity of the facts themselves as to a naturally rhapsodical and turbid mind. As a writer he is exuberant and disordered, but not obscure or vague. Even at his most rapt he is not somnambulistic or self-intoxicated; he does not, even in his most lyrical moments, fly from the facts to an ideal heaven, like the German metaphysical poets of his time, Gleim or Uz or Klopstock or even Goethe on occasions. Great scientists and philosophers have often made their impact by violently exaggerating their original insights. But Herder cannot let go of what he sees, feels, hears, learns. His sense of the texture of reality is concrete, while his analytical powers are feeble. The three original theses which form the subject of this study display this again and again, and have consequently often been a source of irritation to tidier, clearer, logically more gifted thinkers.

III

Let me begin with Herder's Populism, or the idea of what it is to belong to a group. Everyone seems agreed that Herder began as a typical, almost routine defender of the great ideals of eighteenth-century Enlightenment, that is, as a humanitarian, a cosmopolitan, and a pacifist. Later, so it seems to be assumed, he moved towards a more reactionary position, the subordination of reason and intellect to nationalism, Gallophobia, intuition, uncritical faith and belief in tradition. Was this not, after all, the evolution in some degree of other thinkers of his and the succeeding generation in Germany? Almost without exception, they began by welcoming the French Revolution rapturously, planting trees of liberty, and denouncing as obsolete and brutally oppressive the rule of the three hundred German princes, until, horrified by the Terror and wounded by the military humiliation of Germany by the armies of Revolutionary France and, still more, those of Napoleon, they turned into patriots, reactionaries, and romantic irrationalists. Was not this the path pursued by Fichte (above all Fichte), Görres, Novalis and the Schlegels, Schleiermacher and Tieck, Gentz and Schelling, and to some degree even by the great libertarian Schiller? Were not Goethe and Humboldt (and Georg Forster, though he died before the reaction set in) almost alone in their unswerving fidelity to reason, toleration, and the unity of mankind, and in their freedom from nationalism and, in common with Kant and Hegel, in their loathing for all forms of collective emotional afflatus? Is it not reasonable to assume that this process of retreat from reason took place in Herder too? True, he died before the most crushing defeats had been inflicted by Napoleon on the German armies and princes; yet was it not the case that Herder began as a cosmopolitan and ended as a nationalist? Here too then, so it would seem, wounded national pride and perhaps age and the cooling of youthful utopianism had had their inescapable effect. Yet this view seems to me untenable. Whatever may have been the evolution of Fichte or Friedrich Schlegel, Herder's form of nationalism remained unaltered throughout his life. His national feeling was not political and never became so, nor did he abandon or modify the peculiar brand of universalism with which he had begun, whether or not the two tendencies were consistent (the least of his concerns), throughout his long and voluminous intellectual activity.

As early as 1765, in an address composed in Riga, where at the age of twenty-one he occupied the post of a Lutheran preacher in that officially Russian city, in answer to the question 'Have we still a republic and a fatherland like the Ancients?'[1] Herder declared that this was no longer the case. In Greece the strength and the glory of the *polis* were the supreme goals of all free men. Religion, morals, tradition, every aspect of human activity stemmed from, and were directed to, maintaining the city, and any danger to it was a danger to all that these men were and lived by; if it fell, everything fell with it. But then, he went on to say, Christianity came and the horizons of mankind became immeasurably wider. Christianity, he explained, is a universal religion: it embraces all men and all peoples; it transcends all local and temporary loyalties in the worship of what is universal and eternal.[2]

This thesis was highly characteristic of the Christian humanism of the German *Aufklärung*, and, despite all that has been said to the contrary, Herder never abandoned this point of view. His central belief was expressed towards the end of his life in words similar to those of his early writings: 'To brag of one's country is the stupidest form of boastfulness. A nation is a wild garden full of bad plants and good, vices and follies mingle with virtues and merit. What Don Quixote will break a lance for this Dulcinea?'[3] Patriotism was one thing, nationalism another: 'An innocent attachment to family, language, one's own city, one's own country, its traditions, are not to be condemned'. But he goes on to say that 'aggressive nationalism' is detestable in all its manifestations, and wars are mere crimes. This is so because 'All large wars are essentially civil wars, since men are brothers, and wars are a form

---

[1] I, 13-28.   [2] *Ibid.*   [3] XVII, 211.

of abominable fratricide'.[1] A year later he adds: 'We must have nobler heroes than Achilles, loftier patriots than Horatius Cocles'.[2] And many years later, in 1794 he repeats this: 'One fatherland ranged against another in bloody battle is the worst barbarism in the human vocabulary'. These views can scarcely be due merely to the fact, by which they are sometimes explained, that political nationalism would have been too unrealistic an outlook in a feeble and divided country governed by several hundred hereditary despots; so that even to look for it there demonstrates a lack of historical sense. Yet the Italians, who were no less divided and politically impotent, had developed a distinct craving for political unification which dated back at least to Machiavelli, even though the prevailing social and political conditions in Italy were not so very unlike those of eighteenth-century Germany.

Herder's attitude is clearly the normal enlightened attitude of his time; the point, however, is that he did not abandon it. He believed in kinship, social solidarity, *Volkstum*, nationhood, but to the end of his life he detested and denounced every form of centralization, coercion, and conquest, which were embodied and symbolized both for him, and for his teacher Hamann, in the accursed state. Nature creates nations, not states.[3] 'The State is an instrument of happiness for a group',[4] not for men as such. There is nothing against which he thunders more eloquently than imperialism—the crushing of one community by another, the elimination of local cultures trampled under the jackboot of some conqueror. He vies with Justus Möser in his tenderness towards long-lived traditions and institutions embodied in particular forms of life that have created unity and continuity in a human community. He cares nothing for *virtù* in the Renaissance sense of the term. Alexander the Great, Julius Caesar, Charlemagne are not heroes for him. The basis of the state is conquest, the history of states is the history of violence, a bloodstained story of aggression. The state is Ixion's wheel and calls for meaningless self-immolation. 'Why should hundreds suffer hunger and cold to satisfy the whim of a crowned madman, or the dreams bred by the fancy of a *philosophe*?' This may be directed specifically at

---

1 XVII, 319.   2 XVIII, 86.

3 XIII, 340, 375, 'Millions' of people on the globe live without states . . . father and mother, man and wife, child and brother, friend and man—these are natural relationships through which we become happy; what the *state* can give us is an artificial contrivance; unfortunately it can also deprive us of something far more important—rob us of ourselves (XIII, 340-41).   4 XIII, 333 ff.

Frederick the Great and his French advisers, but the import of it is universal. All rule of men over fellow men is unnatural. True human relations are those of father and son, husband and wife, sons, brothers, friends, men; these terms express natural relations which make people happy. All that the state has given us is contradictions and conquests[1] and, perhaps worst of all, dehumanization ('What pleasure is there in being a blind cog in a machine?'[2]). God has divided the world by mountains and oceans in order to prevent some fearful Nimrod from conquering the whole. The *Ideen* anticipate socialist historians in representing the history of conquerors as the history of man-hunters. Despite his vow to look with a sympathetic, or at least impartial, eye upon all cultures and all nations, he cannot bring himself to forgive Rome for crushing the cultures of the peoples it had conquered, not even that of Carthage. There may be merit in efficiency and unity, but it is for him more than offset by the tragedy of the destruction; that is, by the evil of the barbarous disregard of so many spontaneous, natural forms of human self-expression: 'Whom nature separated by language, customs, character, let no man artificially join together by chemistry'.[3] This is what the Romans tried to do and how the whole Roman Empire was held together. And its 'Holy' successor was no better— it was an unnatural monster—an absurd clamping together of disparate cultures—'a lion's head with a dragon's tail, an eagle's wing, a bear's paw, ['glued together'] in one unpatriotic symbol of a state'.[4] The Jews, 'parasitic money-lenders' now,[5] were at least not self-worshippers; they are praised for not having made Palestine the source and centre of the world, for not having idealized their ancestors, and for not deriving their genealogy from gods and demigods (it is this last that has enabled them to survive the Diaspora).[6] Empires, especially multi-national ones ('a wild mingling of various tribes and

---

[1] XXX, 333 ff. [2] *Ibid.* [3] XVIII, 206. [4] XIII, 385. [5] XIV, 65.

[6] Herder was fascinated by the survival of the Jews; he looked upon them as a "most excellent example" of a *Volk* with its own distinct character (X, 139). 'Moses bound the heart of his people to their native soil' (XII, 115). Land, common language, tradition, sense of kinship, common tradition, common law as a freely accepted 'covenant'—all these interwoven factors, together with the bond created by their sacred literature, enabled the Jews to retain their identity in dispersion— but especially the fact that their eyes remained focused upon their original geographical home (XII, 115; VIII, 355; and XVII, 312)—historical continuity, not race, is what counts (XII, 107). This is what creates historical individuality (XII, 123, and XXXII, 207). On this entire subject, and especially the view of the

peoples under one sceptre'), rest on force; they have feet of clay and must collapse. Theocracies that are founded upon some non-political principle, a spiritual or religious force—China or Egypt, for example, to take only non-Christian faiths—have proved correspondingly more durable. The sword of the spirit is better than mere brute force: not even the acutest poverty, the deepest squalor, still less ambition and love of power, entitle men to have recourse to violence. Like Möser, Herder laments the fact that the Germans are poor, hungry, and despised; that Luther's widow had to beg for help from the King of Denmark; that Kepler died of hunger; that men of German speech have been scattered and exiled to England, America, Russia, Transylvania; that gifted artists and inventors are compelled to leave their country and lavish their gifts upon foreigners; that Hessians are sold and bought like 'Negro slaves' while their families starve and perish. Nevertheless, conquest is not the answer. He dwelt on the folly and cruelties of imperialism all his life.

In his first essay on the philosophy of history (*Auch Eine Philosophie*, of 1774) he speaks of Roman conquerors as a compound of 'blood, lust, sinister vices—a trail of blood'. Twenty and thirty years later, and, indeed, in the last years of his life, he continues to denounce the inhumanity of colonial rule, ancient and modern: 'Foreign peoples were judged [by Rome] in terms of customs unknown to them'; imposed by violence, this 'distorted the character of the conquered' until 'the Roman eagle . . . pecked out their eyes, devoured their innards, and covered their wretched corpses with its feeble wings'. 'It was not a happy day when the bloody tyranny of Rome became united with Christianity . . .'. Rome ruined Greece and the Teutonic Knights and recently converted Poles exterminated the Prussians and enslaved 'the poor Balts and peaceful Slavs'.[1] 'Can you name a land', he asks in his *Letters on the Advancement of Mankind* (1793-7), 'where Europeans have entered without defiling themselves forever before defenceless, trusting mankind, by the unjust word, greedy deceit, crushing oppression, diseases, fatal gifts they have brought? Our part of the earth

---

'Jewish problem', not as religious, but national and political, needing what later came to be known as the Zionist solution, see the interesting article by Professor F. M. Barnard, 'Herder and Israel', contributed to *Jewish Social Studies*, which the author has kindly allowed me to read before publication. See also the same author's 'The Hebrews and Herder's Political Creed' (*Modern Language Review*, vol. LIV, 1959).   [1] XVI, 2 and 6.

should be called not the wisest, but the most arrogant, aggressive, money-minded: what it has given these peoples is not civilization but the destruction of the rudiments of their own cultures wherever they could achieve this'. This is what the English have done in Ireland, in the Scottish Highlands, and Europeans have done in their colonies, the natives of which have 'developed a passion for fire-water, whereby they were considered ripe for conversion to our faith'.[1] In 1802, in his periodical *Adrastea*, he imagines a conversation between an Asian and a European: in the course of it the Asian (an Indian) says, ' "Tell me, have you still not lost the habit of trying to convert to your faith peoples whose property you steal, whom you rob, enslave, murder, deprive of their land and their state, to whom your customs seem revolting? Supposing that one of them came to your country, and with an insolent air pronounced absurd all that is most sacred to you—your laws, your religion, your wisdom, your institutions, and so on, what would you do to such a man?" "Oh, but that is quite a different matter", replied the European, "we have power, ships, money, cannon, *culture*" '.[2] On this topic Herder remained uncompromising and passionate: ' "Why are you pouring water over my head?" asked a dying slave of a Christian missionary. "So that you can go to Heaven". "I do not want to go to a heaven where there are white men", he replied, and turned on his side and died'.[3] 'By this means we, Europeans, are engaged in forging the chains with which they will bind us'. Herder is as certain as Karl Marx that those who oppress and exploit others and force their own institutions on others are acting as their own grave-diggers—that one day 'the victims will rise against us and use our catchwords, our methods and ideals to crush us'.[4]

The German mission is not to conquer; it is to be a nation of thinkers and educators. This is their true glory.[5] Sacrifice—self-sacrifice—not

---

[1] Quoted by V. M. Zhirmunsky in *Iogann Gotfrid Gerder* (Gikhl, Moscow/Leningrad, 1959, p. xlix).

[2] *Op. cit.*

[3] *Briefe zur Beförderung der Humanität* (1793-7), Letter 114.

[4] V, 576, 579. See Barnard, *Herder on Social and Political Culture* (Cambridge University Press, 1969, pp. 13-15).

[5] The most eloquent statement of Herder's conception of the German's earthly miseries and spiritual task is to be found in his epistle in verse, *German National Glory*, written in 1792 but published posthumously in 1812 (XVIII, 214-16) when the mood of many of his countrymen, whipped into a frenzy of nationalism by Jahn, Arndt, Körner and Görres, was wholly different.

the domination of one man over another, is the proper end of man. Herder sets his face against everything that is predatory, against the use of force in any cause but that of self-defence. The Crusades, no matter how Christian in inspiration, are hateful to him, since they conquered and crushed other human communities. Yet consent for him is a false basis of society, for consent is ultimately a form of yielding, however rational or voluntary, to strength, whereas human relations must rest upon respect, affection, kinship, equality, not fear or prudence and utilitarian calculation. It is when religions forget the ends of man and turn into empty, mechanical cults, that they develop into a source of unintelligible mystification and their ceremonies decay into a recital of dead formulas, while the priests, who no longer understand their own faith, become instruments of other forces—in particular of the state and the men who control it. For him, as for Nietzsche, the state is the coldest of all cold monsters. Nothing in the whole of human history is more hateful to him than Churches and priests who are instruments of political power; of these he speaks with the same voice as Voltaire or Holbach; as for the state (he says in words that could have been Rousseau's), it robs men of themselves.[1] The state becomes a drug with the help of which men seek to forget themselves, a self-generated method of escaping from the need to live, create, and choose. Furthermore, the sheer exercise of bureaucratic activity is a form of self-intoxication, and he speaks of it as a kind of opium by which men are metamorphosed into mechanical functionaries. Profound differences, both personal and literary, came to divide Herder from Goethe and Schiller, but when, in their jointly written *Xenien*, they say

Deutschland? aber wo liegt's, Ich weiss das Land nicht zu finden.
Wo das Gelehrte beginnt, hört das Politische auf.
(Das Deutsche Reich)

or again

Zur Nation euch zu bilden, Ihr hoffet es, Deutsche, vergebens;
Bildet, Ihr könnt es, dafür, freier zu Menschen euch aus,
(Deutscher National Charakter.)

they speak for Herder too. The state is the substitution of machinery for life, a prospect, and a reality, that frightened him no less than it did Rousseau.

[1] XIII, 341.

What then is the right life for men? They should live in natural units, that is, in societies united by a common culture. Nature creates nations, not states,[1] and does not make some nations intrinsically superior to others. Whatever the qualities of the ancient Germans, 'to look on them, for this reason, as the European people chosen by God, to which He has, in virtue of its native ability, accorded the right to own the entire world and to be served by other peoples—that would be the ignoble vanity of barbarians'.[2] There is no *Favoritvolk*.[3] A nation is made what it is by 'climate', education, relations with its neighbours, and other changeable and empirical factors, and not by an impalpable inner essence or an unalterable factor such as race or colour. All this, said late in his life, is the pure milk of the doctrine of the Enlightenment. Herder protests, not without a certain malicious satisfaction (as Hamann also did, with equally ironical pleasure), that the great liberal Kant in his *Anthropologie* emphasized race and colour too much. He is equally indignant about Kant's proposition that men need a master; he replies that 'animals need a master, not men',[4] and he denounces Kant's philosophy of history, according to which it is the vices of mankind—desire for power and mastery over the scarce resources of the earth—that stimulate competition, struggle, and thereby progress, with the corollary that the sufferings of the individual are indispensable to the improvement of the species (a doctrine that was destined to reach its richest development in Hegel, and in another form in Spencer's evolutionary doctrine and the vagaries of social Darwinism). Herder repudiates these doctrines in the pure spirit of liberal, individualist, Weimar cosmopolitanism. Indeed, the perception that cruel and sinister implications are contained in any doctrine that preaches the sacrifice of individuals on the altar of vast abstractions—the human species, society, civilization, progress (later thinkers were to say, race, state, class, and a chosen élite)—has its true beginnings here. Kant's unconcealed lack of sympathy for Herder's sweeping and imprecise generalizations, and his complaints that these were never supported either by adequate evidence or rigorous argument, may in part account for Herder's deliberate choice of the famous champion of the inexorable voice of

---

[1] XIII, 340, 375.   [2] Zhirmunsky, *op. cit.* XVII, 212.

[3] XVIII, 247, 248. 'There must be no order of rank; ... the negro is as much entitled to think the white man degenerate, as the white man is to think of the negro as a black beast.' I owe this quotation to Barnard, *op. cit.*

[4] XIII, 383.

duty, the moral equality of men, and the infinite value of the individual, as the butt of his own passionate anti-racialism and anti-imperialism and of his defence of the right of all men and nations to develop along their own, self-chosen, lines. Variety does not, for Herder, entail conflict. He does not see why one community absorbed in the development of its own native talent should not respect a similar activity on the part of others. The Kant of the *Grundlegung* or of *Zum ewigen Frieden* might have agreed; but the Kant of the *Anthropologie* and the other essays on universal history evidently did not. Kant drew a sharp line of division between, on the one hand, individual morality, universal, absolute, free from internal conflict, based on a transcendent rationality wholly unconnected with nature and history and empirical reality, and, on the other, the disharmonies of the processes of nature, the aim of which was the preservation of the species, and the promotion of progress by competition and strife. Herder would have none of this. He found such dualism totally unintelligible. The hard and fast distinctions between orders of experience, mental and corporeal faculties, reason and imagination, the world of sense and the worlds of understanding or of the ethical will or *a priori* knowledge, seemed to him so many artificial partitions, 'wooden walls' built by philosophers to which nothing corresponded in reality. His world is organic, dynamic, and unitary: every ingredient of it is at once unique, and interwoven with every other by an infinite variety of relationships which, in the end, cannot be analysed or even fully described. 'Similarities, classes, orders, stages', he wrote in 1775, 'are only . . . houses of cards in a game. The creator of all things does not see as a man sees. He knows no classes; each thing only resembles itself'.[1] 'I am not sure that I know what "material" and "immaterial" mean. I do not believe that nature erected iron walls between these terms . . . I cannot see them anywhere . . .'.[2] He is anxious not to lose any part of reality, not to obliterate or elide or smooth out irregularities in order to fit them into a system, get them neatly covered by a general formula. He inherits from his teacher Hamann the desire to seize the whole in its fullness, in all its peculiar, complex, historically changing manifestations (this is what fascinated and permanently influenced the young Goethe when they met in 1770), and goes a good deal further than Montesquieu, who raised the banner of revolt against '*les grands simplificateurs*'. The

1 VIII, 315.   2 VIII, 177.

springs of life are mysterious, hidden from those who lack the sense of the inwardness of the spirit of a society, an age, a movement—a sensibility killed by the dissection practised by French *lumières* and their academic German imitators. Like Hamann he is convinced that clarity, rigour, acuteness of analysis, rational, orderly arrangement, whether in theory or practice, can be bought at too high a price. In this sense he is the profoundest critic of the Enlightenment, as formidable as Burke, or de Maistre, but free from their reactionary prejudices and hatred of equality and fraternity.

IV

As for Herder's doctrine of Expression, it is for him profoundly connected with the ways in which and by which men live. What determines the units in which it is 'natural' for men to live? Despite his tendency to look upon the family and patriarchal institutions as the basic forms of human association, Herder does not explicitly affirm Aristotle's (and Rousseau's) doctrine that a 'natural' or satisfactory human society is constituted only by small human groups in which men can know each other face to face and where (in Aristotle's phrase) one herald can be heard by all. Human groups, large and small, are products of climate, geography, physical and biological needs, and similar factors; they are made one by common traditions and common memories, of which the principal link and vehicle—indeed, more than vehicle, the very incarnation—is language. 'Has a nation anything more precious than the language of its fathers? In it dwell its entire world of tradition, history, religion, principles of existence; its whole heart and soul.'[1] It is so because men necessarily think in words or other symbols, since to think is to use symbols; and their feelings and attitudes of life are, he maintains (as Vico did before him), incorporated in symbolic forms—worship, poetry, ritual. This is so whether what they seek are pleasures or necessities; the dance, the hunt, primitive forms of social solidarity expressed and preserved by myth and formalized representation, in fact, the entire network of belief and behaviour that binds men to one another, can be explained only in terms of common, public symbolism, in particular by language. Herder had derived from Hamann his notion that words and ideas are one. Men do

---

[1] XVII, 58.

not think, as it were, in thoughts and ideas and then look for words in which to 'clothe' them, as one looks for a glove to fit a fully formed hand. Hamann taught that to think was to use symbols, and that to deny this was not so much false as unintelligible, because without symbolism one was led fallaciously to divide the aspects of a single experience into separate entities—the fatal doctrine of Descartes, who spoke of mind and body, thought and its object, matter and mind, as though they were independent existents. Such distinctions as we draw between thought and feeling (and their 'objects'), physical sensation and intellectual or moral or aesthetic awareness are, according to Hamann (where one can understand him), an attempt to draw attention now to this, now that facet of a single experience; a tendency which, pushed too far, tends to separate and abstract one facet from another, and, pushed further still, to invent imaginary abstract objects—or idealized entities—to transform reality into a collection of artificial figments. This springs from a craving for tidy scientific classification, but it distorts the facts, congeals the continuous flow of the living sense of nature and of God into dead fragments, and kills the sources of the true sense of reality—the imagination, consciousness of divine revelation, direct acquaintance with reality, obtained through the senses, which men, unspoiled by the logic and metaphysics of rationalism, always have. Hamann was a Christian touched by mysticism: he looked upon the world, upon nature and history, as the speech of God to man; God's words were hieroglyphs, often tormentingly dark, or they were allegories, or they were symbols which opened doors to the vision of the truth which, if only men saw and heard aright, answered the questions of their heads and hearts.[1] Hamann was not himself a visionary. He had had no special revelation; but when, in the midst of an acute spiritual crisis, he turned to the Bible, he was overwhelmed by the realization that the history of the Jews embodied a universal, trans-historical truth: for it symbolized his own—and every man's—painful quest for God. Men were made in God's image, but as Hamann's Pietist ancestors had taught, man was sinful and weak, he stumbled and fell and rose again as he sought to hear the voice of his father and master, the Christ within and without him, who alone could make him whole. Man was healed only by surrendering himself to the unity of life, by

[1] The sources of this view in Christian mysticism and Neoplatonism, and its form in other philosophical systems—for instance, that of Berkeley—have not as yet been sufficiently investigated.

allowing his entire being—spirit and flesh, mind, will, and above all senses—to take in that which God was saying to him directly in Holy Writ, and also signified by means of the working of Nature and by the pattern of human history. Nature and history were symbols, cryptograms, of the Logos, for those who were not perverted by metaphysical subtleties to read. Sin was denial of divine grace and of what God had given man: passions, desires, love, a sense of joy in every manifestation of life, of sensuous nature, of creation and procreation in all forms. The existence of this reality could not, indeed, be proved. Hume was right; no facts or events can be demonstrated to exist by reason. Yet we accept them because we cannot help it, because it is animal faith in the external world, given in sense perception, which alone makes it possible for us to think or act at all. God, the world of the senses, the meanings of words—all are directly given and intimately present to any man if only he will let himself see, hear, be.

Herder remained free from mysticism. It was Hamann's rejection of rationalist analyses, and his unabashed sensualism and empiricism as well as his simple Christian faith that influenced Herder, and not the peculiar mystical nominalism which led Hamann to seek to understand God's hidden purposes in the occult significance of the individual Hebrew or Greek words of Holy Writ. Hamann's doctrine of language —that language alone was the central organ of all understanding and all purposive action, that men's fundamental activity was to speak to others (to men or God or themselves), and that only through language could individuals, or groups, and the meanings that they embodied in poetry or ritual, or in the network of human institutions and ways of life, be understood—this great revelation became an article of faith for Herder. To understand men was to understand what they meant, intended, or wished to communicate. Creation is communication. During the great debate in the eighteenth century about the origins of human speech he acquired a European reputation by saying that language was neither a sudden miraculous gift of God, as Süssmilch and other orthodox Christian writers maintained, nor a deliberate invention of particular men at a specific moment of time, a tool for the improvement of life, like the wheel or the compass, as the French scientists—Maupertuis and Condillac—came near to saying, and Monboddo explicitly maintained. Language was a natural growth, no more and no less mysterious than any other form of natural development which, if one believed in a creative God, was divine, inasmuch as God had given man a nature capable of mental activity; the power of generating symbols, of communication, of intentionality, was intrinsic to its development. At other times—recalled, perhaps by Hamann, to his beliefs as a Lutheran clergyman—he was, after all, the clerical head of the Grand Duchy of Weimar—Herder recanted and conceded that language was indeed implanted in, or taught to, man by God, by a specific creative act. But he could not rest in this belief. How could creatures not spiritually developed enough to use language suddenly come to be capable of doing so? And what is it to be spiritually developed, if not to be capable of thought (i.e. the use of symbols, whether images or gestures or words)? Defying the strict Lutherans, towards the end of his life Herder returned openly to the belief that language was an essential part of the natural process of the growth of consciousness, indeed, of human solidarity, which rests on communication between men; for to be fully human is to think, and to think is to communicate; society and man are equally inconceivable without one another. Hence 'Mere intelligence without the expression of language is on earth a mere Utopia'.[1] Herder means that it is inconceivable rather than improbable. Words, by connecting passions with things, the present with the past, and by making possible memory and imagination, create family, society, literature, history. He declares that to speak and think in words is to 'swim in an inherited stream of images and words; we must accept these media on trust: we cannot create them'. The notion of a wholly solitary—as opposed to an artificially self-isolated—man is to him as unintelligible as it was to Aristotle or some linguistic philosophers of our own time. Mere contemplation yields no truth; it is only life, that is, action with or against others, that does this. For Herder man is shaped by, and must be defined in terms of, his association with others. We can purify and reform a language, but we cannot create one out of nothing; for to create a language is to think, and to think is to use language. This circle cannot be broken. The relation of particular words or groups of words to specific things is not logically or metaphysically necessary, but causal or conventional. Particular words are used in communicating particular experiences, either as a result of natural influences—environmental factors—collectively called 'climate', after Montesquieu; or of psychological ones; or of mere chance; or of the decisions of human beings

[1] XII, 357.

who, acquiring some terms by 'natural' means (in some pre-rational state) invent others as they please, arbitrarily. That is why the doctrine of real essences—the Wolffian plan of discovering the truth by the analysis of concepts—is a chimaera. Locke was right: we have no insight into 'essences'. Only experience can tell us if the expression X in a particular text means the same as the expression Y. The dogmatic certainty of fanatical sectarians about what this or that sacred text must mean is therefore irrational and groundless. Knowledge of philology—the historical development of languages—alone yields the story of changing uses and meanings. Herder is anti-mechanistic: but he is an empiricist, in direct descent from Occam and the English naturalists. Only assiduous historical research, sympathetic insight into the purpose of the speaker, a grasp of the machinery of communication whereby human beings understand each other, whether directly, or across the centuries, can bridge the chasms between different, yet never wholly divorced, civilizations. 'Language expresses the collective experience of the group'.[1]

'Has a nation anything more precious? From a study of native literatures we have learned to know ages and peoples more deeply than along the sad and frustrating path of political and military history. In the latter we seldom see more than the manner in which a people was ruled, how it let itself be slaughtered; in the former we learn how it thought, what it wished and craved for, how it took its pleasures, how it was led by its teachers or its inclinations.'[2] Hence Herder's stress on the importance of genetic studies and the history of language, and hence, too, the great impulsion that he gave to studies of comparative linguistics, comparative anthropology and ethnology, and above all to the great philological movement that became the pride of German scholarship towards the end of his life and in the century that followed. His own efforts in this direction were no less suggestive or speculative than those of Vico. After declaring, in language borrowed from Lavater, that 'the physiognomy of language is all important', he insisted, for example, that the languages which preserved genders (e.g. Russian, with which he came into contact during his Riga years) implied a vision of a world different from the world of those whose languages are 'sexless'; so too did particular uses of pronouns. He insisted that

[1] XI, 225. See also XVII, 59; XVIII, 346; XXX, 8.
[2] XVIII, 137.

verbs—connected with action—came before nouns connected with contemplation of objects; that active nations employ different linguistic modes from passive ones; that nuances of language are pointers to differing forms of experience (*Weltanschauungen*). Logic for him is only an abstraction from languages living or dead. There is no 'deep' logical structure 'presupposed' by all forms of rational thought; in his *Sprachphilosophie*, logic is an approximation to what is common in iso-morphic languages, which themselves point to a high degree of simi-larity in the experiences of their users. Anthropology, not metaphysics or logic, whether Aristotelian or Leibnizian or Kantian, is for Herder the key to the understanding of human beings and of their world. It is the history of language that most clearly and continuously reveals such phenomena as social growth—the cycles of infancy, youth, maturity, decay—that are common to individuals and nations. The relation of language to thought, although in a sense they are one, is an ambivalent one. At any rate, the art of writing, the incorporation of thought in permanent forms, while it creates the possibility of a continuity of social self-awareness, and makes accessible his own and other worlds to an individual, also arrests and kills. What has been put down in writing is incapable of that living process of constant adaptation and change, of the constant expression of the unanalysable and unseizable flow of actual experience, which language, if it is to communicate fully, must possess. Language alone makes experience possible, but it also freezes it. Hamann spoke of the valley of dry bones which only 'a prophet' (such as Socrates, St Paul, Luther, and perhaps himself) could cover with flesh. Herder speaks of corpses—forms of linguistic petrifaction —against which, in due course, men revolt. The history of linguistic revolutions is the history of the succession of cultures, the true revolu-tions in the history of the human race. Was there once a language common to all men? He does not wish to assert this. On the one hand, he clings to the notion of one world, one basic human personality, the 'organic' interrelation of everything; he insists on the folly and danger of abstraction, of fragmentation, of splitting the human personality into separate faculties, as not only Wolff but Kant, too, had done in their psychologies and in their strict division of body from soul, nature from spirit, the empirical from the *a priori*, the historical from the eternal. Yet he is a Christian, too, and he is committed to the Aristotelian and biblical doctrine of natural kinds. Man is unique; Lord Monboddo and the naturalists must be mistaken. That, no doubt, is why language had to be a direct gift of God, and not the product of a gradual process of emergence of rational beings out of some pre-rational state of nature —from the animal kingdom and subhuman forms of sentience, or even from insentience.[1] The contradiction is never reconciled.

The only identification that Herder never abandons is that of thought and action, language and activity. Poetry, particularly early epic poetry, is for him pure activity. He was taken in by Ossian, like many of his contemporaries. It is probably from these poems rather than from Homer—although he speaks of the Homeric poems as improvisations, not a 'dead artefact'—that he derives his notion of poetry as activity. Poetry, particularly among early peoples, is, he maintains, magical in character; it is not cool description of nature or of anything else: it is a spur to action—to heroes, hunters, lovers; it stimulates and directs. It is not to be savoured by the scholar in his armchair, but is intelligible only to those who have placed themselves in situations similar to the conditions in which such words sprang into existence. During his voyage from Riga to Nantes, he observed the sailors during rough seas. These dour men under a savage discipline who lived in terror of, and in constant intimate contact with, the elements which they sought to dominate, resurrected for him the dark world of Skalds and Vikings and the Eddas,[2] a world scarcely intelligible to tranquil philologists in their studies or detached literary epicures who turn over the pages idly, without the power to re-create the world of which these works are the vision and the voice. Words, rhythms, actions are aspects of a single experience. These are commonplaces today, but (despite Vico) they were far from being such in Herder's time.

'The more savage, that is, the more alive and freedom-loving a people is (for that is the single meaning of the word), the more savage, that is, alive, free, sensuous, lyrically active, its songs must be, if it has songs', he wrote in 1773. He compares 'the living presentness of the imagery' of such songs with 'songs written for paper'. 'These arrows of a savage Apollo pierce hearts and carry souls and thoughts with them'. 'All unpolished peoples sing and act; they sing about what they do, and thus sing histories. Their songs are the archives of their people, the treasury of their science and religion . . . a picture of their domestic life in joy and in sorrow, by the bridal bed and the graveside.' 'Here

[1] Mr G. A. Wells in his *Herder and After* (*op. cit.*) advances this view, which seems to me very illuminating.

[2] See below, pp. 186-7.

everyone portrays himself and appears as he is.'[1] Language, content, tone, tell us more about the outlook, beliefs, origins, history, mingling of nations than travellers' tales. Then artifice begins. When the words were divorced from music, when 'the poet began . . . to write slowly in order to be read', art may have gained, but there was a loss of magic, of 'miraculous power.'[2] What do our modern critics, the 'counters of syllables', 'specialists in scansion', masters of dead learning, know of all this? 'Heart! Warmth! Blood! Humanity! Life!'[3] 'I feel! I am!'[4] These are Herder's mottoes; no wonder that the poets of the *Sturm und Drang* recognized themselves in his writings.

He dreams of a visit to the Northern seas reading 'the story of *Utal* and *Ninetuma* in sight of the very island where it all took place'. His voyage to France, which took him past the shores of Scandinavia and England, transported him: 'This was a living and creative Nature, between the deeps of sea and sky', very different from the world in which he was living, where 'we scarcely see or feel, only reflect and reason', in which poets invent imaginary passions and qualities of soul unknown to them or anyone, and 'compare verses about objects about which one cannot think or feel or imagine anything at all'. He feels a kindred spirit in the English scholar Robert Wood, who gazed upon the ruins of Troy, a volume of Homer in hand.[5] He must go to the Scottish Highlands, to see the places described by the great Ossian himself and 'hear the living songs of a living people'. After all, 'the Greeks, too . . . were savage . . . and in the best period of their flowering far more of Nature remained in them than can be descried by the narrow gaze of a scholiast or a classical scholar'. Homer goes back to ancient sagas, Tyrtaeus to ballads, Arion and Orpheus are 'noble Greek shamans', Sappho's songs are like nothing so much as 'the songs of a Livonian girl of our own time'.[6] Our scholars and translators have

---

[1] *Correspondence on Ossian and the songs of ancient peoples;* these quotations are taken from the translations in *The Rise of Modern Mythology* by Burton Feldman and Robert D. Richardson, Jr. (Indiana University Press, Bloomington/London, 1972, pp. 229-30).

[2] *Über die Wirkung der Dichtkunst auf die Sitten der Völker in alten und neuen Zeiten,* 1778, published 1781.

[3] V, 538.

[4] VIII, 96.

[5] *Von deutscher Art und Kunst* of 1775, in which his essay on Ossian was published.

[6] *On the Similarity of Medieval English and German Poetry,* in *Deutsches Museum,* 1777.

no inkling of this: consider the translation of a Lapp song by the minor poet Christian Ewald Kleist. 'I would willingly give up for this song a dozen of Kleist's imitations. Do not be surprised', he writes to his bride Caroline, 'that a Laplandic youth who knew neither school nor writing, and scarcely knows God, sings better than Major Kleist. After all, the Lapp improvised his song while he was gliding with his reindeer over the snow, and time dragged so slowly on the way to Lake Orra where his beloved lived'.[1] Swiss and English scholars had celebrated Homer, Dante, Shakespeare, Milton. Hurd, Young, Percy, Lowth and Blackwell revived the study of ancient poetry. Enthusiasm for the achievements of the collective genius of primitive societies, under the impulsion of Rousseau, was transformed into a European movement by Herder's passionate advocacy.

All genuine expressions of experience are valid. They differ because lives differ: perhaps because the earth's axis is inclined by twenty-four degrees. This generates different geophysical 'climates', different experiences, different societies. Anything that seems to Herder authentic delights him. He has his preferences: he prefers the Greeks, the Germans and the Hebrews to the Romans, the ancient Egyptians, or the Frenchmen of his own time or of the previous century. But, at least in theory, he is prepared to defend them all; he wishes and thinks he is able to penetrate—'feel himself' (*Einfühlen* is his invention, a hundred years before Lipps or Dilthey or Croce)—into their essence, grasp what it must be like to live, contemplate goals, act and react, think, imagine, in the unique ways dictated by their circumstances, and so grasp the patterns of life in terms of which alone such groups are to be defined. The central concept here is that of natural growth, biological, emotional, intellectual. Nature *is* growth—what Bodmer and Breitinger had spoken of, perhaps echoing Vico's *nascimento*, as *Naturwüchsigkeit*—spontaneous natural growth, not the static 'true nature' of Boileau's aesthetics, or Batteux's *la belle nature*, which the artist must learn to discern and reveal from the welter of mere experience.

Everything that is natural is valuable. The notion (for example, the Marquis de Sade's) that vices or decadence or aggression are not less natural than the rich and harmonious development of all human potentialities is not allowed for. In this respect Herder is a true child

---

[1] Letter to Caroline Flachsland in 1771.

of the Enlightenment at its most naïve as well as at its most imaginative and penetrating. The late Professor Arthur Lovejoy was surely right when he included Herder among the thinkers (perhaps the majority in the West) who identified the 'must' of natural laws that caused things to be as they are and governed the world inexorably with the 'ought' of the normative rules, derived, apparently, from the self-same nature, obedience to which alone conducts men towards happiness and virtue and wisdom. But this consensus has its limits. Herder sharply differs from the central thought of the French Enlightenment, and not only in the respects that all his commentators have noted. What is usually stressed is, in the first place, his relativism, his admiration of every authentic culture for being what it is, his insistence that outlooks and civilizations must be understood from within, in terms of their own stages of development, purposes and outlooks; and in the second place his sharp repudiation of that central strain in Cartesian rationalism which regards only what is universal, eternal, unalterable, governed by rigorously logical relationships—only the subject matter of mathematics, logic, physics and the other natural sciences—as true knowledge.

But Herder rebelled against the *Aufklärung* in an even profounder way, by rejecting the very notion of impassable barriers in nature or experience—barriers between types of consciousness or faculties or ideas or natural objects. What repels him equally in such deeply disparate thinkers as Descartes and Kant and the French *philosophes* is their common insistence on rigid divisions between 'faculties' and types of experience, which they seem to him to have introduced merely to make it possible to classify and generalize. He admires Leibniz more than Kant: he recognizes the logical gulf between mathematical truths and those of fact, but he regards the former (probably following Hume) as tautologies, statements unconcerned with nature.[1] He is a thoroughgoing empiricist in matters of epistemology. Kant's transcendental categories, which claim to determine experience *a priori*, seem to him a monstrous conflation of analytic and synthetic: he rejects the 'synthetic *a priori*' as a hideous confusion.[2] Reality for him admits of no *a priori* laws; Kant's attempt to distinguish contingent from necessary judgments about experience seems to him to be far more misleading than the distinction between intuited necessities and ob-

---

[1] XXI, 36.   [2] XXI, 38.

served contingencies out of which Spinoza and Leibniz built their systems. Categories, rigorous distinctions of kinds of truth about the nature of reality—like the similar distinctions drawn between words and concepts—distort judgment not only in epistemology and logic, but in politics and ethics and the arts, and indeed all regions of experience. All activities, he insists, express the whole and undivided man whom Descartes and Kant, in their several ways, have done their best to carve up into compartments with their faculty psychology of 'reason', 'imagination', 'intuition', 'feeling', 'will'.[1] He declares that he knows of no criteria for distinguishing such Kantian faculties as *Erkennen*, *Empfinden*, *Wollen*—they are indissolubly united in the organic personality of living men.[2]

The attack on Kant in the *Metakritik* of 1799 merely summarizes a lifelong attitude. The black-and-white terms these neo-scholastics use to describe man—an inexhaustibly complex organization—seem to Herder wilfully absolute and arbitrary. Instead, for example, of asking themselves how free men are, free from or for what, and where and when, and in what respects, or what renders them more or less free, these thinkers dogmatically pronounce man to be free, wholly free in some absolute sense, as against animals who are wholly mechanical, or at least wholly lack freedom. They speak of man as distinguished by his possession of reason (not as being less or more rational), and define him in terms of selected properties that one must either possess wholly, or not possess at all; they describe him in terms of sharp, artificial dichotomies that arbitrarily break up the interwoven, continuous, at times irregular, fluid, shapeless, often unanalysable, but always perceptible, dynamic, teeming, boundless, eternal multiplicity of nature,[3] and so provide distorting lenses both to philosophers and historians. Attempts to bring manifestations so complex and so various under some general law, whether by philosophers seeking knowledge, or by statesmen seeking to organize and govern, seemed to Herder no better than a search for the lowest common denominator—for what may be least characteristic and important in the lives of men—and, therefore, as making for shallowness in theory and a tendency to impose a crippling uniformity in practice. Herder is one of the earliest opponents of uniformity as the enemy of life and freedom. One of the central doctrines of the Western tradition, at any rate since Plato, has maintained that the good is one,

[1] *This footnote is printed on p. 216.*   [2] XXI, 18.   [3] See XIII, 194.

while evil has many faces; there is one true answer to every real question, but many false ones. Even Aristotle, for whom Plato's ideal of an unchanging, wholly unified society is too rigid, since it does not allow for the variety of human characters and wishes, merely reports this as a fact, not as something desirable in itself. The central current in ethics and politics, as well as metaphysics and theology and the sciences, is cast in a monist mould: it seeks to bring the many into a coherent, systematic unity. Herder is an early and passionate champion of variety: uniformity maims and kills. The 'ferment' of the Middle Ages did at least, he wrote in 1774, 'hold at bay the devouring jaws of despotism' whose tendency is 'to crush everything into deadly uniformity. Now is it better, is it healthier and more beneficent for mankind to produce only the lifeless cogs of a huge, wooden, thoughtless machine, or to rouse and activate lively energies? Even if institutions are not perfect, even if men are not always honest, even if there is some disorder and a good deal of disagreement, it is still preferable to a state of affairs in which men are forced to rot and decay during their own lifetime. . . .'.[1] Even Montesquieu, so widely praised for his novel sense of the differences between societies and of the 'spirit' that animates their laws and institutions, has tried to press these teeming varieties of human life and culture into the straitjacket of three basic types: 'three wretched generalizations! . . . the history of all times and peoples, whose succession forms the great, living work of God, reduced to ruins, divided neatly into three heaps. . . . Oh, Montesquieu!'[2]

All regionalists, all defenders of the local against the universal, all champions of deeply rooted forms of life, both reactionary and progressive, both genuine humanists and obscurantist opponents of scientific advance, owe something, whether they know it or not, to the doctrines which Herder (with a far wider and more magnificent sweep than Möser or Burke or Ferguson) introduced into European thought. Vico might have achieved something of this. But he was (and is) not read; as Savigny remarked, he came into his own too late to have a decisive influence.

However much lip service Herder may have paid to 'natural kinds', in general he conceived of nature as a unity in which the *Kräfte*—the mysterious, dynamic, purpose-seeking forces, the interplay of which

---

[1] Taken from the translation provided by Professor F. M. Barnard in *Herder on Social and Political Culture* (*op. cit.*, 1969), p. 191.

[2] *Ibid.*, p. 217.

constitutes all movement and growth—flow into each other, clash, combine, coalesce. These forces are not causal and mechanical as in Descartes; nor insulated from each other as in the *Monadology* of Leibniz; his notion of them owes more to neo-Platonic and Renaissance mysticism, and, perhaps, to Erigena's *Natura naturans* than to the sciences of his time. For Herder reality is a kind of symbiosis of these *Kräfte* (whose character remains obscure) with an environment that is conceived in somewhat static terms; if the environment is altered too abruptly, the result is some kind of collapse. Herder found more and more evidence for this. Transplanted flowers decay in unsympathetic climates; so do human beings. Greenlanders do not thrive in Denmark. Africans are miserable and decay in Europe. Europeans become debilitated in America. Conquest crushes, and emigration sometimes leads to enfeeblement—lack of vital force, the flattening out of human beings, and a sad uniformity.[1] The *Ideen* is full of such examples. Like Fourier after him, Herder believed in the complete realizability of all potentialities ('All that can be, will come into being'), since everything fits somewhere. Only artificiality is destructive, in life as in art. Marriages of convenience, coldly entered into, ruin children, and are worse for them than pure animality. The patriarchs at times exercised severe and cruel authority: but at least this is more 'natural'—and therefore less harmful—than the artificial reasonings of philosophers. Herder harbours a Rousseau-like suspicion of 'reasoning'. He does not think that Voltaire's desiccated maxims or Wolff's syllogisms are better for children than the stern but natural behaviour of primitive men. Anything is preferable to a system which imposes the ideal of one culture on another and arranges, adjusts, makes for uniform 'physiognomies', as opposed to a condition which is 'natural', in a state of 'creative disorder', where alone individuality and freedom live and grow. Hence his condemnation of all theories which over-categorize men—into racial types, for example, or social orders—and thereby divide them from each other. Centralization and *dirigisme* are the enemies: even some degree of inefficiency is preferable to 'a condition in which men are made to rot and decay in their lifetime'. And, in the same spirit, 'political reform must come from below' for 'even when man abuses his freedom most despicably he is still king; for he can still choose, even if he chooses the worst; he can rule over himself, even if he legislates himself into a beast'.[2] His differences from his fellow

[1] See on this p. 197.   [2] *Ibid.*, p. 20; Herder, XIII, 146-7.

opponents of the French *lumières*—Möser, Kant, Rousseau, Burke— are obvious enough.

He condemns the anthropologies which treat men in general and leave the individual drained of too many differentiating characteristics. Even tradition, which otherwise acts as a preservative of the most vital characteristics of human groups, can be a danger when it becomes too mechanical and acts as a narcotic, as it seems to him to have done in Asia, which it put to sleep by eliminating too many of the other in- gredients of a healthy life, too many other *Kräfte* that are indispensable to life and activity. This thought is incapable of precise formulation; but, as always with Herder, it is suggestive and has a clear general direction. 'The savage who loves himself, his wife and his child . . . and works for the good of his tribe as for his own . . . is in my view more genuine than that human ghost, the . . . citizen of the world, who, burning with love for all his fellow ghosts, loves a chimera. The savage in his hut has room for any stranger . . . the saturated heart of the idle cosmopolitan is a home for no one'.[1] He repeats throughout the *Ideen* that originality, freedom of choice and creation, is the divine element in man. When a savage speaks with vigour and precision he is superior to 'the civilized man who stands on a pedestal built by others'. There is much talk in the *Ideen* (this is later echoed by Fichte) about men who live on other men's accounts: they are viewed as 'dead cosmo- politans', men whose feelings have been drained away, dehumanized creatures, victims of nature or history, moral or physical cripples, para- sites, fettered slaves.

How do men come to lose their humanity? By living on others and by the labour and ideas of others. Herder, in opposition to the primi- tivists, welcomed invention—the arts and sciences are fruits of the creative powers of man, and through them he rises to the full height of his purposive nature. Inventions as such do not corrupt (in this Herder differs from the Rousseau of the First and Second Discourses); only if one lives on the inventions of others does one become mechanical and devitalized.[2] Here, too, as in the writings of Mably, Rousseau and

---

[1] XIII, 339.

[2] In his essay on Ossian, Herder speaks of this as the source of the fatal division of labour which creates destructive barriers among men, classes and hierarchies and the division of spiritual from manual labour which robs men of their humanity. Material progress may march hand in hand with cultural decline; this theme is taken up by Goethe and Schiller and developed by Marx and Marxists. I owe this point to Professor Roy Pascal.

Karl Friedrich von Moser,[1] begins that lament, still more characteristic of the following century, and perhaps even more often heard in our own, for the youth that is gone for ever—for the lost virtues of an earlier, more vigorous epoch in the life of mankind. Herder, no less than Mill or Carlyle or Ruskin, speaks with gloom about the triviality and lifelessness of modern men and modern art, in contrast with the full-blooded, doughty, independent human beings of the morning hours of humanity—the creators of the great epics and songs, of an anonymous but more robust age. Before Henri de Saint-Simon he draws a contrast between the creative and the relatively sterile epochs in the history of culture. Herder has his optimistic moments, when he supposes that a renewal is possible: that if man can only 'cease to be in contradiction with himself' and 'return to himself', and if peoples can only 'find themselves' and 'learn not to think in other people's thoughts',[2] they can recover and revive and create new works of art, in modern terms, as noble and expressive of their true nature as anything that men have created in the past. There is only one course against which Herder sets his face absolutely: that is any attempt to return to the past. Here there is no salvation. To sigh after the Greeks and wish to return to them, of which he suspects Winckelmann, is absurd and impossible: his idealization of the Greeks as the originators of art which among them attained to a sublime height never reached by, say, the Egyptians, is wholly unhistorical and nothing but a 'terrible delusion'.[3]

The dangers to free development are many. In the first place, there is the centralized state; it can rob us of something essential: it can rob us of ourselves. There are foreign cultures that 'devour German folk song like a cancer'—folk song that is a response to the deepest human

[1] Especially in Moser's *Von dem Deutschen Nationalgeist*, published in 1765-6, which speaks of the Germans as despised, disregarded, mocked, and preyed upon by everyone.

[2] Such phrases are almost verbally exact echoes of Hamann's sentences, dealing with what much later came to be called the problem of 'alienation.'

[3] Johann Gottfried Herder, *Werke in Zwei Bänden*, ed. Karl Gustav Gerold (München, 1953), II, 117, 128. Also see pp. 658 and 663. Compare the following from *Auch Eine Philosophie*: 'there is no country the civilization of which has been able to take a backward step, and become for the second time what it has once been. The path of destiny is as inflexible as iron. Can today become yesterday? ... The Ptolemies could never again create an Egypt, nor the Hadrians a Greece, nor the Julians a Jerusalem'. These cultures have had their day. 'The sword is worn out, the empty scabbard lies in pieces.' Quoted by F. M. Barnard, *op. cit.*, pp. 216-17.

cravings, to collective desires that seek to embody common experiences in symbolic forms not dreamed of in Voltaire's philosophy. There is the more specific danger of foreign languages: 'I am able to stammer with immense effort in the words of a foreign language; its spirit will evade me'. Yet 'to this we devote the best years of our life!'[1] But we are not Greeks; we are not Romans; and we cannot become such. To wish to return is to be dominated by a false vision, a crippling illusion as fatal as any for which it attempts to be the cure. Imitation is a terrible curse: human nature is not identical in different parts of the world . . . the worlds of things and sounds are different. . . .[2] What then must we do? We must seek to be ourselves. 'Let us be characteristic of our nation, language, scene, and posterity will decide whether or not we are classical.' Perhaps Klopstock's *Messias* was less successful than it might have been because it was not 'national' enough.[3] It is here that Herder utters his most ardently nationalist sentiments: 'I cry to my German brothers . . . the remnants of all genuine folk songs are rolling into the abyss of oblivion . . . the night of so-called culture is devouring all about it like a cancer'.[4] 'We speak the words of strangers and they wean us from our own thought . . .'[5] He sees no merit in 'peasants in wigs', much as Hamann talks of 'false noses'. He appeals to the Germans to know themselves, to understand their place and respect their role in the cosmos, in time and in space.

v

Is this nationalism? In an obvious sense it is. It is anti-French—the voyage to Nantes and Paris (like the later journey to Rome) depressed Herder acutely. He met some of the most distinguished of the *philosophes*, but evidently failed to achieve any degree of communication with them. He suffered that mixture of envy, humiliation, admiration, resentment and defiant pride which backward peoples feel towards advanced ones, members of one social class towards those who belong to a higher rung in the hierarchy. Wounded national feeling—this scarcely needs saying—breeds nationalism, but it is important to

---

[1] IV, 388.

[2] *Kritische Wälder*, No. 4, unpublished in Herder's lifetime.

[3] Professor Rouché is understandably surprised by the spectacle of a Christian clergyman complaining that the central theme of Christian religion is perhaps too foreign a topic for a German poem.

[4] XXV, 11.   [5] IV, 389.

realize that Herder's nationalism was never political. If he denounces individualism, he equally detests the state, which coerces and mutilates the free human personality. His social vision is antagonistic to government, power, domination. Louis XIV and Frederick the Great (like Caesar and Charlemagne before them) represent a detestable ideal. Herder does not ask for power and does not wish to assert the superiority of his own class or culture or nation. He wishes to create a society in which men, whoever they are, can live full lives, attain to free self-expression, 'be someone'; and he thinks that the less government they have the better. We cannot return to the Greek *polis*. This may, indeed, have been the first stage of a development destined in its later stages to become nationalistic and chauvinistic in the full, aggressive sense. Whether or not this is historically and sociologically true, it is clear that Herder did not himself harbour these sentiments. Even though he seems to have coined the word *Nationalismus*, his conception of a good society is closer to the anarchism of Thoreau or Proudhon or Kropotkin, and to the conception of a culture (*Bildung*) of which such liberals as Goethe and Humboldt were proponents, than to the ideals of Fichte or Hegel or political socialists. For him *die Nation* is not a political entity. He is repelled by the claims of contemporary Celtomaniacs and Teutomaniacs who rhapsodized over the ancient Gaels or Northmen. He celebrates German beginnings, because they are part of, and illuminate, his own civilization, not because German civilization ranks higher than that of others on some cosmic scale. 'In the works of the imagination and feeling the entire soul of a nation reveals itself most clearly.'[1] This was developed by Sismondi, Michelet, and Mazzini into a full-scale political-cultural doctrine; but Herder stands even closer to the outlook of Ruskin or Lamennais or William Morris, to populists and Christian socialists, and to all of those who, in the present day, are opposed to hierarchies of status or power, or to the influence of manipulators of any kind. He stands with those who protest against mechanization and vulgarization rather than with the nationalists of the last hundred years, whether moderate or violent. He favours autarky, but only in personal life; that is, in artistic creation and the rights of natural self-expression. All his invocations of the *Nationalgeist* (an expression probably coined by Karl Friedrich von Moser), and of its many aliases —the *Geist des Volkes, Seele des Volkes, Geist der Nation, Genius des*

---

[1] XVIII, 58.

Volkes and the more empirical *Nationalcharakter*[1]—are intended to stress what is ours, not theirs, even though theirs may intrinsically be more valuable, viewed on some vaster scale. Herder admits no such scale: cultures are comparable but not commensurable; each is what it is, of literally inestimable value in its own society, and consequently to humanity as a whole. Socrates is for him neither the timeless cosmopolitan sage of the Enlightenment, nor Hamann's destroyer of pretentious claims to knowledge whose irony and self-confessed ignorance opened the path to faith and salvation. Socrates is, above all, an Athenian of the fifth century; and that age is over. Aristotle may be more gifted than Leibniz, but Leibniz is ours, Aristotle is not; Shakespeare is ours, other great geniuses, Homer or Moses, are not. Individuality is all; artificial combinations of old and new, native and foreign, lead to false ideas and ruinous practice.[2] 'Let us follow our own path ... let men speak well or ill of our nation, our literature, our language: they are ours, they are ourselves, and let that be enough.'[3] Better Germans, whatever they are, than sham Greeks, Frenchmen, Englishmen.[4] But when he says, 'Awake, German nation! Do not let them ravish your Palladium!',[5] declares that fearful storms are coming and warns men not to lie asleep like Jonah in the tempest, and when he tells men to take warning from the terrible example of partitioned Poland,[6] and says, 'Poor torn, crushed Germany, be hopeful!' and 'Germans, speak German! Spew out the Seine's ugly slime!'[7], it is difficult to avoid the thought that this may indeed have fed the sinister nationalism of Görres and Jahn, Arndt and Treitschke, and their monstrous modern successors. Yet Herder's own sentences refer to purely cultural self-determination; he hates '*policirte Nationen*'. Nationality for him is purely and strictly a cultural attribute; he believes that people can and should defend their cultural heritage: they need never give in. He almost blames the Jews, despite his passionate addiction to their antiquities, for not preserving a sufficient sense of collective honour and making no effort to return to their home in Palestine, which is the sole place where they can blossom again into a *Nation*. He is interested, not

---

[1] I, 263; II, 160; III, 30; V, 185, 217; VIII, 392; XIII, 364; XIV, 38, 84; XXV, 10, and *passim*.

[2] VIII, 207, 314, 315; XIV, 227; XV, 321; XVIII, 248 (I owe these and several other references to Professor F. M. Barnard).

[3] Quoted by H. Lévy Bruhl, *L'Allemagne depuis Leibniz* (Paris, n.d.), pp. 168-9.

[4] I, 366, 367.   [5] XVII, 309.   [6] XXIX, 210.   [7] XXVII, 129.

in nationality but in cultures, in worlds, in the total experience of peoples; and the aspects of this experience that he celebrates are personal relationships, friendship and enmity, attitudes to nature, war and peace, art and science, ways in which truth, freedom and happiness are pursued, and in particular the relations of the great civilizing leaders to the ungrateful mob. He fears organization as such, and, like the early English Romantics, like Young or Henry and Joseph Warton, he wants to preserve what is irregular and unique in life and in art, that which no system can wholly contain.

His attack on political centralization and intellectual polarization springs from the same source. When he imagines the world as a garden which can contain many flowers, and when he speaks of the possible and desirable harmony between all the national cultures, he is not simply ignoring the aggressive potentialities of nation states or blandly assuming that there is no reason for conflict between various nationalisms. Rather, he is deeply hostile to the growth of political, economic, military centralization, but sees no reason why culturally autonomous communities need clash. It may, of course, be unrealistic and unhistorical to suppose that one kind of autarky need not lead to other and more dangerous kinds. But it is not the same kind of unrealism as that with which he, and the Enlightenment generally, are usually charged. His faith is not in nationalism, collectivism, Teutomania, or romantic state worship, but in something that is, if anything, incompatible with these ideals. He is the champion of those mysterious *Kräfte* which are 'living and organic'. For him, as for Shaftesbury (one of those English thinkers who, like Young and Carlyle, influenced the Germans far more than his own compatriots), there is, in the end, only one great creative *Kraft*: 'what is alive in creation is, in all forms, shapes, channels, one spirit, one single flame'.[1] This is scarcely an empirical or scientific notion. He sings paeans to the *Seele des Volkes* which is the social incarnation of the Leibnizian *vis viva*, 'unique, wonderful, inexplicable, ineradicable, and as old as the *Nation*'.[2] Its most vivid expression is, of course, not the state, but 'the physiognomy of its speech'.[3] The point that I wish to stress is that the true heir of this doctrine is not power politics but what came to be called populism. It is this that acquired such momentum among the oppressed people of Eastern Europe, and later spread in Asia and Africa. It inspired not *étatistes*,

---

[1] VIII, 178. [2] XIV, 38. [3] XIII, 364.

but believers in 'grass roots'—Russian Slavophiles and *Narodniks*, Christian Socialists and all those admirers of folk art and of popular traditions whose enthusiasm assumed both serious and ridiculous shapes, still not unfamiliar today. Populism may often have taken reactionary forms and fed the stream of aggressive nationalism; but the form in which Herder held it was democratic and peaceful, not only anti-dynastic and anti-élitist, but deeply anti-political,[1] directed against organized power, whether of nations, classes, races or parties. I have called it populism because this movement, whether in Europe or outside it, seems to me the nearest approximation to Herder's ideal. It is, as a rule, pluralistic, looks on government as an evil, tends, following Rousseau, to identify 'the people' with the poor, the peasants, the common folk, the plebeian masses,[2] uncorrupted by wealth or city life; and, to this day, animates folk enthusiasts and cultural fanatics, egalitarians and agitators for local autonomy, champions of arts and crafts and of simple life, and innocent utopians of all brands. It is based on belief in loose textures, voluntary associations, natural ties, and is bitterly opposed to armies, bureaucracies, 'closed' societies of any sort.

Historically, populism has, of course, become closely interwoven with real nationalism, and it has, indeed, often provided the soil in which blind xenophobia and irrationalism grew to dangerous heights; and this is no more accidental than the alliances of nationalism with democracy or romanticism or liberalism at various points in the nineteenth century. Nevertheless, it is a historical and moral error to identify the ideology of one period with its consequences at some other, or with its transformation in another context and in combination with other factors. The progeny of Herder in, let us say, England or America are to be found principally among those amateurs who became absorbed in the antiquities and forms of life (ancient and modern) of cultures other than their own, in Asia and Africa or the 'backward' provinces of Europe or America, among professional amateurs and collectors of ancient song and poetry, among enthusiastic and sometimes senti-

---

[1] 'As you know, I do not concern myself with political matters', he wrote to Goethe from Paris, late in the century, and spoke the truth.

[2] This strain is strong in Herder, particularly in his early years: e.g. 'Philosopher and plebeian, write in order to be useful!' (quoted by Zhirmunsky, *op. cit.*, p. viii, who dates it as written in 1765, when Herder was twenty-one). There is also his insistence that political reform must always come 'from below' (Barnard, *op. cit.*, p. 5, etc.).

mental devotees of more primitive forms of life in the Balkans or among the Arabs; nostalgic travellers and exiles like Richard Burton, Doughty, Lafcadio Hearn, the English companions of Gandhi or Ibn Saud, cultural autonomists and unpolitical youth movements, as well as serious students and philosophers of language and society.

Perhaps Herder's most characteristic descendants were to be found in Russia, in which he took so abiding an interest. In that country his ideas entered the thought of those critics and creative artists who not merely developed national and pseudo-national forms of their own native art but became passionate champions of all 'natural', 'spontaneous', traditional forms of art and self-expression wherever they manifested themselves. These admirers of ethnic colour and variety as such, Mussorgsky, Stassov, and some of the musicians and painters whom they inspired, so far from supporting authority and repression, stood politically on the left, and felt sympathy for all forms of cultural self-expression, especially on the part of persecuted minorities — Georgians, Poles, Jews, Finns, and also Spaniards, Hungarians, and other 'unreconstructed' nations. They denounced, however unjustly and intemperately, such 'organ grinders' as Rossini and Verdi, or neo-classical schools of painting, for alleged cosmopolitanism, for commercialism, for a tendency to destroy regional or national differences in favour of flat and mechanical forms of life, in short, for rootlessness (a term which afterwards became so sinister and ominous in the mouths of obscurantists and chauvinists), heartlessness, oppression, and de-humanization. All this is typically Herderian.

Something of this kind, too, may have entered Mazzini's ideal of the Young Italy which was to live in harmony and mutual understanding with Young Germany — and the 'Youth' of all nations — once they had thrown away the shackles of oppressive imperialism, of dynastic autocracies, of the denial of the rights of all 'natural' human units, and attained to free self-determination. Such views may have been thoroughly utopian. But if they were nationalistic, they were so in a sense very different from the later — and pejorative — sense of the word. Populism may have been in part responsible for isolationism, provincialism, suspicion of everything smooth, metropolitan, elegant and socially superior, hatred of the *beau monde* in all its forms; but with this went hostility to centralization, dogmatism, militarism, and self-assertiveness, or, in other words, all that is commonly associated with the full-grown nationalism of the nineteenth century, as well as with deep antipathy to mobs—Herder carefully distinguishes the *Pöbel auf die Gassen* ('the rabble') from *Das Volk* (i.e. 'the body of the nation'), however this is done[1]—and with a hatred of violence and conquest as strong as any to be found among the other Weimar humanists, Goethe, Wieland and Schiller. The faithful followers of Herder may often have been—and can still be—confused, sentimental, impractical, ineffective and sometimes ridiculous, but not managerial, calculating or brutal. No one made more of this profound contrast than Herder himself.

VI

In this connection it is worth considering Herder's attitude to three great eighteenth-century myths which fed the stream of nineteenth-century nationalism. The first is that of the superiority of a particular tribal culture. His denunciation of patriotic boastfulness—the *Favorit-volk* doctrine—has already been referred to. One of the most quoted sentences from *Yet Another Philosophy of History* tells us that 'every nation has its own inner centre of happiness, as every sphere its own centre of gravity'.[2] This is what the historian, the critic, the philosopher must grasp, and nothing is more fatal than the attempted assimilation of the *Mittelpunkt* of one culture with those of others. 'One must enter the time, the place, the entire history[3] [of a people]; one must "feel oneself [*sich einfühlen*] into everything".[4] This is what contemporary historians [he is referring to Schlözer] conspicuously fail to do.'[5] To understand the Hebrew scriptures it is not enough, he tells us, to see it as a sublime work of art, and compare its beauties with those of Homer, as the Oxford scholar, Robert Lowth, had done; we must transport ourselves into a distant land and an earlier age, and read it as the national poem of the Jews, a pastoral and agricultural people, 'written in ancient, simple, rustic, poetic, not philosophical or abstract, language. . . .' 'Be a shepherd with shepherds, a peasant in the midst of an agricultural people, an oriental among the primitive dwellers of the East, if you wish to enjoy these creations in the atmosphere of their birth . . .'.[6] Germans are not ancient Hebrews; biblical images are

---

[1] XXV, 323. [2] V, 509. [3] V, 502. [4] V, 502. [5] V, 436-38.

[6] This is less than fair to Lowth, who, a good deal earlier than his critic, spoke of biblical verse as words that 'burst forth in sentences pointed, earnest, rapid and tremulous' and declared that 'we must see all things with their eyes . . . to read Hebrew as Hebrews would have read it . . .' (*De sacra poesi Hebraeorum prae-lectiones*, 1753, Lecture 5. Quoted by Burton Feldman and Robert D. Richardson, *op. cit.*, p. 149).

drawn from a world alien to them. 'When the poet of the Bible speaks of the snows of Lebanon or the pleasant vineyards of Carmel . . . these are empty words to a German poet . . .'; 'the dreadful storms from the sea passing over their land to Arabia, were for them thundering steeds bearing the chariot of Jehovah through the clouds . . .'.[1] He says that it would be better for a contemporary poet to sing of electric sparks than copy these Judaean images; for the Bible the rainbow is the footstool of the Lord's House; for the Skalds it is a fiery bridge over which the giants sought to storm heaven.[2] All this is at best only half intelligible to us. The Germans are not biblical Jews, nor are they classical Greeks or Romans either.[3] Every experience is what it is. To understand it is to grasp what it meant to those who expressed it in the monuments through which we try to read it. All understanding is necessarily historical. The *Aufklärer*—Gottsched, Lessing, and Moses Mendelssohn—not only lack all historical perspective, they tend to grade, to give marks for moral excellence. Herder, in this (what he would regard as a Spinozan) mood, warns, at any rate in *Auch eine Philosophie* of 1774, against moral evaluation (prone though he was to it himself, then and later), and urges the critic above all to understand that if one must condemn and praise, this should be done only after an exercise of sympathetic insight—of one's capacity for *einfühlen* ('empathy'). *Auch eine Philosophie* contains the most eloquent description of the newly discovered sense of history, with its uncanny resemblance to that of Vico, whom, so far as we can tell, Herder did not read until twenty years later: 'How unspeakably difficult it is to convey the particular quality [*Eigenheit*] of an individual human being and how

[1] X, 14 (written in 1780-81).

[2] *Ueber die neue deutsche Literatur, Fragmente* (pt. III), 1767.

[3] *Ibid.* 'Oh accursed word "classical"! It has transformed Cicero for us into a classical school rhetorician, Virgil and Homer into classical poets, Caesar into a pedagogue, Livy into a phrasemonger. It has divided expression from thought, and thought from the event that has generated it . . . this word has become a wall between us and all true education which would have seen the ancients as living exemplars . . . this word has buried many a genius beneath a heap of words . . . crushed him under a millstone of a dead language . . . when a German poet is described as a second Horace . . . as a new Lucretius, a historian as a second Livy, that is nothing to be proud of; but it would be a great, rare, enviable glory for us if one could say about such writers: "this is how Horace, Cicero, Lucretius, Livy, would have written if they were writing about this topic, at this particular stage of culture, at this particular time, with this particular purpose, for this particular people, with its particular outlook and its own language." '

impossible it is to say precisely what distinguishes an individual, his way of feeling and living; how different and how individual [*anders und eigen*] everything becomes once his eyes see it, once his soul grasps, his heart feels, it. How much depth there is in the character of a single people, which, no matter how often observed (and gazed at with curiosity and wonder), nevertheless escapes the word which attempts to capture it, and, even with the word to catch it, is seldom so recognizable as to be universally understood and felt. If this is so, what happens when one tries to master an entire ocean of peoples, times, cultures, countries, with one glance, one sentiment, by means of one single word! Words, pale shadow-play! An entire living picture of ways of life, or habits, wants, characteristics of land and sky, must be added, or provided in advance; one must start by feeling sympathy with a nation if one is to feel a single one of its inclinations or acts, or all of them together.'[1]

Greece, he continues, was not Athens. It was inhabited and ruled by Athenians, Boeotians, Spartans, Corinthians. Egyptians were traders no less than Phoenicians. Macedon was a conqueror like Rome. The great Greek thinkers had speculative minds as sharp as those of moderns. Yet (Herder repeats in and out of context) they were Egyptians, Romans, Greeks, Macedonians, and *not* inhabitants of our world. Leibniz is ours; Plato is not. Similarity is not identity; one must see both the wood and the trees, although only God can do this completely. All history is an unending conflict between the general idea and the particular; all general ideas are abstractions, dangerous, misleading, and unavoidable. One must seek to see the whole, however unattainable this goal may be. Exceptions and deviations will amaze only those who insist upon forcing an idealized image on the manifold of reality. Hume and Voltaire, Robertson and Schlözer, are denounced for using the measuring rod of their own time. All civilizations are incommensurable.[2] The critic must, so far as he is able, surrender to his author and seek to see with the author's eyes. Herder disagrees with Diderot's justly celebrated theory of the actor who is inwardly detached from it when he plays a role.[3] The true interpreter must seek to penetrate—lose himself in—the original which he, as it were, recreates even if he can never wholly achieve this. Genuine translation

---

1 V, 502.   2 V, 509.

3 'Nous sentons, nous; ils observent...' (*Oeuvres*, ed. Assézat et Tourneux. VIII, 170-71).

from one language—that is, way of life—into another is, of course,
impossible; no real idiom is literally translatable: the olives sacred to
Minerva that grew round the Academy cannot be taken beyond the
frontiers of Athens. 'Even when Sparta ravaged Athens, the goddess
protected her grove. So no one can take the beauties of our language
from us: beauties woven into its texture, glimmering like Phryne's
bosom beneath her silken veil.'[1] To translate is—for better or for worse
—to create; the translation must be an *Originalarbeit* by a *Schöpferisches
Genie*;[2] and, of course, because the creator is what he is, and not someone or somewhere else, a great deal is, and must be, lost. Egypt must not
be judged by Greek criteria, or by Shaftesbury's modern ones; the
schoolboy is not joyless because he takes no pleasure in the avocations
of a grown man, nor were the Middle Ages worthless because they
do not please Voltaire: there is more in the great ferment of the Dark
Ages than the absurdities of Ripuarian or Salic laws. The mediaeval
culture of the West must be seen as a great revolt against the suffocating
centralization of Rome, a 'rewinding of the gigantic, run-down clock.'
To denounce and idealize it is equally absurd: 'I am by no means
disposed to defend the constant migrations and devastations, the feudal
wars, the hordes of monks, the pilgrimages, the crusades. I only want
to explain them: to show the spirit that breathed through it all, the
seething of human forces'. This was original enough in 1774. The
Middle Ages are not a corridor to the Renaissance, nor is paganism
an ante-room of Christianity. One culture is never a mere means to
another; even if there is a sense in which mankind as a whole is advancing,[3] each of the stages is an end in itself: men are never means to ends
beyond themselves. No less than his opponent Kant, he fervently
preaches the doctrine that only persons and societies, and almost all
of these, are good in themselves—indeed they are all that is good,
wholly good, in the world that we know. These maxims, which now
(at least in the West) seem so platitudinous, were antinomian heresies
in the middle of the eighteenth century in Paris and its intellectual
dependencies.

So much for the myth of the Dominant Model. Still bolder was

[1] II, 44.
[2] I, 173; I, 178.
[3] Herder does not make clear what he means by the progress—*Fortgang*—
of mankind: relativism is, on the face of it, incompatible with belief in objective
progress. But see pp. 190-4 below.

Herder's rejection of the historical myths of the century;[1] of the French myth of classical culture created by the Gallo-Romans, in which lay the true soul of France, and which the barbarians destroyed, and equally of the counter-myth of the superiority of the Frankish conquerors, to which support had been given by Montesquieu, Mallet, and Boulainvilliers. Similarly Herder has no truck with the Renaissance myth of the sunlit pagan world killed by the gloomy, pleasure-destroying Christian religion; he uses harsh words about the monks who suppressed the old German songs; but this does not mean that the Middle Ages are the dark haunt of the 'demons, slaves, diabolical priests and tyrants' painted by Voltaire, Gibbon, Hume, and later still, Heine and all the neo-pagans. But neither does he uphold the growing German-Protestant legend of the uncorrupted, fearless, Cheruscan warrior Hermann canonized by Klopstock as Arminius, and then, in the shape of the young Siegfried, placed by Wagner in the German nationalist pantheon. These fantasies offer no avenue of escape. All attempts to flee, whether to modern Paris or the dark German woods, are condemned by Herder as being equally deluded. Those who, for whatever reason, will not face reality are doomed.

The third great myth of the eighteenth century was that of steady progress, if not inevitable, at least virtually certain; with consequent disparagement of the benighted past, which entailed the view of all earlier centuries as so many steps toward the superior life of the present and the still more wonderful life of the future. Herder rejects this completely. 'Each [culture] is a harmonious lyre—one must merely have the ear to hear its melodies.' Those who seek to understand must learn to grasp the respects in which Abraham or Leonidas or Caesar are not men of our time—to see change as it occurs, not in juxtaposed segments which can be detached, compared, and awarded marks for merit, for the degree to which they approach our standards of enlightenment. Is there, then, no progress? Are all cultures equally valuable? This is not Herder's view. There is *Fortgang*, but this is not the same as the notion of progress enunciated by, say, Turgot or Condorcet, or, in particular, by Voltaire (for example, in *La Philosophie d'histoire par feu l'Abbé Bazin*), against whom, together with the Swiss philosopher of history, Iselin, Herder's thunderbolts are specifically directed. Theirs is a shallow, unhistorical delusion. Diversity is everything. This

---

[1] M. Rouché (*op. cit.*) deals with this far more faithfully than Herder's better known German commentators.

is the central thesis of, to give it its full title, *Auch eine Philosophie der Geschichte zur Bildung der Menschheit*, as of almost all Herder's early writings. 'The general, philosophical, philanthropic temper of our age seeks to extend "our own ideal" of virtue and happiness to each distant nation, even to the remotest ages in history. . . . Those who have thus far taken it upon themselves to explain the centuries of progress, have mostly cherished the notion that it must lead to ever increasing happiness. In support of this they have embroidered or invented facts, played down or suppressed facts that belie it . . . taken words for works, enlightenment for happiness, and so invented the figment of "the general progressive improvement of the world".' Others realized that this was a dangerous delusion, and fell into hopeless scepticism like Montaigne, Bayle, Hume, and ultimately even Voltaire and Diderot. This rests on a misconception of what progress is. It lies in a variety of cultures, incommensurable with each other and incapable of being arranged on some single scale of progress or retrogression. Each society, each culture, develops in its own way. 'Each age is different, and each has the centre of its happiness within itself. The youth is not happier than the innocent, contented child; nor is the peaceful old man less happy than the vigorous man in the prime of life.' The Middle Ages are full of 'abominations, errors, absurdities', but also possess 'something solid, cohesive and majestic' which our age, with its 'enervated coldness and human misery', can scarcely understand. 'Light does not nourish men', order and affluence are not enough; still less technical accomplishment 'in the hands of one person, or of a few, who do the thinking' for everyone. There are many ways of life and many truths — to believe that 'everything is either true or false' is 'a wretched general illusion' of our progressive age. True *Fortgang* ('advance') is the development of human beings as integrated wholes and, more particularly, their development as groups — tribes, cultures, and communities determined by language and custom, creating out of the 'totality of their collective experience',[1] and expressing themselves in works of art that are consequently intelligible to common men, and in sciences and crafts and forms of social and political and cultural life that fulfil the cravings (conscious and unconscious) and develop the faculties of a given society, in its interplay with its alterable, but not greatly alterable, natural environment. 'To bind and interrogate this Proteus, which is usually called national character and which shows

----

[1] XI, 225; XVII, 59; XVIII, 346; XXX, 8.

itself certainly not less in the writings than in the usages and actions of a nation—that is a high and beautiful philosophy. It is practised most surely in poetry; for in the works of imagination and feeling the entire soul of nations reveals itself most freely.'[1] This is what the classical Greeks succeeded in doing so marvellously. Despite all Hamann's anathemas, Herder cannot refrain from expressing his passionate admiration for the culture of Athens—a feeling that he shared with Goethe and Hegel, Hölderlin and Schiller, and, indeed, with the majority of the civilized Germans of his time, romantic and anti-romantic alike. Herder thinks the Greek achievement is in part due to the beauty of nature in Greece, a beauty which inspired principles that those fortunate inhabitants (mistakenly but excusably) regarded as objective and universally valid. But there must be no *Favoritvolk*; he hastens to add to the list Kashmiris and Persians, Bokharans and Circassians, who also lived in beautiful natural surroundings, grew handsome themselves and produced beautiful cultures (unlike the Hebrews, whose merits are not aesthetic). The Greeks advanced; they developed their own faculties harmoniously and triumphantly, because nature was propitious and because no great natural accidents arrested this development. But they are not a hallway to the Romans, whose civilization must be judged in terms of its own internal criteria, its own 'centre of gravity'. What he calls *Fortgang* is the internal development of a culture in its own *habitat*, towards its own goals; but because there are some qualities that are universal in man, one culture can study, understand, and admire another, even though it cannot return to it and will only make itself foolish if it tries. At times Herder speaks like Bossuet: as if history were not an episodic story but a vast drama; as if the finger of God guided the destinies of humanity in some teleological fashion, a play in which each great cultural epoch was an act. He does not develop this notion, which led Bossuet to see each act as in some degree a link between its predecessor and its successor. More often he speaks as if history were indeed a drama, but one without a *dénouement*: as if it were like a cosmic symphony of which each movement is significant in itself, and of which, in any case, we cannot hear the whole, for God alone does so. The later movements are not necessarily closer to, or a prefiguring of, some ultimate goal and, therefore, superior to the earlier movements. Life is not a jigsaw puzzle of which the fragments must

[1] XVIII, 57-8.

fit into some single pattern in terms of which alone they are all intelligible, so that what seems, taken in isolation, irrational or ugly, is seen to be an indispensable ingredient in the great harmonious whole—the world Spirit come to full self-consciousness of itself, in Hegel's famous image. Herder believes in the development of each movement of the symphony (each act of the drama) in terms of its own ends, its own values, which are none the worse or less morally valuable because they will pass or be destroyed and be succeeded by others. There is a general purpose to be achieved by human life on earth, which he calls *Humanität*. This is a notoriously vague term, in Herder and the *Aufklärung* generally, connoting harmonious development of all immortal souls towards universally valid goals: reason, freedom, toleration, mutual love and respect between individuals and societies, as well as physical and spiritual health, finer perceptions, dominion over the earth, the harmonious realization of all that God has implanted in His noblest work and made in His own image.[1] This is a characteristically all-inclusive, general and optimistic formula of Weimar humanism, which Herder does, indeed, adopt, particularly in his later works, but which he does not seem to have used (for it has no precise connotation) as a universal criterion either of explanation or of value. He wants above all to be comprehensive and fair. He dislikes Gothic architecture despite the eloquence with which he made so deep an impression on Goethe in Strasbourg; he is repelled by chivalry, by mediaeval values in general, but he defends them against Voltaire, against caricatures. He placed no great value, particularly towards the end of his life, upon primitivism as such, and in this respect differed from its true admirers in the eighteenth century. Yet colonial subjugation of native populations, ancient and modern, in and outside Europe, is always represented as being morally odious and as a crime against humanity. If paganism requires to be defended against Christian attack, and Homer against Klotz and the *Encyclopédie*, so must Christianity be defended against Holbach, Voltaire, and the Sinophiles, and the Chinese and Mongols in their turn against the arrogance of Europeans. The shamans of central Asia, he insists, are not just deceivers; nor are myths simply false statements about reality invented by wicked priests to bamboozle and acquire power over the masses, as Bayle and Voltaire had made the world believe; nor are the inventions of poets merely intended to give pleasure or to instruct. Here he stands with Vico, some time before he read him;

[1] See the remarks on *Humanität* in XIII, 154.

one wonders whether he ever more than merely glanced at his work. Shamans express in the form of myth and superstition objects of men's natural wishes—a vision of the world from which poetry naturally springs and which it expresses. Whole worlds are created by such poetry, worlds worthy of man and his creative powers, worlds not commensurable with other worlds, but all equally worthy of our interest and in need of our insight, because they are worlds made by men; by contemplating them we may succeed in grasping what we, in our turn, can be and create. We do this not by learning the lessons of the past (he sometimes says that the past repeats itself, but his central doctrine, in opposition to Hume or Voltaire, is that each page is unique), but rather because the vision of past creation inspires us to find our own centre of gravity, our own *Mittelpunkt* or *Schwerpunkt* or that of the group—nation, region, community—to which we belong. Without such belonging there is no true creation and no true realization of human goals. Hence to foist a set of alien values on another *Nation* (as missionaries have done in the Baltic provinces, and are doing, for example, in India) is both ineffective and harmful.[1] Worst of all are those who have no group, because they are exiled or self-exiled, physically or spiritually (for Herder the two are not very different), and are doomed to sterility. Such disintegration seemed to him to threaten the Germans in his own day. Indignantly some of his modern critics point out that he condemned France—the France of the eighteenth and nineteenth centuries!—as being an exhausted society. But whatever his failings as a prophet (and he speaks with many voices, some of them far from distinct and often uttering contradictory sentiments), as a social psychologist he rose above his generation; more clearly than any other writer, he conceived and cast light upon the crucially important social function of 'belonging'—on what it is to belong to a group, a culture, a movement, a form of life. It was a most original achievement.

VII

'It is the composer's duty, as a member of society, to speak to and for his fellow human-beings.'

'I believe in roots, in associations, in backgrounds, in personal relationships . . . My music has its roots in where I live and work.'

BENJAMIN BRITTEN, on receiving the first Aspen Award, 1964.

[1] VII, 210, 303.

The notion of belonging is at the heart of all Herder's ideas. His doctrine of the unity of theory and practice, like that of his populism, is intelligible only in terms of it. To belong is not a passive condition, but active co-operation, social labour. 'Complete truth is always only the Deed.'[1] Whether one reads the last books of his *Ideas about the Philosophy of History of Mankind*, the earlier treatise *On Hebrew Poetry*, the essays on Shakespeare, Ossian, Homer, the critical 'Groves', or the late *Adrastea* or *Kalligone*, one finds that what dominates them all is the notion that there are central patterns in terms of which each genuine culture—and the human beings who constitute it—can, and indeed must, be identified. For Herder, to be a member of a group is to think and act in a certain way, in the light of particular goals, values, pictures of the world: and to think and act so is to belong to a group. The notions are literally identical. To be a German is to be part of a unique stream of which language is the dominant element, but still only one element among others. He conveys the notion that the ways in which a people—say, the Germans—speak or move, eat or drink, their handwriting, their laws, their music, their social outlook, their dance forms, their theology, have patterns and qualities in common which they do not share, or share to a notably lesser degree, with the similar activities of some other group—the French, the Icelanders, the Arabs, the ancient Greeks. Each of these activities belongs to a cluster which must be grasped as a whole: they illuminate each other. Anyone who studies the speech rhythms, or the history or the architecture, or the physical characteristics of the Germans, will thereby achieve a deeper understanding of German legislation, music, dress. There is a property, not capable of being abstracted and articulated—that which is German in the Germans—which all these diverse activities uniquely evince. Activities like hunting, painting, worship, common to many groups in widely differing times and places, will resemble each other because they belong to the same genus. But the specific quality which each type of activity will show forth will have more in common with generically different activities of the same culture[2] than with specifically similar activities of another culture. Or, at the very least, that which the various activities of the same culture will have in common—the

---

[1] 'Die vollstaendige Wahrheit ist immer nur That', he wrote in 1774, long before Fichte or Hegel (*Uebers Erkennen und Empfinden in der Menschlichen Seele*, VIII).

[2] This notion is to be found in Hamann.

common pervasive pattern in virtue of which they are seen to be elements in one and the same culture—is more important, since it accounts for the characteristics of these activities at a deeper level, than their more superficial resemblances to the corresponding activities of other cultures and other human groups. In other words, what German epic poetry has in common with German family life, or German legislation, or German grammar, determines the patterns of these activities—runs through them more deeply—than that which German poetry has in common with Hindu or Hebrew poetry. This common property is not occult; no special non-empirical faculty is needed to detect it; it is a natural attribute and open to empirical investigation. Despite his theology, his belief in the primacy of religion, and his use of such metaphysical notions as the collective 'soul' and 'spirit', despite the mysterious *Kräfte*, despite occasional lapses into acceptance of the dogma of natural kinds, Herder was far more of an empiricist from the beginning to the end of his life than Leibniz, Kant, or even Helvétius. This was obscured by the fact that the following generation of German metaphysicians whom he influenced dealt freely in transcendent formulas. Yet in his own day he was at times suspected by the stricter among his fellow churchmen of inclining dangerously toward materialistic heresies. The heart of his empiricism lay in the importance that he attributed to the discovery of patterns in history and nature. It is this directly perceptible, but literally unanalysable, pattern quality in virtue of which what Germans think or do or say is, as a rule, characteristically and unmistakably German, it is this *Gestalt* quality[1] that, in his view, makes us attribute the doer and the deed, the thinker and the thought, to a specific German culture at a specific stage of its development. To fit into such a pattern is to belong: it is for this and no other reason that a German exiled from the milieu of his fellow Germans, perhaps a Saxon or a Prussian forced to live elsewhere, will not feel at home there; and whoever does not feel at home cannot create naturally, freely, generously, unself-consciously, in the manner that Schiller called 'naïve', and that Herder, whether he admits it or not, most admires and believes in. All his talk about the national character, the national genius, the *Volksseele*, the spirit of the people and so forth, in the end comes to this alone. His notion of

[1] Since originally writing this, I was glad to find it strongly confirmed by Professor H. B. Nisbet (*Herder, Goethe and the National Type*, Publications of the English Goethe Society, 1967, pp. 267-283).

what it is to belong to a family, a sect, a place, a period, a style, is the foundation of his populism, and of all the later conscious programmes for self-integration or re-integration among men who felt scattered, exiled, or alienated. The language in which he speaks of his unfortunate fellow countrymen, driven through poverty or the despotic whims of their masters to Russia or Transylvania or America to become 'blacks and slaves', is not simply a lament for the material and moral miseries of exile, but is based on the view that to cut men off from the 'living centre'—from the texture to which they naturally belong—or to force them to sit by the rivers of some remote Babylon, and to prostitute their creative faculties for the benefit of strangers, is to degrade, dehumanize, destroy them.[1] No writer has stressed more vividly the damage done to human beings by being torn from the only conditions in which their history has made it possible for them to live full lives. He insists over and over again that no one milieu or group or way of life is necessarily superior to any other; but it is what it is, and assimilation to a single universal pattern, of laws or language or social structure, as advocated by the French *lumières*, would destroy what is most living and valuable in life and art. Hence the fierce polemic against Voltaire, who, in his *Essai sur les Moeurs*, declared that 'Man, generally speaking, was always what he is now'.[2] or that 'morality is the same in all civilized nations'. Hence, by definition, it seemed to follow that the rest were barbarous or stupid: 'Gauls are a disgrace to nature'.[3] Hence, too, the attack on Sulzer for demanding a universal philosophical grammar, according to the rules of which one would be enabled to judge of the degree of the perfection of a people's language, and, if need be, correct its rules in the light of the universal rules. Needless to say, this for Herder was both false in principle and the death of poetry and the springs of all creative power. Every group has a right to be happy in its own way. It is terrible arrogance to affirm that, to be happy, everyone should become European.[4]

[1] 'No Tyrtaeus', he wrote in 1775, 'will follow our brothers who have been sold to America as soldiers, no Homer will sing of this sad expedition. When religion, people, country, are crushed, when these very notions are grown shadowy, the poet's lyre can yield only muted, strangled sounds' (quoted from *Die Ursachen des gesunkenen Geschmacks bei den verschiedenen Völker da er geblühet*).

[2] *Essai sur les Moeurs et l'Esprit des Nations*, Paris, 1785, p. 32.

[3] *Op. cit.*, p. 53 (quoted from 'Voltaire's Philosophy of History' by Jerome Rosenthal, *Journal of the History of Ideas*, XVI, April, 1955, No. 2, pp. 151-79).

[4] *Ideen zur Philosophie der Geschichte der Menschheit*, VIII, ch. 5.

This is so not because, as Voltaire maintained, other cultures may be superior to ours, but simply because they are not comparable. 'No man can convey the character of *his* feeling, or transform my being into his.'[1] 'The negro is as much entitled to think the white man degenerate as the white man to think the former a black beast. . . . The civilization of man is not that of the European; it manifests itself, according to time and place, in every people.'[2] There is no *Favoritvolk*. Herder assumes only that to be fully human, that is, fully creative, one must belong somewhere, to some group or some historical stream which cannot be defined save in the genetic terms of a tradition, a milieu and a culture, themselves generated by natural forces—the *Klima* (i.e. the external world) and physical structure and biological needs which, in interplay with every individual's mind and will, create the dynamic, collective process called society.

This theory entails no mythology. For Herder all groups are ultimately collections of individuals; his use of 'organic' and 'organism' is still wholly metaphorical and not, as in later, more metaphysical thinkers, only half metaphorical. There is no evidence that he conceived of groups as metaphysical 'super-individual' entities or values. For Herder this is no mystique of history, or of a species to which individuals were to be sacrificed, still less of the superior wisdom of the race, or of a particular nation or even of humanity as a whole. Nevertheless, to understand men is to understand them genetically, in terms of their history, of the one complex of spiritual and physical 'forces' in which they feel free and at home. This notion of being at home, and the corresponding notion of homelessness ('nostalgia', he once remarked, 'is the noblest of all pains') which lies at the heart of his reflections on the emptiness of cosmopolitanism, on the damage done to men by social barriers, oppression by strangers, division, specialization—like the connected concepts of exploitation, and of the alienation of men from each other, and, in the end, from their own true selves—derives from his one central conception. Those who have grasped the notion that men are made miserable not only by poverty, disease, stupidity, or the effects of ignorance, but also because they are misfits or outsiders or not spoken to, that liberty and equality are nothing without fraternity; that only those societies are truly

---

[1] *Ideen zur Philosophie der Geschichte der Menschheit*, VIII, ch. 5.

[2] XVIII, 247-9, see F. M. Barnard, *op. cit.*, p. 24, from whom I have adapted this translation.

human which may follow a leader but obey no master,[1] are in possession of one of Herder's *idées maîtresses*. His writings radically transformed the notion of relations of men to each other. Hegel's famous definition of freedom as *bey sich selbst seyn*, as well as his doctrine of *Anerkennung*—reciprocal recognition among men—seem to me to owe much to Herder's teaching. The proposition that man is by nature sociable had been uttered by Aristotle and repeated by Cicero, Aquinas, Hooker, Grotius, Locke and innumerable others. The depth and breadth of Herder's writings on human association and its vicissitudes, the wealth of concrete historical and psychological observation with which he developed the concept of what it is for men to belong to a community, made such formulas seem to be thin abstractions and drove them permanently out of circulation. No serious social theorist after Herder dared advance mechanical clichés of this type in lieu of thought. His vision of society has dominated Western thought; the extent of its influence has not always been recognized because it has entered too deeply into the texture of ordinary thinking. His immense impact, of which Goethe spoke and to which J. S. Mill bore witness, is due principally to his central thesis—his account of what it is to live and act together—from which the rest of his thought flows, and to which it constantly returns. This idea is at the heart of all populism. And it has entered every subsequent attempt to arrive at truth about society.

VIII

So much for Herder's specific contribution to the understanding of men and their history. There are two implications of his conception of men that have received little attention from his interpreters. These are, first, his doctrine of the indivisibility of the human personality and, as a corollary of this, his conception of the artist and his expressive role in society; and secondly, his pluralism and the doctrine of the incompatibility of ultimate human ends. Herder was, as everyone knows, much occupied with aesthetic questions and tried to seek out

---

[1] 'The man who needs a master is an animal; as soon as he becomes human, he no longer needs any master at all' (XII, 383). This is specifically directed against Kant's statement, 'men, like animals, need masters', in the *Idea for a Universal History from a Cosmopolitan Point of View* (Prussian Academy edition, 1923, VIII, 23). But see also Kant's *Was ist Aufklärung?* and Herder's letter to Hamann of February 14, 1775.

all manifestations of art in their richest and fullest forms. He tended to find them in the creations of the early ages of man. For Herder art is the expression of men in society in their fullness. To say that art is expression is to say that it is a voice speaking rather than the production of an object—a poem, a painting, a golden bowl, a symphony, all of which possess their own properties, like objects in nature—independently of the purposes or character or *milieu* of the men who created them.[1] By the very appropriately called *Stimmen der Völker in Liedern*, and by explicit argument, Herder seeks to demonstrate that all that a man does and says and creates must express, whether he intends it to do so or not, his whole personality; and, since a man is not conceivable outside a group to which, if he is reasonably fortunate, he continues to belong (he retains its characteristics in a mutilated state, even if he has been torn from it), he conveys also the 'collective individuality'[2]—a culture conceived as a constant flow of thought, feeling, action, and expression. Hence, he is bitterly opposed to the view, influential in his day as in ours, that the purpose of the artist is to create an object whose merits are independent of the creator's personal qualities or his intentions, conscious or unconscious, or of his social situation. This is an aesthetic doctrine that reigned long before the doctrine of art for art's sake had been explicitly formulated. The craftsman who makes a golden bowl is entitled, according to this view, to say that it is no business of those who acquire or admire his creation to inquire whether he is himself sincere or calculating, pious or an atheist, a faithful husband, politically sound, a sympathetic boon companion or morally pure. Herder is the true father of the doctrine that it is the artist's mission, above others, to testify in his works to the truth of his own inner experience;[3] from which it follows that any conscious falsification of this experience, from whatever motive—indeed any attempt merely to satisfy the taste of his customers, to titillate their senses, or even to offer them instruction by means that have little to do with his own life or convictions, or to use techniques and skills as a detached exercise, to practise virtuosity for its own sake or for the sake of the pleasure it brings—is a betrayal of his calling. This was implicit in the artistic movement which came to be called *Sturm und Drang*, of which

---

[1] A doctrine maintained, so it seemed to Herder, by such despotic Paris arbiters of artistic beauty as the disciples of Boileau—the abbés Du Bos, Batteux and the like.

[2] V, 502.   [3] But cp. p. 88, n. 1.

Herder was one of the leaders. To view oneself as a professional who in his works of art plays a role, or performs with a specialized part of himself, while the rest of him is left free to observe the performance; to maintain that one's behaviour as a man—as a father, a Frenchman, a political terrorist—can be wholly detached from one's professional function as a carpenter, doctor, artist, this view, to which Voltaire, if he had considered it, could scarcely have offered any objection, is, for all the writers of the *Sturm und Drang*, a fatal misapprehension and distortion of the nature of man and his relations with other men. Since man is in fact one and not many (and those who are genuinely divided personalities are literally no longer sane), it follows that whether a man be an artist, a politician, a lawyer, a soldier, anything that he does expresses all that he is. Some among the *Stürmer* remained individualistic —Heinse, for example, or Klinger. But Herder is uncompromisingly hostile to such egomania. The individual, for him, is inescapably a member of some group; consequently all that he does must express, consciously or unconsciously, the aspirations of his group. Hence, if he is conscious of his own acts (and all self-consciousness is embryonic assessment and therefore critical), such awareness, like all true criticism, is inevitably to a high degree social criticism, because it is the nature of human beings to be socially aware: expression is communication. Herder feels that all history shows this to be so. To divide (and not merely to distinguish as facets or aspects of one substance) body and soul, science and craft or art, the individual and society, description and evaluation, philosophical, scientific, or historical judgment, empirical and metaphysical statements, as if any of these could be independent of one another, is for Herder false, superficial, and misleading. The body is the image, the expression, of the soul, not its tomb or instrument or enemy. There are no 'iron planks between body and soul';[1] everything can pass into everything else by the insensible transitions of which Leibniz had spoken in his *Nouveaux Essais*. 'Once upon a time men were all things: poets, thinkers, legislators, land surveyors, musicians, warriors.' In those days there was unity of theory and practice, of man and citizen, a unity that the division of labour destroyed; after that 'Men became half thinkers, half feelers'.[2] There is, he remarks,

[1] VIII, 256-62.

[2] *Ibid.* The celebrated description in the introduction to Karl Marx's *German Ideology* of what a full human life could be, seems to be a direct echo of this doctrine.

something amiss about moralists who do not act, epic poets who are unheroic, orators who are not statesmen, and aestheticians who cannot create anything. Once doctrines are accepted uncritically—as dogmatic, unalterable, eternal truths—they become dead formulas, or else their meaning is fearfully distorted. Such ossification and decay lead to nonsense in thought and monstrous behaviour in practice.[1]

This doctrine was destined to have a great flowering, not merely in the application of the concept of alienation in the writings of the young Marx and his friends in their Left-Hegelian phase, and among those who have used these ideas in our own time, but more particularly among pre-Marxist Russian radicals and revolutionaries. No body of men ever believed so devoutly and passionately in the unity of man as the Russian intelligentsia of the last century. These men—at first dissident members of the nobility and gentry, later members of many classes—were united by a burning faith in the right and duty of all men to realize their creative potentialities (physical and spiritual, intellectual and artistic) in the light of the reason and the moral insight with which all men are endowed. What the eighteenth-century French *philosophes* and the German Romantics preached, these men sought to practise. Light to them came from the West. And since the number of literate—let alone well-educated—men in Russia was infinitesimal compared to the number who lived in ignorance, misery, hopeless starvation and poverty, it was plainly the first duty of any decent man to give all he could to the effort to lift his brothers to a level where they could lead a human existence. From this sprang the conception of the intelligentsia as a sacred order called upon by history to dedicate their lives to the discovery and use of all possible means—intellectual and moral, artistic and technological, scientific and educational—in a single-minded effort to discover the truth, realize it in their lives, and with its aid to rescue the 'hungry and the naked', and make it possible for them to live in freedom and be men once more. Man is one and undivided; whatever he is and does flows from a single centre; but at the same time he is as he is within a social web of which he is a constituent; to ignore it is to falsify the nature of man. The famous doctrine that the artist, and above all the writer, has a social obligation to express the nature of the milieu in which he lives, and that he has no right to isolate himself artificially, under the cover of some theory about the need for moral neutrality, or the need for specialization, the purity of

1 XIII, 195.

art, or of its specifically aesthetic function—a priestly task that is to be kept uncontaminated, especially by politics—this entire conception, over which such ferocious battles were fought in the following century, stems from Herder's doctrine of the unity of man.

'Everything that a man undertakes, whether it be produced in action or word or anything else, must spring from his whole united powers; all separation of powers is to be repudiated.'[1] These words of Hamann's, so much admired by Goethe, formed Herder, and became (through Schiller and Friedrich Schlegel) the creed of the Russian radical critics. Whatever a man does, if he is as he should be, will express his entire nature. The worst sin is to mutilate oneself, to suppress this or that side of oneself, in the service of some false aesthetic or political or religious ideal. This is the heart of the revolt against the 'pruned' French garden of the eighteenth century. Blake is a passionate spokesman of this faith no less than Hamann or Herder or Schleiermacher. To understand any creator—any poet or, for that matter, any human being who is not half dead—is to understand his age and nation, his way of life, the society which (like nature in Shaftesbury) 'thinks in him'. Herder says over and over again that the true artist (in the widest sense) creates only out of the fullness of the experience of his whole society, especially out of its memories and antiquities which shape its 'collective individuality'; and he proceeds to speak of Chaucer, Shakespeare, Spenser, as being steeped in their national folk-lore. About this he may be mistaken, but the direction of his thought is clear enough. Poetry—and, indeed, all literature and all art—are the direct expression of uninhibited life. The expression of life may be disciplined, but life itself must not be so. As early poetry was magical, a spur to 'heroes, hunters, lovers', men of action, a continuation of experience, so, *mutatis mutandis*, it must be so now also. Society may have sadly disintegrated since those days, and Herder concedes that the rhapsodical Klopstock may now be able consciously to express only his own individual, rather than the communal, life; but express he must whatever is in him, and his words will communicate the experience of his society to his fellow men. 'A poet is a creator of a people; he gives it a world to contemplate, he holds its soul in his hand.'[2] He is, of course,

---

[1] Quoted from Goethe's *Dichtung und Wahrheit*, Bk. 6, Ch. 12, by Professor Roy Pascal, in *The German Sturm und Drang* (Manchester University Press, 1953), who gives an admirable account, the best in English, of this entire movement.

[2] VIII, 33.

to an equal extent created by it.[1] A man lives in a world of which, together with others, he is in some sense the maker. 'We live in a world we ourselves create.'[2] These words of Herder's were destined to be inflated into extravagant metaphysical shapes by Fichte, Schelling, Hegel, and the Idealist Movement in philosophy; but they are equally at the source of the profoundest sociological insights of Marx and the revolution in the historical outlook that he initiated.[3]

Herder may be regarded as being among the originators of the doctrine of artistic commitment—perhaps with Hamann the earliest thinker consciously to speak (as one would expect of the founder of populism) in terms of the totally *engagé* writer, to see the artist as *ipso facto* committed and not permitted to divide himself into compartments, to separate body from spirit, the secular from the sacred, and, above all, life from art. He believed from the beginning to the end of his life that all men are in some degree artists, and that all artists are, first and last, men—fathers, sons, friends, citizens, fellow worshippers, men united by common action. Hence the purpose of art is not to exist for its own sake (the late *Adrastea* and *Kalligone* are the most ferocious attacks on this doctrine which he suspected both Kant and Goethe of advancing) or to be utilitarian, or propagandist, or 'social realist'; still less, of course, should it seek merely to embellish life or invent forms of pleasure or produce artefacts for the market. The artist is a sacred vessel which is shaped by, and the highest expression of, the spirit of his time and place and society; he is the man who conveys, as far as possible, a total human experience, an entire world. This is the doctrine that, under the impulsion of German romanticism and French socialism, profoundly affected the conception of the artist and his relation to society, and animated Russian critics and writers from the late eighteen-thirties until, at any rate, *Doctor Zhivago*. The theory of art as total expression and of the artist as a man who testifies to the truth—as opposed to the concept of him as a purveyor, however gifted and dedicated, or as a priest of an esoteric cult—entered the practice of the great

---

[1] II, 61.   [2] VIII, 252.

[3] It is odd that one of Hamann's most fruitful observations—that the poetry of Livonian peasants in the country round Riga and Mitau which he knew well, was connected with the rhythms of their daily work, evidently made no impression on his disciple. Herder is fascinated by the intimate relation of action and speech, e.g. in his theory of why it is that (as he supposed) verbs precede nouns in primitive speech, but ignores the influence of work. This was made good much later under Saint-Simonian and Marxist influence.

Russian novelists of the nineteenth century, even of such 'pure' writers as Turgenev and Chekhov. Through their works it has had a great, indeed a decisive influence, not only on the literature and criticism, but on the moral and political ideas and behaviour of the West, and indeed of the entire world. Consequently, Herder was perhaps not altogether mistaken when he so confidently proclaimed the part to be played by the artist in the world to come. Whether as an aesthetic critic, or as a philosopher of history, or as a creator of the notion of the non-alienated man, or as the most vehement critic of the classifiers and dividers, Herder (with Hamann) emerges as the originator of the doctrine of the unity of art and life, theory and practice. He is the most eloquent of all the preachers of the restoration of the unbroken human being by the growth of civilization, *Humanität*, whether by an act of spiritual water-divining whereby the buried stream of the true humanist tradition may be found and continued, or, as Rousseau demanded, by some social transformation that will destroy the shackles that crib and confine men, and will allow them to enter or re-enter the Garden of Eden which they lost when they yielded to the temptation to organize and dominate one another. Once the walls that separate men are knocked down, walls of state or class or race or religion, they will 'return to themselves' and be men and creative once again. The influence of this part of his teaching on the ideas of others, who spoke more articulately and acted with greater political effect, has been very great.[1]

[1] Like other passionate propagandists, Herder pleaded for that which he himself conspicuously lacked. As sometimes happens, what the prophet saw before him was a great compensatory fantasy. The vision of the unity of the human personality and its integration into the social organism by 'natural' means was the polar opposite of Herder's own character and conduct. He was, by all accounts, a deeply divided, touchy, resentful, bitter, unhappy man, in constant need of support and praise, neurotic, pedantic, difficult, suspicious, and often insupportable. When he speaks about the 'wholly irreplaceable feeling of being alive' (XIII, 337) and compares it with the carefully tended, over-arranged world of, say, the critic Sulzer, he is evidently speaking of an experience which he longed for but must often have lacked. It has frequently been remarked that it is tormented and unbalanced personalities—Rousseau, Nietzsche, D. H. Lawrence—who celebrate with particular passion physical beauty, strength, generosity, spontaneity, above all unbroken unity, harmony and serenity, qualities for which they had an insatiable craving. No man felt less happy in the Prussia of Frederick the Great, or even in the enlightened Weimar of Goethe and Wieland and Schiller, than Herder. Wieland, the most amiable and tolerant of men, found him maddening. Goethe said that he had in him something compulsively vicious—like a vicious horse—a desire to bite and hurt. His ideals seem at times a mirror image of his own frustrations.

IX

Finally, I come to what is perhaps the most revolutionary of the implications of Herder's position, his famous rejection of absolute values, his pluralism. Men, according to Herder, truly flourish only in congenial circumstances, that is, where the group to which they belong has achieved a fruitful relationship with the environment by which it is shaped and which in turn it shapes. There the individual is happily integrated into the 'natural community',[1] which grows spontaneously, like a plant, and is not held together by artificial clamps, or soldered together by sheer force, or regulated by laws and regulations invented, whether benevolently or not, by the despot or his bureaucrats. Each of these natural societies contains within itself (in the words of *Yet Another Philosophy of History*) the 'ideal of its own perfection, wholly independent of all comparison with those of others'. If this is so, how must we answer the question, put by men throughout recorded history and settled with such clarity and authority by the great *lumières* of the eighteenth century, namely: What is the best life for men? And, more particularly, What is the most perfect society? There is, after all, no dearth of solutions. Every age has provided its own formulas. Some have looked for the solution in sacred books or in revelation or in the words of inspired prophets or the tradition of organized priesthoods; others found it in the rational insight of the skilled metaphysician, or in the combination of scientific observation and experiment, or in the 'natural' good sense of men not 'scribbled over' by philosophers or theologians or perverted by 'interested error'. Still others have found it only in the uncorrupted heart of the simple good man. Some thought that only trained experts could discover great and saving truths; others supposed that on questions of value all sane men were equally well qualified to judge. Some maintained that such truths could be discovered at any time, and that it was mere bad luck that it had taken so long to find the most important among them, or that they had been so

---

1 This is the real community which was later (even before Tönnies) contrasted with the artificial *Gesellschaft*; e.g. Fichte's *Totum* as contrasted with his *Compositum*. But in Herder there are still no explicitly metaphysical overtones: the *Kräfte* realized in communal life—the dynamic forces which he probably derives from Leibniz—are neither discovered nor act in any *a priori* or transcendent fashion: but neither are they described as being susceptible to scientific tests; their nature, a puzzle to his commentators, evidently did not seem problematic to Herder.

easily forgotten. Others held that mankind was subject to the law of growth; and that the truth would not be seen in its fullness until mankind had reached maturity—the age of reason. Some doubted even this, and said men could never attain to such knowledge on earth; or if they did, were too weak to follow it in practice, since such perfection was attainable only by angels, or in the life hereafter. But one assumption was common to all these views: that it was, at any rate in principle, possible to draw some outline of the perfect society or the perfect man, if only to define how far a given society or a given individual fell short of the ideal. This was necessary if one was to be able to compare degrees of imperfection. But this belief in the final objective answer had not been absolutely universal. Relativists held that different circumstances and temperaments demanded different policies: but, for the most part, even they supposed that, though the routes might differ, the ultimate goal—human happiness, the satisfaction of human wishes—was one and the same. Some sceptical thinkers in the ancient world—Carneades, for example—went further and uttered the disquieting thought that some ultimate values might be incompatible with one another, so that no solution could logically incorporate them all. There was something of this doubt about the logic of the concept of the perfect society not only among the Greeks, but in the Renaissance too, in Pontano, in Montaigne, in Machiavelli, and after them in Leibniz and Rousseau, who thought that no gain could be made without a corresponding loss. Something of this, too, seemed to lie at the heart of the tragedies of Sophocles, Euripides, Shakespeare. Nevertheless, the central stream of the Western tradition was little affected by this fundamental doubt. The central assumption was that problems of value were in principle soluble, and soluble with finality. Whether the solutions could be implemented by imperfect men was another question, a question which did not affect the rationality of the universe. This is the keystone of the classical arch which, after Herder, began to crumble.

If Herder's view of mankind was correct—if Germans in the eighteenth century cannot become Greeks or Romans or ancient Hebrews or simple shepherds, still less all of these together; and if each of the civilizations into which he infuses so much life by his sympathetic *Einfühlen* are widely different, and indeed uncombinable—then how could there exist, even in principle, one universal ideal, valid for all men, at all times, everywhere? The 'physiognomies' of cultures are unique: each presents a wonderful exfoliation of human potentialities in its own time and place and environment. We are forbidden to make judgments of comparative value, for that is measuring the incommensurable. And even though Herder himself may not always be consistent in this respect, since he condemns and praises entire civilizations, his doctrine, at least in his most original works, does not permit this. Nor can it be doubted that he himself made valiant efforts to live up to his earlier principles: for all his dislike of the rigidly centralized Egyptian establishment, or Roman imperialism, or the brutal chivalry of the Middle Ages, or the dogmatism and intolerance of the Catholic Church, he sought to be not merely fair to these civilizations, but to represent them as each realizing an ideal of indefeasible validity which, as an expression of a particular manifestation of the human spirit, was valuable in itself, and not as a step to some higher order. It is this rejection of a central dogma of the Enlightenment which saw in each civilization either a stepping-stone to a higher one, or a sad relapse to an earlier and lower one, that gives force, sense of reality, and persuasive power to his vast panoramic survey. It is true that in the *Ideen* he enunciates the general ideal of *Humanität* towards which man is slowly climbing, and some of Herder's interpreters have faithfully attempted to represent his earlier relativism as a phase of his thought which he 'outgrew', or else to reconcile it with his hazy notion of a single progressive movement towards *Humanität*. Thus, Professor Max Rouché thinks that Herder conceives of history as a drama, each act, perhaps each scene, of which can and should be understood and evaluated independently; which does not prevent us from perceiving that, taken together, these episodes constitute a single progressive ascent.[1] Perhaps Herder did come to believe this, or to believe that he believed it. But it remains a vague conception; his skill and imagination, even in the *Ideen*, go into the evocation of the individual cultures and not of the alleged links between them. The whole thrust of the argument both in such early works as the *Älteste Urkunde des Menschengeschlechtes*, *Von deutscher Art und Kunst*, *Vom Geist der Ebräischen Poesie*, the *Kritische Wälder*, and in the late and mildly worded *Briefe zu Beförderung der Humanität*, and the *Ideen* itself, not to speak of his classical statement of historical relativism in *Auch Eine Philosophie der Geschichte*, is to show and celebrate the uniqueness, the individuality, and, above all, the incommensurability with one another of each of the

---

[1] Rouché, *op. cit.*, Introduction.

civilizations which he so lovingly describes and defends.[1] But if all these forms of life are intelligible each in its own terms (the only terms there are), if each is an 'organic' whole, a pattern of ends and means which cannot be resurrected, still less amalgamated, they can scarcely be graded as so many links in a cosmic objectively knowable progress, some stages of which are rendered automatically more valuable than others by their relationship—say, proximity to, or mirroring of—the final goal towards which humanity, however uncertainly, is marching. This places Herder's *Weltanschauung*, so far as it is consistent at all, despite all the insights that it shares with them, outside the 'perfectibilian' philosophies of modern times, as remote from the divine tactic of Bossuet (or even Burke) as from the doctrine of progress determined by the growth of reason preached by Lessing or Condorcet, or of Voltaire's *bon sens*, or from the ideal of progressive self-understanding and self-emancipation, spiritual or social, Hegelian or Marxist.

If Herder's notion of the equal validity of incommensurable cultures is accepted, the concepts of an ideal state or of an ideal man become incoherent. This is a far more radical denial of the foundations of traditional Western morality than any that Hume ever uttered. Herder's ethical relativism is a doctrine different from that of the Greek sophists or Montesquieu or Burke. These thinkers were agreed, by and large, that what men sought was happiness; they merely pointed out that differences of circumstance and the interplay of environment—'climate'—with men's nature, conceived as fairly uniform, created different characters and outlooks and, above all, different needs which called for dissimilar institutional means of satisfying them. But they recognized a broad identity or similarity of purpose in all known forms of human activity, universal and timeless goals of men as such, which bound them in a single human species or Great Society. This would, at least in theory, enable a socially imaginative and well-informed universal despot, provided he was enlightened enough, to govern each society with a due regard to its individual needs; and to advance them all towards a final universal harmony, each moving by its own path toward the self-same purpose—happiness and the rule of wisdom, virtue

---

[1] Meinecke discusses this in *Die Entstehung des Historismus* (II, 438) and his conclusions are subjected to penetrating criticism by G. A. Wells in *The Journal of the History of Ideas* (XXI, Oct.-Dec. 1960, 535-36). Despite Mr Wells's strictures, Meinecke's central thesis—that the heart of Herder's doctrines is a systematic relativism—still seems to me, for the reasons given above, to be valid.

and justice. This is Lessing's conception, embodied in the famous parable of the three rings in *Nathan the Wise*.[1]

Herder had deep affinities with the *Aufklärung*, and he did write with optimism and eloquence about man's ascent to ideal *Humanität* and uttered sentiments to which Lessing could have subscribed, no less Goethe. Yet, despite the authority of some excellent scholars,[2] I do not believe that anyone who reads Herder's works with the *Einfühlung* for which he asks, and which he so well describes, will sustain the impression that it is this—the ideal of enlightened Weimar—that fills his mind. He is a rich, suggestive, prolix, marvellously imaginative writer, but seldom clear or rigorous or conclusive. His ideas are often confused, sometimes inconsistent, never wholly specific or precise, as, indeed, Kant pointedly complained. As a result, many interpretations can be (and have been) put upon his works. But what lies at the heart of the whole of his thought, what influenced later thinkers, particularly the German Romantics and, through them, the entire history of populism, nationalism, and individualism, is the theme to which he constantly returns: that one must not judge one culture by the criteria of another; that differing civilizations are different growths, pursue different goals, embody different ways of living, are dominated by different attitudes to life; so that to understand them one must perform an imaginative act of 'empathy' into their essence, understand them 'from within' as far as possible, and see the world through their eyes—be a 'shepherd among shepherds' with the ancient Hebrews, or 'sail the Northern seas in a tempest' and read the Eddas again 'on board a ship struggling through the Skagerrak'. These widely differing societies and their ideals are not commensurable. Such questions as which of them is the best, or even which one should prefer, which one would judge to be nearer to the universal human ideal, *Humanität*, even subjectively conceived—the pattern most likely to produce man as he should be or as one thinks he should be—are, therefore, for a thinker of this type, in the end, meaningless. 'Not a man, not a country, not a people, not a natural history, not a state, are like one another. Hence the True, the Good, the Beautiful in them are not similar either.'[3]

---

[1] It has found an unexpected re-incarnation not long ago in Mao Tse-tung's celebrated image of the many flowers.

[2] E.g., Rudolf Stadelmann, *Der historische Sinn bei Herder* (Halle, 1928); R. A. Fritzsche, *Herder und die Humanität, Der Morgen*, Bk. III (Halle, 1928); H. Vesterling, [*Herders*] *Humanitätsprinzip* (Halle, 1890).   [3] IV, 472.

Herder wrote this in his Journal in 1769. The cloven hoof of relativism, or rather pluralism, shows itself even in his most orthodox discussions of universal ideals; for he thinks each image of *Humanität* to be unique and *sui generis*.[1] It is this strain in his thought, and not the language of commonplace universalism which he shares with his age, that struck, and perhaps shocked, the *Aufklärer*, the Kantians, the progressive thinkers of his time. For this goes directly against the notion of steady progress on the part of mankind as a whole, which, despite difficulties and relapses, must, or at least can and should, go on; a proposition to which the German no less than the French or Italian Enlightenment was fully committed.[2]

Herder is not a subjectivist. He believes in objective standards of judgment that are derived from understanding the life and purposes of individual societies and are themselves objective historical structures, and require, on the part of the student, wide and scrupulous scholarship as well as sympathetic imagination. What he rejects is the single over-arching standard of values, in terms of which all cultures, characters, and acts can be evaluated. Each phenomenon to be investigated presents its own measuring rod, its own internal constellation of values in the light of which alone 'the facts' can be truly understood. This is much more thoroughgoing than the realization that man is incapable of complete perfection which, for instance, Winckelmann allowed,[3] Rousseau lamented, and Kant accepted; or the doctrine that all gains entail some loss.[4] For what is here entailed is that the highest ends

---

[1] XIV, 210, 217, 230.

[2] Among modern thinkers, Herder's relativism most resembles Wyndham Lewis's protest against what he called 'the demon of progress in the arts'. In the tract which bears this title that acute, if perverse, writer denounced, with characteristically vehement and biting eloquence, the notion that valid universal criteria exist in terms of which it is possible to assert or deny that (I cannot recollect his specific examples) a work of art of one age is or is not superior to one that belongs to an entirely different tradition. What meaning can be attached to, say, the assertion that Phidias is superior or inferior to Michelangelo or Maillol, or that Goethe or Tolstoy represent an improvement on, or decline from, Homer or Aeschylus or Dante or the Book of Job?

[3] E.g. in his *Die Geschichte der Kunst des Altertums*, ed. J. Lessing (Berlin, 1869-70).

[4] Leibniz (ed. Gerhart), II, 589; Boulainvilliers, *Histoire de l'ancien gouverne-ment de la France* (1727), I, 322; Rousseau in the letter to Mirabeau of July 26, 1767; Herder could have come across this in Wegelin's work on the philosophy of history published in 1770.

for which men have rightly striven and sometimes died are strictly incompatible with one another. Even if it were possible to revive the glories of the past as those pre-historicist thinkers (Machiavelli or Mably, for instance) thought, who called for a return to the heroic virtues of Greece or Rome, we could not revive and unite them all. If we choose to emulate the Greeks, we cannot also emulate the Hebrews; if we model ourselves on the Chinese, whether as they are in reality, or in Voltaire's *opéra bouffe* version, we cannot also be the Florentines of the Renaissance, or the innocent, serene, hospitable savages of eighteenth-century imagination. Even if, *per impossibile*, we could choose among these ideals, which should we select? Since there is no common standard in terms of which to grade them, there can be no final solution to the problem of what men as such should aim at. The proposition that this question can, at least in principle, be answered correctly and finally, which few had seriously doubted since Plato had taken it for granted, is undermined. Herder, of course, condemns the very wish to resurrect ancient ideals: ideals belong to the form of life which generates them, and are mere historical memories without them: values—ends—live and die with the social wholes of which they form an intrinsic part. Each 'collective individuality' is unique, and has its own aims and standards, which will themselves inevitably be superseded by other goals and values—ethical, social, and aesthetic. Each of these systems is objectively valid in its own day, in the course of 'Nature's long year' which brings all things to pass. All cultures are equal in the sight of God, each in its time and place. Ranke said precisely this: his theodicy is a complacent version of Herder's theses, directed equally against those of Hegel and moral scepticism. But if this is so, then the notion of the perfect civilization in which the ideal human being realizes his full potentialities is patently absurd: not merely difficult to formulate, or impossible to realize in practice, but incoherent and unintelligible. This is perhaps the sharpest blow ever delivered against the classical philosophy of the West, to which the notion of perfection—the possibility, at least in principle, of universal, timeless solutions of problems of value—is essential.

The consequences of Herder's doctrines did not make themselves felt immediately. He was thought to be a bold and original thinker, but not a subverter of common moral assumptions. Nor, of course, did he think so himself. The full effect was felt only when the Romantic Movement, at its most violent, attempted to overthrow the authority both of reason and of dogma on which the old order rested. The extent of its explosive potentialities was not fully realized until the rise of modern anti-rationalist movements—nationalism, fascism, existentialism, emotivism, and the wars and revolutions made in the name of two among them; that is to say, not until our own time, and perhaps not altogether even today.

X

Herder's works, as might be expected, bristle with contradictions: on the one hand, 'The power which thinks and works in me, is in its nature as eternal as that which holds together the sun and the stars; wherever and whoever I shall be, I shall be what I am now, a force in a system of forces, in the immeasurable harmony of God's world'.[1] Whatever can be, will be. All potentialities will be realized. Herder believes in plenitude, in the great chain of being, in a nature with no barriers. Influenced by the naturalists, by Ritter, by von Haller, he sees man as an animal among animals: man is what he is because of slowly working natural causes, because he walks upright, or because of a cavity in his skull. Yet he also believes, with Aristotle and the Bible, in natural kinds, and in the special act of creation. He believes in a general human essence, a central human character: it is, as Leibniz taught in the *Nouveaux Essais*, like a vein in marble, to be brought out by reason and imagination; men are the Benjamins, the 'darlings of Nature's old age', the peak of the creative process. Yet he also believes that this human essence takes conflicting forms; types differ and the differences are unbridgeable. He makes curious effort to bring together the monistic notion of the logically rigorous interconnection of all real entities, as in Spinoza's world (although in Herder's case it takes the form of something more flexible and empirical), with the dynamic, self-developing individuated entities of Leibniz.[2] There is a tension between Herder's naturalism and his teleology, his Christianity and his enthusiastic acceptance of the findings of the natural sciences; between, on the one hand, respect for some, at any rate, of the achievements of the French Encyclopaedists, who believed in quantitative methods and precision and a unified schema of knowledge; and, on the other, he prefers the qualitative approach of

---

[1] XIII, 16.

[2] This is developed at length in *God: Some Conversations*, in which he defends Spinoza against Jacobi's charges of atheism and pantheism.

213

Goethe and Schelling and their vitalistic followers. Again, there is a contradiction between his naturalistic determinism, which at times is very strong, and the notion that one can and should resist natural impulses and natural forces;[1] for people who do not resist are overwhelmed. The Jews were crushed by the Romans; their disastrous destiny is ascribed to natural factors; yet he holds that it could have been averted; so, too, the Romans are held to have succumbed to vices which they could have resisted successfully. Herder was not sensitive to the problem of free will as, say, Kant was; there are too many conflicting strains in him. He may have believed, like most self-determinists, that men were free when they did what they chose, but that it was, in some sense, idle to ask whether men were free to choose, since they obviously were not; yet his writings give little evidence that he sought escape in this time-honoured, but hardly satisfactory, 'solution'.[2] Again, there are the separate strands of *Humanität* as a general human ideal (to be realized fully, perhaps, only in the world to come) and the *Gang Gottes über die Natur*—a phrase and a concept which Hegel later appropriated—and, on the other side, his more frequent and characteristic pluralism and relativism. There is noticeable tension between his passion for ancient German tribal life, real or imaginary, as he conceived it—spontaneous, creative and free—and his reluctant admiration for Rome, and even more for the Church, with their universalism and order and capacity for rational organization. More far-reaching still is the contrast between, on the one hand, his notion of the continuity of overflowing nature, the *Natura naturans*, the energy that is one in magnetism and electricity, in plants and animals and men, in language and in art—a universal, continuous life force of which everything is a manifestation, of which laws can be discovered in the form both of the physical sciences of his time, and of biology, psychology, and the particular brand of historical geography and anthropology that he favoured; and on the other hand, the crucial role attributed to the unaccountable leaps of genius, miraculous events, sheer chance, the unanalysable process of true creation, and the consequent impossibility of achieving anything great or lasting solely by the application of techniques; and, what goes with this, the incommunicability of the central

[1] See the magnificent paean to human freedom and man's powers of resistance to nature, XII, 142-50.

[2] *Pace* Mr G. A. Wells, who, in his *Herder and After, op. cit.,* argues strongly for this interpretation.

core of what individuates men or cultures and gives them all the colour
and force and value they possess, something that is open only to the
eye of imaginative intuition, incapable of being reduced to com-
municable, teachable scientific method. Finally, there is the ban on
moralizing, but at the same time the impassioned apostrophes to the
great moments of human existence, the curses heaped on the enemies
of human unity and creativity—the bloodstained conquerors, the
ruthless centralizers, the shrivelling of the spirit by narrow and superficial systematizers, with, at the head of them all, the odious Voltaire,
with his devitalizing ironies and pettiness and lack of insight into what
men truly are. All the confusions of his time seem richly reflected in
his shapeless, sprawling, but continuously suggestive works.

XI

Herder is in some sense a premonitory symptom, the albatross before
the coming storm. The French Revolution was founded on the notion
of timeless truths given to the faculty of reason with which all men
are endowed. It was dedicated to the creation or restoration of a static
and harmonious society, founded on unaltering principles, a dream of
classical perfection, or, at least, the closest approximation to it feasible
on earth. It preached a peaceful universalism and a rational humani-
tarianism. But its consequences threw into relief the precariousness of
human institutions; the disturbing phenomenon of apparently irresistible
change; the clash of irreconcilable values and ideas; the insufficiency of
simple formulas; the complexity of men and societies; the poetry of
action, destruction, heroism, war; the effectiveness of mobs and of
great men; the crucial role played by chance; the feebleness of reason
before the power of fanatically believed doctrines; the unpredictability
of events; the part played in history by unintended consequences; the
ignorance of the workings of the sunken two-thirds of the great human
iceberg, of which only the visible portion had been studied by scientists
and taken into account by the ideologists of the great Revolution. This,
too, could be said of the Russian Revolution. Its ideals are too familiar
to rehearse; and its results, too, threw doubts, whether justified or not,
on the effectiveness of the kind of democracy for which liberals and
radicals in the nineteenth century had pleaded; on the ability of rational
men to allow for and control the forces of unreason; on revolution as
an instrument for the promotion of freedom, a wider culture and social
justice. It awakened men forcibly to the effectiveness of resolute con-

215

spiracies by disciplined parties; the irrationality of the masses; the weakness of liberal and democratic institutions in the West; the force of nationalist passions. As Durkheim, Pareto, and Freud stand to the Russian Revolution—with their views on the uncritical use of such general terms as democracy and liberty, and their theories of the interplay of rational and irrational factors in making for social cohesion and disintegration, ideas which have deeply influenced thought and action in our day—so Herder stands to the events of 1789. The craving for fraternity and for self-expression, and disbelief in the capacity of reason to determine values, dominated the nineteenth century, and even more our own. Herder lived until 1803. He did not attempt to draw the moral of his own doctrines in relation to the fate of Germany or Europe, as Saint-Simon and Hegel and de Maistre, in their very different fashions, had attempted to do. Perhaps he died too early in the century. Nevertheless, he, more than any of his contemporaries, sensed the insecurity of the foundations of faith in the Enlightenment held by so many in his time, even while he half accepted it. In this sense, those who thought of him as endowed with special powers—we are told that he was sometimes called a magician and was a model for Goethe's Faust—did him no injustice.[1]

---

[1] E.g., by Günter Jacobi in *Herder als Faust* (Leipzig, 1911). Goethe himself detested such identifications (for a discussion of this, see Robert T. Clark, Jr., *Herder: His Life and Thought*, University of California Press, Berkeley and Los Angeles, 1955, pp. 127 ff).

Footnote 1 to Page 175:

[1] According to Herder the soul evolves a pattern from the chaos of things by which it is surrounded, and so 'creates by its own inner power a One out of the Many, which belongs to it alone' (*vide XIII*, 182, and *XV*, 532, and cp. H. B. Nisbet, *Herder and the Philosophy and History of Science* [*op. cit.*, p. 63]). That the creation of integrated wholes out of discrete data is the fundamental organizing activity of human nature is a belief that is central to Herder's entire social and moral outlook: for him all creative activity, conscious and unconscious, generates, and is, in turn, determined by, its own unique *Gestalt*, whereby every individual and group strives to perceive, understand, act, create, live. This is the idea which dominates his conception of social structure and development of the nature of an identifiable civilization, and, indeed, of what men live by (*vide V*, 104). Professor Nisbet seems to me entirely justified in describing Herder as a forerunner of *Gestalt* Psychology. (On this see also Martin Schütze's articles, 'Herder's Psychology', in *The Monist*, 35 (1925), pp. 507-554, and 'The Fundamental Ideas of Herder's Thought' in *Modern Philology*, 18, 19, 21 [1920-4].)

Index

INDEX

Dante Alighieri, 64, 77, 173
Darwin, Charles, 146
Degérando, J. M., 93
Della Porta, G. B., 118-19
Dennis, John, 103
Descartes, René, and causality, xiv; exaggerations in, xxiv, 97; Vico reads, 8, 9; Vico opposes, 8-12, 20, 21, 72, 84, 87; and humane learning, 10, 12, 18, 18*n*; on criterion of truth, 10-12, 87-8; on knowledge, 10, 11, 19, 20, 126; on cognition, 25; on human nature, 34; on natural law, 34, 65, 87, 135, 140, 142, 177; on wisdom in history, 71, 129; on reason, 72; precursor of Enlightenment, 72; fear of heresy, 78; idealises physics, 101; influence on Vico, 117; on metaphysics, 119; on natural science, 121; against reverence for past, 150; and dis-unity, 166, 175; Hamann attacks, 166; Herder attacks, 174-5, 177
Diderot, Denis, 145, 155, 188, 191
Dilthey, Wilhelm, and historical fact, xiii, xxvii; influenced by Vico, 4, 27*n*, 137; and historical understanding, 32*n*, 97, 106-7; and empathy, 173
Diodorus Siculus, 78
Donne, John, 103
Doughty, Charles M., 185
Draco, 38, 55, 86
Du Bos, Jean Baptiste, 148-9, 200*n*
Dumoulin, Charles, 130, 132, 134*n*
Duni, E., 78, 141*n*
Duns Scotus, 16*n*
Durkheim, Emile, 56, 88, 216

Einfühlen see Empathy
Einstein, Albert, 76*n*
Empathy (*Das Einfühlen*), Herder on, 154-5, 171-4, 186-8; Vico's description of, 187; and plurality of values, 207, 210; and variety of human outlooks, 211-12, 215

Engels, Friedrich, 123
Ennius, 60
Epicurus, 69, 70, 78
Equality of races and cultures, Herder's belief in, 164-5, 182, 186-8, 190, 192, 194, 198
Erigena, 177
Euripides, 78, 207
Expressionism, 153, 165-72; Herder on poetry as, 169-73; all forms valid, 173; and fullness of life, 177, 186-9, 192; and patterns of culture, 195-9; and nature of art, 200-205; *see also* Aesthetic theory

Fassò, Luigi, 117
Fauriel, Claude, 93
Ferguson, Adam, 150, 176
Feuerbach, Ludwig, 4, 61
Fichte, Johann Gottlieb, 106, 157, 178, 181, 204, 206*n*
Ficino, Marsilio, xv, 16*n*, 25, 71, 93, 103, 117
Filangieri, G., 90
Finetti, Francesco, 78
Fisch, M. H., xiv, 4*n*, 26*n*, 83*n*, 92*n*, 95*n*, 114, 116, 117, 125, 130
Flachsland, Caroline, 173
Flaubert, Gustave, 93
Flint, Robert, 94-5
Fontenelle, Bernard de, 150
Forster, Georg, 156
Foscolo, Ugo, 94
Fourier, Charles, 68, 177
Franklin, Julian H., 128*n*
Frederick II (the Great) of Prussia, 159, 181
Freedom, Hegel defines, 199
French Revolution, 156, 215-16
Freud, Sigmund, xxiv, 54, 56, 83, 211, 216

Gaius, 133
Galiani, Ferdinando, 90
Galileo, 9
Gans, Edward, 94
Gassendi, P., 34

219

exaggerations, xxiv, 97; on utility of historians, 1; as innovator, 3; life and works, 5-8; on discoveries, 7; learning, 8; obscurity, 8, 67-8, 95, 99; and natural sciences, 9, 12, 18-24, 83-4, 89-90, 100, 122, 123; revolt against Cartesian rationalism, 9-12, 96; and humane learning, 10, 11, 17, 24, 82, 89-90; on knowledge and truth, 11-29, 99-100, 105-13; on mathematics, 14-21, 26, 87; and Hobbes, 19, 26-7, 58; on proving existence of God, 20; on anthropomorphism, 22-3; on mental activity, 24; and Renaissance thought, 25, 125-37; and historical understanding, 26-38, 41, 47-9, 56-72, 89, 97, 112-13; attacks natural law theorists, 27, 34, 37-41, 58-60, 64-5, 85-8, 103, 124, 126, 139; early influences on, 30; religious beliefs, 30, 70, 77, 79-81; and imaginative understanding (*fantasia*), 30-32, 58-9, 103, 107-12, 114, 124, 136; criticises unhistorical thinking, 34, 71-2; and culture, 35, 109-10; Platonism, 36; on Providence, 36-7, 52; attacks abstract thinkers, 37; on Jews, 38*n*, 39*n*, 53*n*, 77, 105; on social contract, 39-40; on language, 42-8, 50-52, 56, 77, 88, 101, 169; fear of heresy, 43*n*, 78-9; on metaphor, 46, 103-4; three stages of social growth, 47-8, 61-7; on ancient wisdom, 49-51, 59; on myth, 44, 52-6, 86, 88, 193; on Homer, 55, 150; transcendentalism in *New Science*, 58-9; on primitive man and social evolution, 59-64, 68-73, 78, 80, 84-90, 109; on alienation and reification, 61; cyclical theory of history and human spirit, 64-7, 73, 76-7, 113; on internal knowledge, 67; opposed to Enlightenment, 72-3, 140-41; anticipates romantics, 72,

88*n*; importance of enquiries, 73; relativism, 74; heterodoxy, 77-90; as jurist, 83-4, 123-5, 137, 140; on art, 88*n*; influence and importance, 89-98; classification of knowledge (*verum/certum*), 100, 105-10, 112-13, 123; and human purposiveness, 109-14, 117, 140-41; sources of ideas, 114-42; and Herder, 115, 147-8, 171, 193; Professor Badaloni on, 117-23, 136; conservatism, 122; and travellers' tales, 124; and contemporary historicism, 125; debt to jurists, 135-8; and 16th century historiography, 137-8

Vignier, Nicolas, 136

Virgil, 44, 187*n*

Voltaire, on Locke, xv; and Herder, xxiii, 116, 148, 177, 193, 197, 215; and history, xxv, 137, 138*n*, 140, 147-8, 188-9, 194; on wisdom in history, 70, 71; Vico and, 123; and exotic societies, 124, 139, 148, 212; on human nature, 142, 197; rationalism, 145, 177; contempt for Dark Ages, 149, 189, 190, 193, 197; on State, 162; on progress, 190, 191; scepticism, 191; anti-Christian, 193; on morality of other cultures, 197-8; and *bon sens*, 209

Voss, Gerhard Jan, 6

Wagner, Richard, 49*n*, 146, 190

Warton, Henry *and* Joseph, xxi, 150, 183

Weber, Max, 56, 97, 106, 138

Wegelin, J. R., 147, 211*n*

Weizsäcker, C. F. R. von, 110*n*

Wells, G. A., xv, 171*n*, 209*n*, 214*n*

Whittaker, Thomas, 117

Wieland, C. M., 186, 205*n*

Wilson, Edmund, 95

Winch, P., 32*n*

Winckelmann, J. J., 148, 179, 211